"The Rule of Law, not the Law of justice, and Divine justice *is* Divin[...] theological premise of Pope Francis' *Amoris Laetitia* and then articulates a clear, compelling, effective pastoral application of this foundational Christian teaching to couples trying their best to live a wholly holy life. Something that not only theologians and parish staff will want to study, but married couples and those moving towards married life as well."

—Rev. James T. Bretzke, SJ, John Carroll University

"Gerald J. Bednar, Catholic priest, experienced attorney theologian, and pastor, has provided a much-needed study of *Amoris Laetitia*. 'Mercy is not an alternative to the law. It is a way of applying the law.' Bednar has provided a rich resource for all who seek to understand and to live Jesus' words: 'I have come to call not the righteous but sinners' (Mark 2:17), in the light of the magisterium of Pope Francis."

—Francis J. Moloney, SDB
    Catholic Theological College, University of Divinity,
        Melbourne, Australia

"This is a brilliant book, reflective of the author's training in law and systematic theology as well as teaching for three decades in a major seminary. On every page one detects the skillful theologian-lawyer summarizing and applying the teaching of Pope Francis in *Amoris Laetitia* with precision, respect, and care. The numerous examples from the daily lives of laypersons bring this book to life as Bednar applies the pope's teaching in focused and nuanced ways."

—Msgr. Kevin W. Irwin, The Catholic University of America

"An incisive and illuminating reading of *Amoris Laetitia*, Gerald Bednar's book is pastoral theology at its finest. He utilizes the breadth and depth of Scripture, tradition, and a wealth of ministerial experience in order to argue for the continuity of *Amoris Laetitia* with the Catholic Church's enduring concern for distressed families and marriages. Patient, careful, and measured, this book models the nuance that immediate popular reception of the 2016 apostolic exhortation often lacked."

—Kevin G. Grove, CSC, University of Notre Dame

Mercy and the Rule of Law

A Theological Interpretation of Amoris Laetitia

Gerald J. Bednar

LITURGICAL PRESS
ACADEMIC

Collegeville, Minnesota
www.litpress.org

© 2021 by Gerald J. Bednar
Published by Liturgical Press, Collegeville, Minnesota. All rights reserved. No part of this book may be used or reproduced in any manner whatsoever, except brief quotations in reviews, without written permission of Liturgical Press, Saint John's Abbey, PO Box 7500, Collegeville, MN 56321-7500. Printed in the United States of America.

1   2   3   4   5   6   7   8   9

Library of Congress Cataloging-in-Publication Data

Names: Bednar, Gerald J., 1946– author.
Title: Mercy and the rule of law : a theological interpretation of Amoris Laetitia / Gerald J. Bednar.
Description: Collegeville, Minnesota : Liturgical Press Academic, [2021] | Includes index. | Summary: "An introduction to the concepts and contexts of Amoris Laetitia for the laity, press, and clergy"— Provided by publisher.
Identifiers: LCCN 2021004721 (print) | LCCN 2021004722 (ebook) | ISBN 9780814666555 (paperback) | ISBN 9780814666562 (epub) | ISBN 9780814666562 (mobi) | ISBN 9780814666562 (pdf)
Subjects: LCSH: Catholic Church. Pope (2013- : Francis). Amoris laetitia. | Families—Religious aspects—Catholic Church. | Marriage—Religious aspects— Catholic Church. | Love—Religious aspects—Catholic Church. | Mercy.
Classification: LCC BX2351.C2963 B43 2021 (print) | LCC BX2351.C2963 (ebook) | DDC 261.8/358—dc23
LC record available at https://lccn.loc.gov/2021004721
LC ebook record available at https://lccn.loc.gov/2021004722C

Contents

Preface

Few Catholics today have an adequate notion of what the rule of law actually means. Even fewer Catholics have any passable knowledge of the church's complex history concerning divorce and remarriage. Little wonder then that the promulgation of the apostolic exhortation *Amoris Laetitia* by Pope Francis in 2016 caused such a stir among the laity, the press, some theologians, and even some bishops. This book endeavors to introduce concepts and contexts that will help explain the document and resolve some confusion about it. In focusing on *Amoris Laetitia* and the rule of law, I attempt to address the issues in a way that helps to open a door to further discussion among theologians and clergy whose critical comments have so often missed the point of this important document.

Pope Francis and the bishops who met in synod to help discern the church's teaching have remained faithful to the church and to the Lord's call for mercy. On October 8, 2013, Pope Francis announced that he would convene an Extraordinary Synod the following year to provide a forum for the discussion of the challenges of pastoral care of families.[1] As the synod met and deliberated in October 2014, two opposing groups emerged: those who saw no need to change current practices and those who wanted to enhance the role of mercy in ministry to families, especially to the divorced and remarried. The participants could not reach a consensus. After the pope commended members of

1. Stephen Walford, *Pope Francis, the Family and Divorce: In Defense of Truth and Mercy* (New York: Paulist Press, 2018), 18–24, provides an excellent summary of the events leading to the publication of *Amoris Laetitia*.

the synod for their frankness and appealed to a spirit of collegiality, he called for continuation of the discussion at the Ordinary General Assembly of the Synod of Bishops the following year.

On October 4, 2015, the synod began its deliberations, which lasted for three weeks. The pope had made clear that he did not want any rigid or rigorist interpretation of doctrine to interfere with an effective pastoral application of mercy. This led to suggestions that the synod had been rigged in favor of Cardinal Walter Kasper's proposal that favored a prominent role for mercy. Cardinal George Pell sent Pope Francis a letter signed by thirteen cardinals who expressed their concerns about the working document and the process that would be followed, including the selection of those who would actually draft the document. Different working groups of participants produced a variety of different approaches to the wide array of issues presented to them. The synod approved a Final Report consisting of ninety-four paragraphs. Participants voted on each paragraph separately. The paragraph that addressed the possibility of the sacraments of penance and Eucharist for those in irregular marriages passed by one vote more than the two-thirds majority required by synod rules. The Final Report was presented to the Pope as a guide for the writing of an apostolic exhortation.

Among many other important issues, the 2016 apostolic exhortation *Amoris Laetitia* responds to the question, *"Can a divorced and remarried Catholic receive Communion?"* The answer is "No." Pope Francis keeps that traditional answer in place. But "No" is the correct answer *only in the absence of certain unusual circumstances.*

First, the negative answer assumes that no annulment has been obtained. Obviously, if an annulment has been officially declared, then a divorced and remarried Catholic *can* receive Communion.[2]

Second, the answer also assumes that no dissolution based on the Pauline privilege has been granted. When one of two non-Christian spouses desires baptism and the other spouse refuses to live in peace

---

2. This situation presents no real problem. In the church's eyes, if no marriage ever existed, neither did a divorce. Canon law tribunals in the United States require the couple to obtain a civil divorce before proceeding with a petition for a declaration of nullity. The couple qualifies as "married and divorced" in the civil sense.

with the prospective Christian spouse, the valid marriage between them can be dissolved. After a divorce, the newly baptized Christian may remarry and receive Communion in the church (see canon 1143).

Third, the answer assumes that no dissolution "in favor of the faith" has been granted. According to this favor, sometimes popularly called the "Petrine privilege," a Catholic person in some situations may be divorced, remarry, and continue to receive Communion in the church.[3]

Fourth, the answer assumes that the marriage is based on a valid consent between the parties and has been consummated. If it remains unconsummated, a spouse may petition the pope to dissolve even a sacramental marriage for a just cause (see canons 1142 and 1698). Such a couple must obtain a divorce, and can thereafter marry other partners and receive Communion, all with the official blessing of the church.

Fifth, the negative answer assumes that the couple in question is not living together in a so-called "brother-sister" relationship (that is, abstaining from conjugal relations) to avoid a serious injustice. Church officials allow this practice even though the "brother-sister" relationship objectively violates an existing marital bond. For this reason, the relationship cannot be blessed or recognized in any way in the church. Abstention from sexual relations does not make the "brother-sister" relationship right, nor does it establish chastity, as we will consider at greater length in chapter 3. Church leaders do not permit the relationship; they tolerate it.

Pope Francis points to a sixth unusual circumstance regarding the question of a divorced and remarried couple receiving Communion: some divorced and remarried Catholics may receive Communion if they are caught in a dilemma. If they cannot remain continent while living together, and if it is impossible for them to break apart without grave injustice, they would have no viable alternative. In chapter 8 of *Amoris Laetitia*, the pope gives such irregular couples a process that may lead to Communion for them. As in the "brother-sister" relationship, it can happen by way of tolerance, not by way of permission.

---

3. For example, if a baptized Catholic is married to a non-baptized person and the non-baptized person leaves the marriage, the Catholic spouse may apply for a dissolution of the non-sacramental marriage to enable the Catholic to enjoy a sacramental marriage with another.

In any event, the teaching of *Amoris Laetitia* indicates that Communion is not automatically precluded for all divorced and remarried Catholics. Because of the impossible circumstances of those caught in dilemmas, mercy allows them to make the most generous response they can give to God, tolerates their unfortunate dilemma, and offers penance and Communion to those trapped in such less than ideal circumstances.

How can this be said? That is the subject matter of this small book. Hopefully this short treatise can serve as an introduction to the sometimes-labyrinthine ways taken in Scripture and tradition to reach pastorally sensitive solutions for certain distressed marriages. No doubt the content of this book is not the last word on the subject. Readers can refer to the footnotes to help guide further exploration into the issues that pique their interest.

When *Amoris Laetitia* first became available, I read it eagerly. I quickly noticed that one highlight is its well-informed interpretation of Paul's admonition that Christians must receive the Eucharist "worthily" (see 1 Cor 11:27-29). I emailed my friend at the Australian Catholic University, Fr. Francis Moloney, SDB, who had recently written a book that included an exposition of that passage. We were both overjoyed to see the pope adopt an exegetical approach that took full advantage of modern scholarship. It set the stage for a teaching that more adequately responds to pastoral problems than previously was possible. Frank and I continued to share ideas on the topic. I am most grateful for his guidance, expertise, and encouragement.

My first teacher in systematic theology, Fr. Al Laubenthal, STD, has remained the best of my teachers. He has been of invaluable assistance in reviewing my text and pointing out various implications of my positions and the way that I state them. He has read and offered commentary on every version I produced and has been a most faithful friend and colleague. Fr. George Smiga, STD, professor of Scripture, also took a lively interest in the text and made many helpful suggestions. The late professor of Scripture, Fr. Larry Tosco, CSJ (1942–2019), kindly added his guidance and support from the very early stages of this project. Fr. James Bretzke, SJ, recently and happily assigned to nearby John Carroll University, most generously reviewed my text and made very helpful comments regarding ethics. I feel humbled to have received personalized guidance from such an expert. Msgr. Kevin

Irwin, STD, and Fr. Scott Detisch, PhD, were kind enough to review the chapter on penance and the Eucharist. I am most grateful for their very encouraging remarks. Fr. Gary Yanus, JCD, undertook the nearly impossible task of trying to make sure that my comments regarding canon law did not stray too far from the path. His good nature, competence, and support lifted my spirits. Fr. Damian Ference, currently writing his dissertation in philosophy at the Angelicum, kindly took the time to read through the text on a flight to Rome. His observations helped in solidifying several of my arguments. Msgr. Jeremiah McCarthy, PhD; Fr. Joe Koopman, STD; Beth A. Rath, PhD; and Sr. Lisa Marie Belz, OSU, PhD, also offered most helpful feedback and suggestions. I thank Alan Rome, the librarian at St. Mary Seminary, who has been most accommodating in finding volumes that the seminary collection did not possess. I am most grateful to Martin Cloutier, a parishioner at St. Helen Parish in Newbury, Ohio, who kindly checked my translations from the French originals of several articles and books that I used. Special thanks to Stephanie Lancour at Liturgical Press for coordinating the editing of the manuscript. The editor's insights and suggestions have greatly improved the text.

Any errors in the text belong to me alone. My apologies to those who tried so hard to keep me on target. I welcome correction wherever it is needed. Regardless of its shortcomings, I hope that the text can help to stimulate a more profound discussion among theologians, unburdened by the nastiness that has marred some of the commentary so far. I feel compelled to repeat a request made by Pope Benedict XVI in the first volume of his trilogy, *Jesus of Nazareth*: "I would only ask the reader for that initial good will without which there can be no understanding."[4] Too many readers impatiently liberate themselves from the text of *Amoris Laetitia* so decisively that they offer refutations of positions that the pope does not adopt. Pope Francis has provided a great service to the church and serious thinkers need to build upon his thinking, each from his or her own area of expertise.

Finally, I am grateful to Cleveland's St. Mary Seminary, where I have taught systematic theology for thirty years, and to Fr. Mark Latcovich, PhD, its president-rector, for making available a semester-long sabbatical

---

4. Pope Benedict XVI, *Jesus of Nazareth: From the Baptism in the Jordan to the Transfiguration*, trans. Adrian J. Walker (New York: Doubleday, 2007), xxiv.

in 2019, which enabled me to pursue many of the ideas that make up this book. Rev. John Herman, CSC, the rector at Moreau Seminary, provided a lovely residence at the University of Notre Dame, my alma mater, where I was able to work, reminisce, pray, and enjoy the marvelous hospitality for which the Congregation of Holy Cross is so justly famous.

My blessings to all who contributed to this project and to all who will read this text. May this slim volume serve the glory of God.

Introduction

You tread upon my patience.

—King Henry IV in *King Henry IV, Part I* 1.3.4

Patience.

In contentious times, people grow impatient when others express opinions that contradict what seems obvious to them. Why should people listen to other voices when they can feel the truth so viscerally? That's how the impatience of Henry IV grew. He knew in his gut that a conspiracy formed against him. He soon encounters his opponent, Hotspur, who admits to impatience of his own. When impatience meets impatience, ugly things can happen.

This short treatise presents a theological interpretation of Pope Francis's 2016 apostolic exhortation *Amoris Laetitia* ("The Joy of Love"; hereafter AL) for all those who feel their patience "tread upon" and who have noticed a certain negligence of thought and speech regarding the document. Some members of both the press and the public have reacted precipitously to AL.[1] Contrary to what some may think, Pope Francis does not say that the divorced and remarried can now simply receive absolution and Communion. Far from it. Lacking the leisure to research the issues adequately, hasty commentators usually express their frustration with catch phrases and provocative headlines.

---

1. Cardinal Walter Kasper has expressed some frustration over the careless nature of the discussions surrounding AL and how some people "now declare themselves to be a self-appointed super-magisterium" (*The Message of* Amoris Laetitia: *Finding Common Ground* [New York: Paulist Press, 2019], 5).

They miss the fact that couples are at times caught in *dilemmas*, situations in which all options for moving forward are unacceptable. They seem unaware of the concern of Pope Francis for children. AL attempts to protect not only adults who enjoy the spousal bond but also children who look to their bond with their parents for nurture and security.

Attention has focused on chapter 8 in view of its merciful treatment of irregular marriages, although the apostolic exhortation has many other valuable insights to share on family life. When challenged, many good Catholics tend to revert to what they learned in high school catechism classes. Even trained pastors will use terms like the "absolute indissolubility of marriage," "bigamy," "adultery," and "intrinsic evil" in their critiques simply to catch a hearing. This sort of talk easily leads to the testiness that has infested political discourse in the United States today. Such petulance should not make its way into discussions about the faith. Christian discourse should rise to a higher level.[2]

As an aid to a more helpful discussion among the faithful, chapter 1 begins with an overview of AL. What does it say, and what does it not say? Following Stephen Walford's advice, I give a very brief synopsis of each chapter of the document to provide an overall context, but I save a discussion of chapter 8 for a section of its own, since it calls for a much more detailed analysis than the other chapters.[3] In that eighth chapter, the pope calls attention to the fact that some families have become trapped in irregular marital unions. Caught in a dilemma, whatever choices these divorced parents have, they seem to be problematic in one way or another. They have no legitimate alternative to choose. They must find the least offensive way of proceeding with their lives while giving their children the support they need. Impatient commentators on AL often neglect the dilemmas people face, which constitute the heart of the pastoral concerns of chapter 8. AL insists that the church's ministers need to treat such people with mercy, respect, and love. It does not say that divorce has become acceptable, that the annulment process no longer counts, or that adultery is no longer an intrinsic evil.

---

2. James Heft, SM, has offered a compelling analysis of the situation in his lecture at Loyola University Chicago. See "Is Pope Francis a Heretic?," *Origins* 49, no. 12 (August 1, 2019): 182–86.

3. Stephen Walford, *Pope Francis, the Family, and Divorce: In Defense of Truth and Mercy* (New York: Paulist Press, 2018), 53n51.

Chapter 2 deals with "The Rule of Law, Not the Law of Rules." Many people have a woefully deficient notion of law. They tend to reduce law to a set of rules that need to be applied, quite rigidly at times, to generic situations. Such is not the case either in civil law or in church law. Discussions of AL based on flawed understandings of the nature and function of law are bound to fail. In my estimation, this misunderstanding has contributed most to the impatience and contentiousness on display in some of the discussions of AL. A brief excursus into the realm of civil law will make it easier to understand the sense of how the church applies its own law in the midst of its reliance on mercy. It follows the lead of Jesus. To the surprise of some, Jesus chooses mercy over justice and generosity over fairness at practically every turn in the Gospels. Catholics need to reacquaint themselves with the very unconventional reasoning process of Christ, whose decisions flowed from love and mercy. This leads to a consideration of how Thomas Aquinas treated the application of laws and rules to specific situations. He very carefully distinguishes principles themselves from their application. The application of the law requires the virtue of prudence, a factor often overlooked today. This chapter can yield surprising results for those who consider law as consisting of only the rigid application of so many rules.

Chapter 3 zeroes in on the issues raised in AL's chapter 8. Some thinkers tend to oppose mercy and law. This chapter contradicts that notion and views mercy as a way of applying law. Laws can be enforced mercifully or harshly. The Lord commits the church to the merciful application of the law. This means that it must attend to the concrete circumstances of any case it considers. When this happens, mercy can override a rule without overturning the law, as the Lord did in his ministry.

Chapter 4, "Entering the Field Hospital," invites the reader to take a look at real people caught in real predicaments that produced very real difficulties, even dilemmas. What does conversion require of such couples? What can they do once their decisions have put them in a bind? One case features a woman who simply struggled on her own after divorce. Another concerns a woman who tried the "brother-sister" relationship as a way to satisfy her obligation. A third case presents a situation in which a tribunal denied an annulment to a woman who was nonetheless convinced that her marriage was null. In addition, reports of the experiences of children provoke deep sympathy for those caught in the predicaments of such families. In view of such dilemmas, church leaders judge that sometimes it is lawful to tolerate a lesser moral evil in order to avoid a greater evil or in order to promote a greater good. Pope Francis applies that principle to the dilemmas faced by so many of the divorced and remarried couples in the church today.

By this point, many readers will wonder what sort of Scriptural and historical warrants exist to support the pope's pastoral approach. Chapter 5, "Scriptural Basis and Historical Experience," explores the scriptural foundations and the ways that various popes handled marital dilemmas. It will interest readers to know that scholars can detect the same sort of development within Scripture that continues afterwards in the early church. The church has long had the power to manage marital bonds in the cases that come before it, at least since the days of St. Paul. The power of the keys (Matt 16:19 and 18:18-19) furnishes church leaders with the authority to administer concrete cases as they arise. Popes such as St. Innocent I and St. Leo the Great have exercised that power in ways that Pope Francis now proposes. Those early medieval popes understood the indissolubility of marriage, but those saintly leaders also recognized when to use the power of the keys to advance the merciful ministry that Jesus requires of his leaders.

Chapter 6 will consider the arguments of those who have either publicly questioned AL or give it an unduly restrictive interpretation. Major deficiencies in those works will be noted. Critical works that have appeared prior to the promulgation of AL will receive attention as relevant topics arise in the text and footnotes. The chapter closes with a brief reminder of the place of mercy in the church's ministry.

Finally, chapter 7 deals with the topic of reconciliation and Communion. In what circumstances can those in irregular marital unions receive absolution and come to Communion? Catholics have grown so accustomed to receiving Communion in ordinary circumstances that many do not realize that present doctrine and practice actually permit Communion in certain extraordinary cases, such as those described in chapter 8 of AL. Catholics have learned that they should not take Communion if they know that they have committed a grave sin which they have not yet confessed. Generally this is good spiritual advice. It does not, however, cover all situations, nor has it been taught from the beginning of the church's reflection on eucharistic discipline, as will be shown.

The propositions contained in this text need faithful and serious consideration before anyone undertakes to contradict the pope's apostolic exhortation. Although such reflection takes time, energy, and honesty, the effort will greatly benefit those who try. One quality will reward all readers.

Patience.

CHAPTER ONE

Amoris Laetitia

What It Does and Does Not Say

*A*moris Laetitia exudes the warmth and affection experienced in many families. The document comfortably acknowledges the daily expressions of love and commitment between spouses, the joyful moments of play, and the occasional episodes of discipline with the children (AL 195, 268–269). It concludes with a healthy spirituality of marriage and the family in chapter 9, where it recognizes and encourages the common life of the larger family oriented in love to the world.

Although this study will focus on the controversy that has arisen especially over chapter 8, a more balanced portrait can be achieved only by recalling the surrounding relatively "non-controversial" chapters, which present marriage in its full Christian splendor. By far, the text's most frequently cited authorities are the *Relatio Synodi* (2014) and the *Relatio Finalis* (2015), the statements published by the bishops in connection with the Synod on the Family held in 2014, in preparation for AL's publication during the Year of Mercy.[1] The document presents not only the pope's views, but also generally the views of the bishops who attended the synods.

---

1. A brief history of the synods may be found in the preface.

1. The Non-Controversial Chapters

Anchored in the Bible, Francis's reflection in chapter 1 offers strong hints of St. John Paul II's theology of the body (see esp. AL 9–13).[2] Both Francis and John Paul II begin with the same question: "Have you not read that he who made them from the beginning 'made them male and female'?" (Matt 19:4). Thus, the two can become one flesh, and bear fruit in a way that reflects the Trinity (AL 10–11). God created Adam and Eve, not like the rest of creation, but in God's image and likeness.[3] Francis also reflects in AL his predecessor's thoughts on the dignity of work (AL 23–26). He highlights the tenderness that ought to characterize family experiences by drawing on Psalm 131 and inviting reflection on life in the Holy Family.

Of course, Francis knows the trials and tribulations of modern family life, and he offers his reflections on that topic in chapter 2. Modern social life hardly supports the personal, intimate interchanges that ought to take place among family members. Distorted use of freedom can foster "suspicion, fear of commitment, self-centeredness and arrogance" (AL 33). The church has contributed something to this mess. Francis asserts that at times its ministers have proposed "a far too abstract and almost artificial theological ideal of marriage, far removed from the concrete situations and practical possibilities of real families" (AL 36). In dealing with the difficulties of modern life, couples need guidance through complex situations. Ministers have been called "to form consciences, not to replace them" (AL 37). Narcissism has become a cornerstone of "the culture of the ephemeral" where relationships form in haste and wither away like a wisp of smoke, without a trace (AL 39, 41). The decline of the faith has negatively impacted family life, and often enough the lack of affordable housing and health care also

2. Pope John Paul II first presented what came to be known as his "theology of the body" in a long series of addresses offered at his traditional weekly Wednesday audiences at the Vatican, between September 5, 1979, and November 28, 1984. In the years since then, and especially following his death in 2005, many Catholics have discovered great value in these texts, often with the help of teachers who have simplified and popularized their content.

3. John Paul II, *Man and Woman He Created Them: A Theology of the Body*, trans. Michael Waldstein (Boston: Pauline Books & Media, 2006), especially sections 1:1; 3:3; 18:5; 67:3; 68:4.

weigh heavily on family life (AL 44). Situations of war, persecution, poverty, and injustice drive migrations that severely destabilize family life (AL 46). The church needs to understand the stress that can accompany single mothers who strive to live according to all the rules, but for various reasons cannot (AL 49). Exhaustion takes its toll, at times resulting in decreased communication and even in drug use, alcohol addiction, and gambling (AL 50–51). The church must step forward to strengthen family life for the good of society, especially when secular social movements have lost their way. Modern ideologies that focus on gender fluidity regardless of biological realities can only harm future generations (AL 53–56).

In chapter 3, "Looking to Jesus: The Vocation of the Family," the pope unfolds the implications of the wonderful gift of sexuality. He views the indissolubility of marriage as a divine gift to help the flourishing of married life (AL 62). Jesus restored marriage to the original intention of the Creator, thereby solidifying its part in providing a growing and thriving society (AL 63). He highlights the role of conjugal love in not only developing the intimate union of love enjoyed by married couples but also in providing offspring through responsible parenthood (AL 68). The pope roundly rejects artificial means of controlling conception and declares that children deserve to be born of the love of a mother and father (AL 80–81). Where this is not possible, adoption or foster parenting constitute acts of love that can lift up the child's life (AL 82). The pope also condemns abortion and euthanasia as contrary to the nature of the family as "the sanctuary of life" (AL 83).

The sacrament of matrimony constitutes a sign of Christ's union with the church (AL 71). In the Latin rite, the ministers of matrimony are the man and woman who marry, while the ordained minister plays the role of the official witness of the church (AL 75). Natural marriages between unbaptized people are valid and automatically become sacramental at their baptism as long as the couple does not reject their marriage vows (AL 75). In other words, the church recognizes that the marriages of unbaptized people produce a valid marital bond. A Catholic cannot validly marry a non-Christian partner who previously has been married, even in a civil marriage. Even though that civil marriage is not considered as "sacramental," that is, a marriage between two baptized persons, the church respects the natural bond that has been established between those non-baptized spouses. If the two civilly married spouses become baptized, their civil marriage will be considered as sacramental in the eyes of the church. Their mutual baptisms, in effect, bless their marriage as sacramental.

Nowadays couples often live together without the benefit of the sacrament, by civil marriage only, or by remarriage after civil divorce. It takes no great insight to point out the deficiencies of these irregular unions, but it takes considerable insight and skill to approach such couples in a way that leads to their conversion. Especially where the irregular marriage has attained "a noteworthy stability through a public bond—and is characterized by deep affection, responsibility towards the children and the ability to overcome trials—this can be seen as an opportunity, where possible, to lead them to celebrate the sacrament of Matrimony" (AL 78). The annulment process, for example, can help clear the way for many couples. The process investigates the state of the couple at the time they entered their marriage in order to determine whether an essential element was lacking, such as sufficient maturity or due discretion to make the judgment necessary to enter into a marriage. If an essential element was missing, a church tribunal issues a declaration of nullity, indicating that a true, valid marriage never took place, in spite of all appearances to the contrary. After the issuance of a declaration of nullity, no marital bond stands in the way of a further marriage. Both couples are free to marry. During the process of assessing the validity of a marriage, pastors must "avoid judgments that do not take into account the complexity of various situations, and they are to be attentive, by necessity, to how people experience and endure distress because of their condition" (AL 79). When pastors handle the annulment process well, it can assist in healing many wounds.

In chapter 4, the pope presents "Love in Marriage." In an effort to dislodge the proper notion of love from the romantic ideas that so dominate modern movies and songs, he uses St. Paul's reflection from 1 Corinthians 13:4-7 (AL 89–119). The cultivation of patience can defeat the common tendency to find excuses to take harsh and often hurtful precipitous actions to achieve one's own goals (AL 92). Love is also kind and not jealous, not puffed up or arrogant. It cultivates humility. Love is not rude, impolite or harsh. It looks kindly on the shortcomings of others and treats them generously. The true lover does not become irritable or resentful, nor does love hold grudges. It quickly finds a way to make peace when feelings have been hurt. It values the communion that has been achieved. It shares the joys of others easily, and it "bears all things" without insisting on having the last say in an argument. Others do not have to be perfect to be loved. It can trust enough to allow the other to live freely. It keeps hope alive so as to keep despair away. Americans might be surprised to learn that the largest quotation in the document comes from Martin Luther King, Jr., who urges his followers to love enemies enough not to defeat them, but to defeat only the evil systems in which they have become entangled (AL 118).

One should give special attention to the pope's elaboration of conjugal love where he asserts again that "[m]arriage joins to all this an indissoluble exclusivity expressed in the stable commitment to share and shape together the whole of life. . . . Lovers do not see their relationship as merely temporary. . . . Children not only want their parents to love one another, but also to be faithful and remain together" (AL 123). Every day many couples witness to the fact that indissolubility is not simply an "ideal." If it is, very many couples in fact achieve that ideal. Any healthy couple that embarks on marriage expects the marriage to be indissoluble. In fact, if they did not commit themselves to an indissoluble bond, they would not have a valid marriage. It's part of the package and very much expected.[4] Here the pope reaffirms the natural inclinations that reside in the hearts of all family members. No wonder that he quotes Malachi 2:16: "For I hate divorce, says the Lord." Although such love can be called "natural," it does require cultivation and effort (AL 126).

Again drawing from insights on the theology of the body, Francis refers to the gaze of lovers who "contemplate other persons as ends in themselves" (AL 127).[5] While he advises young couples to avoid marrying hastily, he nonetheless encourages them, when the right time comes, to take the risk, though it involves a "bold gamble" (AL 132). It's an adventure of love. The pope sees marital love as growing under grace with the cooperation of the couple. Indissolubility should not be understood merely as a duty, but should be seen as a

4. Although individual marriage partners should expect their marriage to be indissoluble (and not merely as an ideal), the chances that all the marriages in an entire community will remain indissoluble does smack of the ideal. Has such a community ever existed?

5. See also here John Paul II, *Man and Woman He Created Them*, sections 39–41.

positive quality that deepens day after day as the couple's spousal love
continuously comes to expression. Once again, the pope warns of the
romantic consumerist propaganda that presents married life as easy as
a dream, without sickness, sorrow, hardship, or distress (AL 135). He
also acknowledges the importance of dialogue and the world of emo-
tions, especially when there are hurt feelings (AL 136–146). He treats
the erotic dimension of love as well as temptations to manipulate and
enter violent confrontation (AL 150–157), once again echoing John
Paul II's theology of the body.[6]

In chapter 5, "Love Made Fruitful," the pope traces the development
of the family. Pregnancy presents itself as a "difficult but wonderful
time" (AL 168). Parents must accept what God brings as a gift, even if
the child is different from what was expected or hoped for (AL 170).
He highlights the importance of the love of both the mother and father
together (AL 172–177). The family unit should not set itself apart from
society but should actively go forth to engage the world (AL 182–184).
By that activity, each family can evangelize in its own way.

The pope offers a well-informed reflection on 1 Corinthians 11:17-34,
where St. Paul criticized certain segments of the Christian community as
receiving the Eucharist unworthily because of the way they maltreated
people of lower social classes at eucharistic meals. They created "scandalous distinctions and divisions among its members" (AL 186). This
section of AL will probably challenge many readers. The pope's interpretation of this passage relies on an older understanding, which brings
to light Paul's original intent. It will be treated more fully in chapter 7
below, which takes up the question of who can and cannot receive the
Eucharist and why.

Francis continues by taking up the issue of life in the wider family
(AL 187–198). He encourages the honoring of parents and the elderly
(AL 190–191) and addresses relations between brothers and sisters
where children can learn behaviors that will serve them well in society
(AL 194). The larger family ought to respond with love and support
when family members experience distress such as that which arises
with teenage motherhood, sudden disabilities, addictions, and wid-
owhood (AL 197). Children can only be edified in witnessing the love

6. John Paul II, *Man and Woman He Created Them*, sections 46, 47:3; 60:5, 128.

that responds to those who have made a shipwreck of their lives. The extended family offers support whenever other family members encounter financial or medical distress or other type of emergency. Every marriage encounters a rocky patch from time to time. Couples often take advantage of the grace of God that enables them to grow through those difficulties. The church rejoices as it sees those marriages reach more and more profound depths. The church under Francis continues to admire and support those marriages that face devastating illnesses, poverty, and persecution. Those couples truly understand the commitment that comes with marital vows.

In chapter 6, "Some Pastoral Perspectives," Francis exhorts ministers to show more than a merely generic concern for family life. In their pastoral planning, they must concentrate not only on the rules but also on the values that the rules try to protect (AL 200–201). Marriage preparation must receive renewed attention to ensure that couples receive the support they need (AL 207–211). With preparation undertaken in the proper spirit, they can enter into the sacrament with adequate grounding in faith and a sober realization of the graces couples need for marital success (AL 212–216). The pope encourages ministers to arrange for the accompaniment of young couples throughout the early years of marriage so they can avoid being overwhelmed by unexpected aspects of their new commitment, which ought to include an understanding of what responsible parenthood requires of them (AL 217–230). He offers numerous insights and suggestions concerning the encouragement couples need to sustain their commitment through high points and low (AL 231–258). Among the low points, Francis acknowledges that marital breakdowns can result in abuse, violence, humiliation, exploitation, disregard, and indifference. Vulnerable spouses and children, at times, must separate as a last resort (AL 241). Ministers should support efforts at forgiveness and reconciliation, especially through the Eucharist, but also understand the dire circumstances that can become dangerous for certain family members (AL 242).

Those who have divorced and "entered a new union should be made to feel part of the Church. 'They are not excommunicated' and should not be treated as such, since they remain part of the ecclesial community" (AL 243). Sometimes Catholics mistakenly assume that divorced and civilly remarried couples are automatically expelled from the church. They are not. The list of offenses leading to excommunication does not include divorce and civil remarriage.[7] Care of these people should not be viewed as a weakening of the church's teaching on indissolubility, but as "a particular expression of its charity" (AL 243). In this regard, the synod fathers called special attention to the good of the children, who suffer profoundly from divorce (AL 245). Children should not be used as pawns by parents who can harbor bitterness against their spouses and may feel the temptation to use their children to hurt the other divorced parent (AL 246). Significantly, the pope asks whether people are "becoming numb to the hurt in children's souls" (AL 246). He expresses much concern for the most vulnerable in families: the children. Such concern has not always made such a significant appearance in prior papal documents. The Christian community must "not abandon divorced parents who have entered a new union, but should include and support them in their efforts to bring up their children" (AL 246). This approach relies on the recommendation of the bishops of the synod, and its implications will receive more detailed treatment in chapter 8.

In chapter 7, "Towards a Better Education of Children," the document addresses the formation of children in the family. The pope urges parents to devote time to speaking of important matters to their children and to consider monitoring and limiting their use of television and other electronic devices (AL 260). In undertaking the moral formation of their children, parents need to guide their children in their discernment of desires and values, and in their growing capacity to judge what is right (AL 264–265). Parents must not shy away from correcting and disciplining their children, but never in anger or as if the child were the enemy (AL 268–269). Parents need to apply "patient realism" in nurturing their young through various stages of their growth (AL 271–273). The family can offer a healthy setting in which deferred gratification and self-mastery aid children in developing a Christian sense of hope (AL 275). The family also presents a practical education in how to live with others (AL 276–279). The pope offers guidance in the sensitive area of sex education, which needs to inculcate not only knowledge of facts but also a sensitivity that expresses itself in modesty and ap-

---

7. Canon law reserves excommunication for very particular crimes, including abortion, apostasy, heresy, and breaking the seal of the confessional. See canons 1364–1369, 1398, and 1388.

preciation of differences of others (AL 280–286). Finally he addresses the need to nurture the faith in the children from their earliest years. He admires "mothers who teach their little children to blow a kiss to Jesus or to Our Lady. How much love there is in that!" (AL 287).

The pope devotes chapter 9 to "The Spirituality of Marriage and the Family." Family members should recall that, "The Lord's presence dwells in real and concrete families, with all their daily troubles and struggles, joys and hopes" (AL 315). In fact, their love consists of the "thousands of small but real gestures" (AL 315) that daily make up the communications among family members. A mature spirituality comes to fruition when the couple accepts the normal disillusionment that their spouse loves imperfectly but really (AL 320). The family needs to foster tenderness and mercy as imperfections arise, using Christ as the model (AL 322–333). The apostolic exhortation comes to a fitting close with a prayer to the Holy Family.

By the end of the document, the reader will notice how much it relies on insight into concrete experience and not simply on abstractions. This fidelity to the concrete facts of marriage and family life accounts for the power of its insights. The payoff will become particularly evident in chapter 8.

2. The Controversial Chapter 8, "Accompanying, Discerning and Integrating Weakness"

Pope Francis declares that "everyone should feel challenged by Chapter Eight" (AL 7), and that presumably includes the pope himself. Those who struggle to understand chapter 8 should feel consoled that even the pope feels some discomfort. Indeed, no one should take its guidance glibly. In that chapter, the pope and synod fathers take on the difficult topic of failed and irregular marriages. Some commentators have not understood the context of this chapter and express their frustration with the supposed lack of clarity in the text. Others have simply ignored it.

Throughout chapter 8, the pope does not refer to every divorced and remarried couple but only those who have encountered dilemmas. Some unfortunate couples have become involved in situations from which they have no morally pure way out. They have become trapped in their circumstances, which offer them only evil alternatives. Let's first take a look at what the text says and then consider some of its implications.

A. The Text

The pope begins the chapter with the frank recognition that many in the church experience weakness and participate in the life of the church in an incomplete manner. These people can still perform good and loving acts of kindness. The church must accompany the weak and wounded, and help them to a fuller response to the call of God in their lives. It must act as a field hospital that treats all manner of wartime wounds in the most difficult of circumstances (AL 291).

The pope then gives a definition of Christian marriage, which "reflects the union between Christ and his Church," and "is fully realized" in the free and loving union of spouses who have given themselves to each other faithfully and exclusively until death, being open to children, and consecrated by the sacrament that gives them the grace to become a domestic church and "a leaven of new life for society" (AL 292). While few achieve the full ideal of marriage, many couples realize it in at least partial and analogous ways. Sadly others form unions that flatly contradict such an understanding. They endure painful divorces and hopefully avail themselves of the annulment process where healing can begin.

The pope then enters a discussion of "Gradualness in Pastoral Care," in which he notes that many couples have opted today to marry civilly or simply to cohabit. How should ministers best approach such couples? Pope Francis follows St. John Paul II's advice that the church's ministers need to bring broken people along the path to holiness gradually, not all at once.[8] The minister meets them where they are and assists them in taking the next step along the way. The church can and should accompany those unions that have demonstrated stability, deep affection, responsibility for children and an ability to overcome trials, so they might eventually celebrate the sacrament of matrimony (AL 293). Obviously, pastoral care for such couples must proceed carefully and with sensitivity. Emphasis on the positive qualities that evangelization brings will persuade more readily than a negative judgment about their current status. Respect for the signs of love in their union can help pave the way for the celebration of the sacrament so as to transform their union into the full reality of marriage (AL 294).

---

8. See Pope John Paul II, *Familiaris Consortio* 9.

Ministers ought to approach such situations with the "law of gradualness" (AL 295) that respects a person's stages of growth in the moral life. This law of gradualness does not attempt to declare that those in irregular unions somehow fulfill the law. They do not. The principle of pastoral gradualism does not imply that one should pare back the law to make it fit the temperament and capabilities of weak people. It merely recognizes that people do not grow up overnight. They gradually increase in understanding, appreciation, and strength. Eventually they may acquire the wherewithal to leave a sinful situation and to advance in the acceptance of God's love—in this case, as offered in marriage (AL 295). So far, so good. Few ought to have any difficulties in following the pope's directives thus far.

Francis next considers "The Discernment of 'Irregular' Situations," which begins to challenge some readers. The pope refers to two ways of reacting to irregular situations in marriage: "casting off and reinstating." The church's way has always been "the way of mercy and reinstatement" (AL 296). The pope cautions against any judgments that fail to take into account the complexity of various situations and how people can experience the profound distress that has occurred in their lives. The logic of the Gospel opens doors to salvation; it does not declare one's situation as hopeless (AL 297). Significantly, the pope clarifies, "Naturally, if someone flaunts an objective sin as if it were part of the Christian ideal, or wants to impose something other than what the Church teaches, he or she can in no way presume to teach or preach to others; this is a case of something which separates from the community (cf. Mt. 18:17)." Care for an irregular couple does not attempt to ignore the sin in their lives, rather it shows the couple the way to life in Christ. The church has the responsibility of teaching the faith to irregular couples and of assisting them "so they can reach the fullness of God's plan for them" (AL 297).

The pope offers a couple of examples of the great variety of situations that can face those in irregular unions. One situation is "a second union consolidated over time, with new children, proven fidelity, generous self giving, Christian commitment, a consciousness of its irregularity and of the great difficulty of going back without feeling in conscience that one would fall into new sins" (AL 298).

A man and a woman in an irregular situation at times cannot separate for serious reasons, such as the harm it would inflict on the upbringing of the children. Some have made every effort to save their marriage, but have been unjustly abandoned. Others have entered a second union precisely for the sake of the children's upbringing. Still others may be convinced that their previous union was invalid. Annulment applications may have been denied for lack of evidence. Nevertheless, the previous marriage may really be null. Those people face dilemmas that admit of no adequate solution. Whatever they do is wrong.

The pope notes that such situations are far different from a recent divorce or cases where a spouse "has consistently failed in his obligations to the family" (AL 298). Quoting the synod fathers twice and then Pope Benedict XVI, Pope Francis writes that "the discernment of pastors must always take place 'by adequately distinguishing,' with an approach which 'carefully discerns situations.' We know that no 'easy recipes' exist" (AL 298). Each case must be considered in view of each person's situation and stage of moral growth, their natural strengths and weaknesses at this complex and challenging stage in their lives. Regarding the so-called "brother-sister" relationship that is possible in these difficult situations, the pope shows his awareness of how imperfectly this solution addresses the difficulties of some of those in irregular unions. In footnote 329, he observes, "In such situations, many people . . . point out that if certain expressions of intimacy are lacking, 'it often happens that faithfulness is endangered and the good of the children suffers'" (AL 298). Here he is citing no less an authority than Vatican II.[9] In other words, artificial fixes cannot replace authentic family life. They can accomplish only so much. Chapters 3 and 4 below will address those concerns.

The synod fathers urge pastors to integrate the divorced and civilly remarried more fully into parish life while avoiding scandal (AL 299). The pope agrees that the logic of integration ought to take hold so that such couples may not feel excommunicated but as part of the church. What does this mean for their liturgical participation? It "can be expressed in different ecclesial services, which necessarily requires discerning which of the various forms of exclusion currently practiced in the liturgical, pastoral, educational and institutional framework can

---

9. The quotation is from Vatican II's Pastoral Constitution on the Church in the Modern World *Gaudium et Spes* 51.

be surmounted" (AL 299). It is important that those in irregular marriages understand themselves to be "living members [of the Church], able to live and grow in the Church and experience her as a mother who welcomes them always, who takes care of them with affection and encourages them along the path of life and the Gospel" (AL 299).

At this point, many readers long for a set of specific rules, as if all cases could be boiled down to discrete elements while ignoring many of the concrete dynamics that make each case difficult but also human. Priests need to accompany the divorced and remarried in ways that understand the predicaments they can encounter (AL 300). The pope provides a list of questions to guide an examination of conscience to ascertain the level of fault for a given party and to determine the shape that conversion might take in that particular person's life. The purpose is to present a process that "guides the faithful to an awareness of their situation before God" (AL 300). They need to form a "correct judgment on what hinders the possibility of a fuller participation in the life of the Church and on what steps can foster it and make it grow" (AL 300). Obviously, this discernment must include the "Gospel demands of truth and charity, as proposed by the Church" (AL 300). The objective of the search is "God's will and a desire to make a more perfect response to it" (AL 300).

Priests who are approached by couples experiencing such issues should encourage such couples to meet with them as often as necessary to accompany them in their discernment of various issues. Priests can guide couples in envisioning the course that conversion can take in their lives. Many questions deserve consideration. Have they considered annulments? Has the irregular marriage worked to the advantage of the children? How so? Is the marriage a matter widely known in the parish? Is scandal a concern? How would they describe their relationship with God? Does the conscience of each one seem unsettled? Will they each approach the sacrament of reconciliation?[10]

The pope then considers "Mitigating Factors in Pastoral Discernment." This very important section elaborates the church's stance that allows for a much more compassionate response than simply noting that someone is in an irregular situation and must be held at arm's

10. See James Bretzke, *A Morally Complex World: Engaging Contemporary Moral Theology* (Collegeville, MN: Liturgical Press, 2004), 187–90, for further guidance.

length, as if they automatically were in the state of mortal sin. Subjective guilt is much more subtle than such judgments allow. A person may know the rule but have great difficulty in appreciating its inherent values. Moreover, a person may be in a "concrete situation, which does not allow him or her to act differently and decide otherwise without further sin" (AL 301). In other words, some people become locked in dilemmas which offer no way out that is both virtuous and practicable. They face a situation in which they must choose the lesser of two evils, there being no viable third alternative.[11]

The pope refers to the *Catechism of the Catholic Church*, which mentions factors that can diminish or nullify imputability or responsibility for an action. Among those factors are "ignorance, inadvertence, duress, fear, habit, inordinate attachments, and other psychological or social factors."[12] Other considerations such as "affective immaturity, force of acquired habit, conditions of anxiety or other psychological or social factors" can also "lessen or even extenuate moral culpability."[13] Many synod fathers affirmed together with the pope, "Therefore, while upholding a general rule, it is necessary to recognize that responsibility with respect to certain actions or decisions is not the same in all cases" (AL 302).[14]

This means that pastoral ministers must pay close attention to the conscience of a person caught in irregular circumstances (AL 303). Obviously ministers will need to encourage the fuller enlightenment of the conscience, but not in a heavy-handed way that takes responsibility away from the person. One's conscience, besides being able to recognize that one's life does not correspond to the expectations of the Gospel, "can also recognize with sincerity and honesty what for now is

---

11. Thomas Aquinas gave leeway to those who possess grace and charity, yet lack the ability to outwardly exercise a virtue because their situation is rendered so difficult. See *Summa Theologiae* I-II, q. 65, a. 3, ad. 2 and ad. 3 (hereafter, ST); and *De Malo*, q. 2, a. 2.

12. *Catechism of the Catholic Church*, 2nd ed. (New York: Doubleday, 1997), 1735 (hereafter cited as CCC).

13. CCC 2352.

14. Cardinal Walter Kasper expounds on these principles in *The Gospel of the Family* (New York: Paulist Press, 2014), 26–32, 44–46, and *Message of* Amoris Laetitia, 15–17, 39–45. Bishop Robert Barron also holds this view in *To Light a Fire on the Earth: Proclaiming the Gospel in a Secular Age* (New York: Image Books, 2017), 226–29.

the most generous response which can be given to God, and come to see with a certain moral security that it is what God himself is asking amid the concrete complexity of one's limits, while yet not fully the objective ideal" (AL 303).

In other words, God does not will only the intrinsically good; sometimes God wills the lesser of two evils when only evil alternatives exist. When good alternatives do not exist in a given situation, God wills the least evil alternative that does exist.[15] This involves what theologians call God's "consequent will," which refers to the divine will as it applies to the human situation marred by sin. Prior to sin, God's "antecedent will" dealt only with a good creation.[16] After sin, God deals with the imperfect and limiting situations that sin imposes. Given a situation in which someone has sinned and has created a dilemma from which there is no escape, God wills the lesser of the two evil alternatives. This "is what God himself is asking amid the concrete complexity of one's limits" (AL 303) even though one cannot characterize it as "good." Certainly God does not want the moral actor to take the most evil alternative!

As we will see below, Francis would not preclude some who are divorced and remarried from receiving sacramental penance and Eucharist.[17] Some authors question whether the pope actually permits sacramental sharing of this kind.[18] Other commentators conclude from the text of AL that he indeed envisions sacramental sharing as part of the pastoral care of some of the divorced and remarried.[19] Although

---

15. See Eleonore Stump, *Wandering in Darkness: Narrative and the Problem of Suffering* (Oxford: Clarendon Press, 2010), 428.

16. ST I, q. 19, a. 6, ad. 1.

17. This will be explained in chapter 7.

18. See, for example, José Granados, Stephan Kampowski, and Juan José Pérez-Soba, *Accompanying, Discerning, Integrating: A Handbook for the Pastoral Care of the Family According to* Amoris Laetitia (Steubenville, OH: Emmaus Road, 2017), xv, 76–78. They fail to take into consideration that the objective sin of an irregular couple may not be manifest, nor obstinate, nor might its contradiction to the unity implied in the Eucharist constitute a fatal defect, as will be demonstrated below in chapters 3, 4, and 7.

19. See Kasper, *Message of* Amoris Laetitia, 44–45; James Bacik, *Pope Francis and His Critics: Historical and Theological Perspectives* (New York: Paulist Press, 2020), 73ff.; and Stephen Walford, *Pope Francis, the Family and Divorce: In Defense of Truth and Mercy* (New York: Paulist Press, 2018), 61. The pope himself wrote an admiring preface to Walford's book. Finally, the statement of the Argentine bishops, explicitly approved by the pope, interprets AL in terms of sacramental sharing. See *Basic Criteria for*

the pope's position calls for discernment of the most careful kind, his stance on permitting Communion in appropriate cases seems clear.

Francis then offers a reflection on "Rules and Discernment." Understandably, people rely on laws and rules to guide their actions. Normally, the practice is sufficient to produce a good result, yet it would be reductive to consider only rules (AL 304). The pope again relies on St. Thomas Aquinas to guide the bishops to a more reliable sense in these complex matters of life. Aquinas states, "Although there is necessity in the general principles, the more we descend to matters of detail, the more frequently we encounter defects. . . . In matters of action, truth or practical rectitude is not the same for all, as to matters of detail, but only as to the general principles; and where there is the same rectitude in matters of detail, it is not equally known to all. . . . The principle will be found to fail, according as we descend further into detail."[20]

Francis calls for fraternal charity in dealing with those who have worked themselves into difficult situations (AL 306). He sees this more challenging position in pastoral ministry as upholding the command to deal mercifully with others. Almost all of the pope's critics fail to appreciate that in chapter 8, Francis treats marital dilemmas in which every realistic direction available to a person violates serious obligations of one sort or another.

This leads Francis to consider "The Logic of Pastoral Ministry." The fact that rules cannot respond to every situation does not imply that the rules have changed or that the church has altered its thinking on marriage. Dilemmas do not defeat the truth. They do not promote relativism or depart from the truth proclaimed in the Gospel (AL 307). Dilemmas indicate that mercy needs to preside over impossible situations that are not amenable to rulemaking. Pastoral ministers must accompany with care those whose lives lay in shambles and who struggle to understand God's will in the midst of chaos. The pope recognizes that growth comes progressively and that the Lord's mercy can spur the afflicted on to a more profound life in the faith (AL 308).

---

the Implementation of Chapter VIII of *Amoris Laetitia*, 6 and 7; available at http://www
.cyberteologia.it/2016/09/basic-criteria-for-the-implementation-of-chapter-viii-of
-amoris-laetitia/. The pope wrote a letter of approval to the Argentine bishops on
September 5, 2016.

20. ST, I-II, q. 94, a. 4. Quoted in AL 304.

At that point, Francis addresses "those who prefer a more rigorous pastoral care which leaves no room for confusion" (AL 308). Although the desire for constant clarity is understandable, the church needs to be "attentive to the goodness which the Holy Spirit sows in the midst of human weakness, a Mother who, while clearly expressing her objective teaching, 'always does what good she can, even if in the process, her shoes get soiled in the mud of the street'" (AL 308).

The pope wants ministers to avoid unduly harsh treatment of those who suffer and to apply mercy and tenderness to the profound hurt that has intruded into the lives of those in irregular marriages. Far from being a modern or liberal approach, his thinking conceives of law in terms that have existed since the days of the beginning of the Jewish Scriptures, as we will see in the next chapter. Pastoral care calls for a mature assessment of who Christians are called to be in the midst of the unpredictable turmoil that can arise in anyone's life (AL 310). Abstract principles can advance the matter only so far. When dealing with concrete issues, love responds to exigencies that abstractions are not equipped to handle.

While upholding the integrity of the church's moral teaching, "special care should always be shown to emphasize and encourage the highest and most central values of the Gospel, particularly the primacy of charity . . ." (AL 311). Legal rigorists endanger the Gospel by putting unrealistic conditions on mercy and by thereby diluting the message (AL 311). Francis urges the ministers of the church to "avoid a cold bureaucratic morality in dealing with more sensitive issues" (AL 311). Pastoral discernment needs to include merciful love, understanding, forgiveness, accompaniment, hope, and integration (AL 311).

B. Some Implications

Pope Francis has not changed the church's laws on divorce and remarriage, nor should he. Some Catholics have become concerned because, in their view, AL seems to alter the church's doctrine on the indissolubility of marriage. They fear that his apostolic exhortation departs from accepted teachings and pastoral practices, when, in fact, the pope's teachings and actions are in keeping with similar papal practices from long ago.

The merciful application of the law can appear to change the law. It does not. Francis certainly endorses the indissolubility of marriage

(AL 62, 77). No spouse or couple can simply declare an end to their marriage through civil divorce or any other non-ecclesiastical means. Marriage constitutes a lifelong commitment that needs to weather the storms that come its way.

The pope has chosen to affirm those faithful couples and their families, but at the same time to address the difficulties of those who have entered irregular second marriages through weakness and sin. Certainly distressed couples should explore the possibilities of a declaration of nullity of their marriage. If the attempted marriage was null from the beginning, no marital bond stands in the way of a second attempt at marriage. Although the annulment process can be arduous, it has healing dimensions. It can offer a definitive judgment that frees the parties to marry and to get on with life.

The question posed in chapter 8 concerns what can be done in the present circumstances to help couples trapped in irregular marriages, not whether their past actions were right. For those who cannot simply leave their present circumstances and reunite with their former spouses, the magisterium has recommended that they live in "brother-sister" relationships. Although this may serve many irregular couples best, it may require others to live in fruitless marriages that may frustrate either one or both of the parties. Furthermore, when a man and woman try to live such a truncated marriage, it inevitably has an adverse effect on their children, as Vatican II observed.[21]

Mercy is not an alternative to the law. It is a way of applying the law. Mercy attends to the concrete circumstances of a given case, and it assesses what love requires. Certainly love can require the literal application of the law, but a strict application can also produce a cruel, unnecessarily callous outcome. Laws can be applied mercifully or harshly. Pope Francis insists that the church betrays her mission if her ministers fail to apply laws with mercy. At times, such dedication to mercy makes it appear that he has given up on indissolubility. He has not.

Popular suspicion of AL has become overblown for a number of reasons, including misleading reporting of its contents, the misunderstanding of Scripture, and an ignorance of the history of past and present pastoral practices that involve mercy. Perhaps one overarching

21. See *Gaudium et Spes* 51.

critique would note that the opposition fights against a position that no one holds.[22] Few have appreciated the proper role of mercy. Even fewer have considered that chapter 8 involves dilemmas, not an attack on the doctrine of indissolubility.

With this brief overview of AL, the reader can approach the topics raised in chapter 8 in the greater context of marriage as the church and so many of its members view it: a great blessing and gift from God.

---

22. Chapter 5 will respond to the more serious objections.

CHAPTER TWO

The Rule of Law, Not the Law of Rules

A Gospel Perspective

Before delving directly into the topic of divorce and remarriage, it will help to gain a precise understanding of the rule of law. An awareness of the possibilities afforded by the rule of law will make it easier to appreciate how church leaders could take merciful approaches to those caught in the impossible circumstances that some distressed marriages present.

1. The Rule of Law versus the Law of Rules[1]

Oliver Wendell Holmes observed, "The life of the law has not been logic; it has been experience."[2] That pithy sentence in his 1881 classic, *The Common Law*, clarified the reasoning process employed by the

---

1. Moral theologians usually treat the topics covered in this chapter under the heading of *aequitas*, as it was found in Roman law, or its Greek equivalent, *epikeia*. The canonical usage of those terms differs somewhat in that *epikeia* refers to a private, merciful interpretation, and *aequitas* refers to a juridical authority's power to fill a *lacuna* in the law. I have chosen to develop the simpler language found in the civil courts of equity in the United States. It seems to me to offer a more intelligible entry into a discussion of the Torah and related topics.

2. Oliver Wendell Holmes, *The Common Law* (New York: Holmes Press, 2012), 1.

better judges in the legal world. They do not simply apply rules; rather, they see beyond the rules to discern the American character at its best, which the rules try to express in their own limited but essential way. This has its ecclesiastical equivalent, as we will see. But first it will be helpful to consider the insight of Holmes. He highlighted the difference between what I will call the "rule of law" as opposed to the "law of rules."

The rule of law envisions the relationships between people in a given society. Not just a set of rules, "the law embodies the story of a nation's development through many centuries."[3] In the United States, it describes the American character. Not merely a logically consistent code, the law gives authoritative expression to the experience and expectations of the people. Its nuances must be discerned through the wisdom bestowed by historical research, the distinctions observed in judicial precedent, and knowledge of the culture. When people follow the law, their brand of natural justice will rise among them.[4] Dante likened this natural sense of justice to the natural instincts that guide a bird to build its nest in one way and not another.[5] Just as each species builds its own nest in its own way, each nation produces its own version of the law in which its own notion of justice resides.

The law of rules, on the other hand, assumes that the constitution and its collection of statutes, ordinances, and regulations give full expression to the law. Sometimes rules capture an element of the law very well. At other times, a statute may be so badly drafted that it obfuscates the law it tries to express. Other statutes clearly state their objectives but may contain loopholes that can defeat the purpose of the law. People may also become so skillful at avoiding statutory requirements that they can profit handsomely in their dealings with the unwary. In those cases, upright citizens detect a lack of fairness, even though the rules have been followed to a tee. Therefore, Justice Holmes and others

3. Holmes, *Common Law*, 1.

4. Alasdair MacIntyre, *Whose Justice? Which Rationality?* (Notre Dame, IN: University of Notre Dame Press, 1988), 2, 7, chap. 2. See also Eric Voegelin, *The New Science of Politics* (Chicago: University of Chicago, 1952), 27, 46, 159, where he notes that societies have operative myths that provide the "self-evident" truths against which their constitutions make sense. Holmes's use of the term *law* functions in a fashion similar to Voegelin's term *myth*.

5. *Paradiso*, 18:111.

have concluded that there must be more to the law than rules. Justice must look beyond rules to achieve a fair result.

Despite Holmes's treatise, judges well into the twentieth century still struggled to incorporate properly his insight into their opinions. In 1927, a company sought to foreclose a mortgage that had become past due because of a simple clerical error. A check for $4,219.69 had been sent and cashed, but, due to a miscalculation, it was $401.87 short. When the secretary discovered her error, she immediately notified the mortgagee that the difference would be paid as soon as her boss, the president, who was the only one authorized to write checks, returned from his business trip in Europe. When he returned, she forgot to tell him about the shortage. After twenty days elapsed, the plaintiff filed for foreclosure. Her boss tendered the balance the same day. It was refused, and the matter went to court. In *Graf v. Hope Building Corp.*, Judge O'Brien, writing for the majority, had only to refer to the agreement and to the logic of the rules of contract law to reach his conclusion.[6] Nothing stood in the way of foreclosure. The secretary's mathematical error, her forgetfulness, and the president's immediate tender of the balance due could not override the rule, no matter how innocent or inconsequential the infraction.

Chief Judge Cardozo dissented. He understood the rules very well but thought that the law required a different result. The all-too-human error of the secretary and the immediate offer to pay the full balance owing should not trigger foreclosure. In Cardozo's opinion, the majority ruling simply did not describe how society operates in America. The law favors mercy to those who make an honest mistake in a situation like that. He wrote in his dissent, "In this case, the hardship is so flagrant, the misadventure so undoubted, the oppression so apparent" that the court should require the mortgagee to accept late payment in such circumstances.[7] Cardozo did not want to change the rules; he simply wanted to follow the law. Such judgments require skill to distinguish substantive harm from mere technicalities. St. Thomas More cautioned, "Laws must be applied not mechanically but prudently. . . . Laws, like medicines, can be applied well only by individuals who show

6. 254 N.Y. 1 (1930).
7. 254 N.Y. 14.

prudence, courage and temperance."[8] Good judgment includes the recognition of many subtle factors.[9]

According to the rules, O'Brien was right. According to the law, Cardozo was right.[10] Everyone has an interest in justice and fairness. Unfortunately, at times people equate that interest with an uncritical adherence to the rules.

2. Law as Alive in the Scriptures

The situation described in the civil courts above has its ecclesiastical equivalent. Both clergy and laity apply rules to religious controversies. But they can also confuse the rules with the law and at times mistakenly expect that their uncritical adherence to the rules will produce the graceful result promised by Christ himself.

John Meier notes the complexity of the law: "Coming as it did from Yahweh . . . and comprising as it did both narratives and commandments (but also with elements of prophecy and wisdom), this religious *tôrâ* can roughly be translated as 'divine revelation.'"[11] The Torah needed to be discerned, not simply read as if it were only a set of Rules. Indeed, he notes how fluid the Pentateuch was in Jesus's day. Rewriting certain stories was possible.[12] Not only different interpretations existed, but

8. Thomas More, *The Yale Edition of the Complete Works of St. Thomas More*, vol. 12 (New Haven: Yale, 1976), 225. While a proper implementation of the Law allows for more humane decisions, at times it requires prodigious judicial talents. Some judges can rationalize, innocently or not, in such a way that their rendition of the law can produce decisions that fly in the face of the society's notion of common sense and decency. See the decisions allowing for abortion in *Roe v. Wade*, 410 U.S. 113 (1973); and for the compelled sterilization of women, an opinion in which Justice Holmes himself wrote, "Three generations of imbeciles is enough" (*Buck v. Bell*, 274 U.S. 200 [1927]).

9. Among other things, those factors include historical awareness, research into legal precedents, a knack for identifying relevant facts, appreciation of the richness of human relations as it is expressed in the society's foundational writings, an understanding of the wisdom of its recognized sages, and the benefit of mature experience in the American culture.

10. Although Judge O'Brien would claim that the rules did in fact embody American Law, Cardozo's dissent has been cited approvingly in no fewer than 179 cases. See, for example, *Gottlieb v. Gottlieb*, 25 N.Y.S.3d 90 (2016).

11. John Meier, *A Marginal Jew: Rethinking the Historical Jesus*, vol. 4: *Law and Love* (New Haven: Yale, 2009), 28–29, 30–32.

12. Meier, *A Marginal Jew*, vol. 4, 31.

Meier points out that "at times, knowledgeable 1ˢᵗ-century Jews would claim that the written Law of Moses contained important command-ments that . . . simply are not there in the text."[13] These possibilities cohere nicely if one supposes that the Torah referred not only to the written rules contained in the Pentateuch but also to an unwritten source, the Torah as God intends it and as Jesus understood it. Indeed, rabbinic Judaism eventually recognized that the full Torah existed only in heaven.

Paul respected the law, calling it "holy and just and good" (Rom 7:12), but he also knew the difference between the Torah and its writ-ing. He asserts that God "has made us competent to be ministers of a new covenant, not of letter but of spirit; for the letter kills but the Spirit gives life" (2 Cor 3:6). Indeed, Walter Kasper rightly insists that "the gospel does not mean a book, much less a codex."[14] James Dunn observes, "The point is that *gramma* [letter] is not simply a synonym for *nomos* [law]."[15] Jesus could see the distinction easily, and, after his conversion, so too could Paul.

According to Paul, at one point the law served the function of iden-tifying sin to the people so as to enable them to regulate their lives. However, this led the people to become fascinated with the rules and, therefore, with sin, and they sunk even lower.[16] Furthermore, some-times self-interest distorted their perspective. Many of the Jews in Jesus's day approached the law properly, carefully discerning its require-ments. Others unfortunately used the law to exploit their privileged status as the chosen people. The rule of law became for them the law of rules. They extracted these rules from their context, and manipulated them to prop up their exclusive, exalted status. Biblical theologian Olivier-Thomas Venard, OP, notes that a Christian who reads the Scrip-tures faithfully knows that the letter is "necessary but not sufficient."[17]

13. Meier, *A Marginal Jew*, vol. 4, 32.

14. Kasper, *The Message of* Amoris Laetitia: *Finding Common Ground* (New York: Paulist Press, 2019), 13.

15. Paul regards the Law as a positive force that Christ came to activate in us by purging it of sin so the law might be fulfilled in us. "For the law of the Spirit of life in Christ Jesus has set you free" (Rom 8:2). See James D. G. Dunn, *The Theology of Paul the Apostle* (Grand Rapids: Eerdmans, 1998), 149.

16. See Dunn, *Theology of Paul*, 143–50; and also Rom 2:28 and Gal 3:1-5, 14.

17. Olivier-Thomas Venard, *A Poetic Christ: Thomist Reflections on Scripture, Language and Reality* (New York: T & T Clark, 2019), 101.

The law was given to regulate life, not to increase sin (see Gal 3:21). Christ fulfills the law by infusing it with life, something the law could not do by itself. Indeed, the law of Christ is now written on the heart, as Jeremiah once promised (see Jer 31:33).[18]

Jesus brings the idea of the law to the forefront. He offers the commandments of the love of God and neighbor as a summary statement of the law (see Matt 22:37-40). Paul follows suit: "the one who loves another has fulfilled the law" (Rom 13:8).[19] As in the civil law, the way of the Torah is not always perfectly expressed in each particular rule. Christians need the guidance of Jesus to help them determine what to do on the practical level. Jesus understood the intended sense behind the law and did not hesitate to correct deficient notions as the need arose. "You have heard it said. . . . But I say to you. . ." (see Matt 5:21-48). How could he do this?

John presents Jesus as the incarnate Light of the World (John 1:9, 8:12). Light functioned as a symbol of the Torah in Jesus's day.[20] Jesus embodied the Torah. Francis J. Moloney, SDB, writes that "Jesus claims to be the perfection of the Law. . . . [He] personifies . . . the light of the Law. . . . What once the Law was to Israel, now Jesus is to the world."[21] In effect, Jesus *is* the Torah. He perfects it as it applies to everyone, Jew and Gentile alike.[22] Jesus, therefore, sees beyond the written Torah, right to the Father's will. He fulfills the law and even modifies it as needed.[23] Walter Kasper agrees that "the Word of God is not a kind of travel guide or concrete description of the way, but rather a light for the journey of life (Ps. 119:105)."[24]

---

18. See Dunn, *Theology of Paul*, section 6, esp. 130, 133, 135, 145, 149.

19. The complexity of the New Testament situation eventually results in Matthew's complaint that some Christians teach others that Torah observance makes no difference. Matthew's gospel insists that every letter of the Law retains its importance (see Matt 5:17-19).

20. See, for example, Wis 18:4; Ps 119:105; 84:11; 16:11; and Prov 6:23.

21. Francis J. Moloney, *Signs and Shadows: Reading John 5-12* (Minneapolis: Fortress Press, 1996), 94–95.

22. See Stanley Marrow, *The Gospel of John: A Reading* (New York: Paulist Press, 1995), 251; and Gerald Borchert, *John 12-21, The New American Commentary*, 25 B (Nashville: Broadman & Holman, 2002), 109.

23. See Jacob Neusner, *A Rabbi Talks with Jesus*, rev. ed. (Montreal: McGill-Queens University Press, 2000), especially chaps. 3–6.

24. Kasper, *Message of* Amoris Laetitia, 14.

Theologian Servais Pinckaers notes that Thomas Aquinas considered the law as "a work of wisdom, first engaging the intelligence, and only then the will."[25] While various types of laws are interrelated, the evangelical law represents "the most perfect possible participation in the eternal law that can be found on earth and the closest approximation to our final goal."[26] In other words, the law does not consist in mere precepts, ordinances, and obligations. It needs to be discerned, not simply read. It flows from revelation and penetrates the interior of the human person. Therefore, Pinckaers argues, the law becomes "the very source of the virtues."[27] The law "enlightens the reason as to the nature and character of things."[28] This gives rise to a morality of freedom, a virtue ethics, that integrates the challenge of the Sermon on the Mount into each person's striving for excellence. It indeed represents the rule of law and not the law of rules.

Believers fulfill the law by following Christ. On a practical level, that implies that leaders exhibit a healthy spirituality, intelligent Scriptural exegesis, and a mature theological analysis that takes into account the historical dimension of the church. All this needs to inform one's discernment of the law of the Lord.

Although people often wish Jesus would give more clear-cut rules, he does the opposite. He frequently puts his disciples in positions that require difficult judgments. Paul compares the law to a *pedagogue* (*paidagogos*; Gal 3:24), that is, in Paul's context, a slave who accompanied a child to make sure the child arrived at school, where the teacher would provide the child with its real education and formation. Those who stay only with the pedagogue have not yet found their master. At some point, they need to let go of the pedagogue to encounter their Lord.

It will help to recall how often Jesus's teaching seems foreign to the ways people typically think in twenty-first-century America. For example, one might expect to find ringing endorsements of justice and fairness from Jesus. Yet practically at every turn, Jesus does not side with the rules of justice in its modern American sense; rather, he

25. Servais Pinckaers, *The Sources of Christian Ethics*, trans. Sr. Mary Thomas Noble, OP (Washington, DC: The Catholic University of America Press, 1995), 181.

26. Pinckaers, *Sources of Christian Ethics*, 181. See Thomas Aquinas, ST I-II, q. 106, a. 4.

27. Pinckaers, *Sources of Christian Ethics*, 183.

28. Pinckaers, 420.

sides with mercy. Nor does he side with fairness; rather, he sides with generosity. It's worth taking a closer look at this surprising element of the Gospels.

3. The Advice of the Gospels

First, it should be noted that *justice* in the Gospels means something very different from the way Americans typically use the term today. *Justice* or *justification* refers to a work of God reconciling sinners to himself. It refers to the ability of a believer to walk uprightly with others before God. The gracious will of God produces justification that saves those lost in sin. Paul sees this work as achieved by Christ who reconciles all to the Father (see Eph 2:4-10).[29]

Although this time-honored use of the term *justice* has a long history, Jesus also speaks of justice in its American sense, that is, as ensuring that people receive their due.

A. Not "Justice" but Mercy

One group of sayings that confronts the American sensibilities on justice can be found at Matthew 7:1ff. and Luke 6:37ff. For example, in Luke 7:1 ("Do not judge, so that you may not be judged"), the act of judging itself comes under scrutiny. Luke 7:3 ("Why do you see the speck that is in your neighbor's eye, but do not notice the log in your own eye?") suggests that the only legitimate act of judgment is self-judgment. Rather than attempting to correct another, the Christian must clean his or her own soul first, a never-ending task.

Although people can hunger for justice to be done to and for others, the Gospels continue to question whether any human being is in a position to judge at all. Jesus compares the kingdom of God to a man who sowed seed in a field. During the night, an enemy came and planted weeds among the wheat. As the crops came up, the farmer and his slaves could not separate the weeds from the wheat. The farmer tells them to let both grow to term. Only at the end will they be judged—and then by the reapers at the end of time, not by the slaves who now stand ready to pull the weeds (Matt 13:24-30).

29. See Dunn, *Theology of Paul*, 337, 342–44.

When it comes to judgment, humility and mercy comingle as natural allies in the Scriptures. Indeed, most priests can share stories of those they judged to be a perfect couple during marriage preparation but who divorce rather quickly after the wedding. Likewise they can think of couples for whom they held no hope yet whose marriages endure.

The scribes and Pharisees put the issue of justice front and center as they drag the woman caught in adultery before Jesus (John 7:53–8:11). They cite the command of Moses to stone such a woman. Will Jesus authorize a "just" stoning? Famously, he scribbled on the sand, straightened up, and said to them, "Let anyone among you who is without sin be the first to throw a stone at her." Although the facts and the rules line up perfectly for a conviction, Jesus works cleverly with the law and implements it in a way that results in mercy. In that scene, the law achieves its intended effect.

What if a disciple sins? What should the other disciples do? Jesus answers that they must "rebuke the offender, and, if there is repentance, you must forgive" (Luke 17:3). Although Jesus allows for judgment here, he also calls for mercy, not punishment. Given his prior cautions, judgment can come only as a result of careful discernment under the law. Even if the offender repeats his offense "seven times a day" (Luke 3:4) and asks forgiveness, the disciple must forgive. Mercy never ends, regardless of what justice might otherwise require.

In Matthew 18:23-35, Jesus gives Peter incentive to forgive seventy-seven times. He does so simply by contrasting a life that has received mercy with a life that has not. In the parable, a king, out of the mercy of his heart, forgave his slave an enormous debt of ten thousand talents. Set free, that forgiven slave then encountered a fellow slave that owed him a mere hundred denarii. The debtor slave begged for mercy to no avail and was imprisoned until he could pay back the debt. The king became so enraged at the merciless conduct of the slave he had just forgiven that he gave him a taste of his own medicine and handed him over to the torturers until he paid his entire debt, an impossible task. In telling the parable, Jesus does not indicate that mercy comes to an end, but he rather puts on full display a world made completely unlivable by its unswerving dedication to rules. Once again, the Lord presents mercy as necessary. It produces a much more livable world than justice would allow.

Another pericope that touches on the superiority of mercy over justice comes at Matthew 5:38-42. Justice would seem to require punishment that equals the crime: "An eye for an eye and a tooth for a tooth." Jesus instructs his disciples to do the opposite: "Do not resist an evildoer." This counsel baffles those dedicated to justice. Jesus further instructs the disciples to be generous by going the extra mile and giving not only one's cloak, but one's coat as well. He sets aside the rules of justice and fairness, and commands mercy and generosity instead.

In the Sermon on the Mount, far from counseling that one may claim what is justly due, Jesus forbids even anger (Matt 5:21-22). Justice works in reverse to the American way. An American crying "Give me justice" wants restitution. The scales of justice must be balanced, as if vengeance could erase a felony. But for Jesus, reconciliation constitutes the primary task, *even for the victim* (Matt 5:22). There can be no thought of obtaining justice by sending the criminal to jail. Furthermore, if any disciples wrong another, they cannot offer their gifts at the temple. They must first be reconciled and only then offer their gifts. American courtroom "justice" takes a back seat to mercy.

Finally, Jesus has choice words for lawyers. He pronounces woes to those who attend to the finer points of tithing spices while neglecting "the weightier matters of the law: justice and mercy and faith" (Matt 23:23). The justice Jesus has in mind is the justice by which God justifies the sinner. This brand of justice removes the log from one's own eye. Because the members of his audience have failed to do so, Jesus calls them "blind guides" who manage to "strain out a gnat but swallow a camel!" (Matt 23:24). Once again, justice refuses to adjudicate the guilt of others. It rather tends to one's own shortcomings. Otherwise, woeful lawyers merely "load people with burdens hard to bear" while not lifting "a finger to ease them" (Luke 11:46).

These images capture nicely the pastoral concerns of Pope Francis with regard to applying mercy to couples in irregular situations. But is this fair to other couples?

B. Not "Fairness" but Generosity

Just as the Gospels advocate mercy while giving second-class status to American justice, so too they advocate generosity while making fairness a lesser concern.

Perhaps the clearest story in this regard is found at Matthew 20:1-16. One set of laborers, hired early in the morning, agreed to the usual daily wage. The master finds others at about nine a.m. and others at noon. He hires more at three p.m. and still more at five p.m. Yet at the end of the day, the manager pays everyone a full day's pay. Those who worked all day grumble that the others received exactly the same wage as they, even though they endured the burdens of the entire day. It's not fair! But the landowner insists on his right to be generous. Generosity trumps fairness.

The parable of the Prodigal Son (Luke 15:11-23) constitutes a story that is stunning in its lack of fairness. The younger son takes his inheritance ahead of time and squanders it on a life of gross self-absorption. The older son stays home with his father. The younger son finally returns home out of concern for his own self-preservation. The father adorns the younger son with fine clothes and a ring. To the delight of the father, the household rejoices with a lavish meal complete with music and dancing. The older son understandably cries the age-old complaint of one sibling against another: "No fair!" The father sympathizes with him and assures him of his love and possessions. Nevertheless, the father insists on generosity even if it is not fair.

Something similar could be said of the parable of the rich fool that Jesus told in response to the man who wanted the inheritance that should come to him. After all, what good is it to fill one's barns if one's life will be required of him that very night (Luke 12:20)? In the end, merely receiving one's due pales in comparison to the generosity of God. Fairness as a reliable standard fails again. The same with Jesus's encounter with the tax collector Zacchaeus (Luke 19:1-10). Jesus applauds the tax collector's admission of his lack of fairness, which motivates generosity, not merely a balancing of the scales.

* * *

Both mercy and generosity require discernment, not simply the application of rules. Mercy and generosity do not necessarily produce free passes and plentiful food at every turn. There is nothing automatic about them. One thinks of Paul's admonition that those who would not work should not eat (see 1 Thess 3:10; also 2 Cor 8:11-15) and the Lord's instructions on how to deal with a disciple who gives offense (Luke 17:3-4). Just as rules cannot give adequate expression to justice and fairness, so too the faithful should refrain from turning mercy and generosity into unbending rules. One must discern what mercy and generosity require in each circumstance. The faithful must carefully consider the matter in light of the entire Gospel. In other words, mercy and generosity do not come to adequate expression in abstract rules, but they become apparent only as part of the discernment of the law in concrete circumstances.[30]

So too, in a similar way, pastoral ministers must deal with those in irregular marital situations. The task requires sensitivity, imagination, and creativity. No formula reliably gives solutions to every conceivable case.

4. The Flexibility of Mercy and Generosity

Similar to American civil law and the Torah, the Gospel must be discerned, not simply read. Turning Gospel precepts into rules can flatten the law of love and deprive it of its texture. The merciful and generous treatment of couples in irregular marriages falls squarely within the intent of the Gospel.

Mature believers understand the necessity of rules, but they also appreciate the priority of mercy and generosity. The faithful must avoid making up unbending rules for the application of mercy and generosity (see AL 304). Discernment must guide one's search for the requirements of the Law of Love. Perhaps Jesus stressed mercy and generosity so frequently because he knew the human inclination perversely to find so much comfort in the rules that keep their property safe.

In situations of justice and fairness, believers come to understand that, to paraphrase Holmes, the life of the faith has not been logic, but the Christian experience of the divine mystery as the faithful en-

---

30. Thinkers too often mistakenly identify the manipulation of abstract terms with rationality itself, whereas the Christian strives to foster faithfulness to Christ who calls for attention to the concrete particularities involved in any potential act of mercy. Thus, St. John Henry Newman noted the harm caused by "excessive attachment to system" and the "love of order and regularity." He considered them forms of impatience, which impede philosophical investigation. Reason makes progress like a "clamberer up a steep cliff, who, by quick eye, prompt hand and firm foot, ascends how he knows not himself, by personal endowments and by practice, rather than by rule, leaving no track behind him, and unable to teach another" (*Fifteen Sermons Preached Before the University of Oxford Between A.D. 1826 and 1843* [Notre Dame, IN: University of Notre Dame Press, 1997], I:10 and XIII:7 [pp. 9 and 257]). See also Malcolm Bull, *On Mercy* (Princeton: Princeton University Press, 2019), 119.

counter God through Christ and in the Spirit. This means accepting the occasionally difficult responsibility to achieve a subtle and flexible understanding of the requirements of the law in the Spirit of Jesus Christ. Yes, this is sometimes challenging and even perplexing, but it is always a grace-filled exercise aimed at the closest one can come to the peace of Christ in one's circumstances.

Pope Francis employs the understanding of law in use ever since God first revealed the Torah. Law is something to be discerned in the context of mercy and love, not something to be applied in an ideologically rigid fashion. Laws and rules give us direction. They point the way. They do not fully embody the response that would be appropriate in every circumstance that life presents.

Revelation comes in a person, Jesus Christ, not in a book. It remains for Christians to discern the presence of Christ through the Holy Spirit and to react accordingly. Francis uses the law in such a way in chapter 8, where he considers the dilemmas that people can enter—sometimes through their own fault and sometimes through the fault of others. Rules alone do not suffice in such situations. They lack the required human discernment, the human touch. They lack faith.

In other words, a principle is one thing; its application is quite another. Principles do not apply themselves. It takes human judgment, prudence, and discernment to know which facts are relevant in what way and how a principle may apply in a given concrete circumstance. Nor can a correct concrete judgment be made into a rule. Much more is involved in making these complex judgments.

Pastors sometimes dream of simply applying a rule to a generic situation and being done with it. They might even feel virtuous for imagining themselves as promoting the true faith while holding someone else's feet to the fire. But the pope likens those dreams to using laws as if they were stones to throw at people (AL 305). Those actions actually betray the faith. Referencing a document prepared by the Vatican's International Theological Commission, Francis notes that natural law is not a pre-established "set of rules that impose themselves *a priori* on the moral subject; rather, it is a source of objective inspiration for the deeply personal process of making decisions."[31]

---

31. International Theological Commission, *In Search of a Universal Ethic: A New Look at Natural Law* (2009), 59, cited in AL 305.

Pastors who resist this sort of thinking wish that guidance of the faithful were a much simpler task than it is. Pastors must not retreat from duties that call for profundity; they are called to love their people enough to grapple with the real issues that life brings. Francis notes that a person may well be in an objective situation of sin, but still might "be living in God's grace." Such a person "can also grow in the life of grace and charity, while receiving the Church's help to this end" (AL 305). Here he reminds priests that the confessional is not to be turned into a torture chamber, nor the Eucharist into a prize for the perfect.[32]

5. Aquinas on Laws and Rules

Pope Francis cites Aquinas in his effort to escape an approach to morality based solely on rules (AL 304). Although his approach has drawn criticism (which will be addressed in chapter 6 below), Francis properly cites the Angelic Doctor for pastoral purposes. He hopes to dissuade those who might inappropriately use Aquinas's thought to criticize couples who have no morally pristine alternatives to pursue. The pope finds support in Aquinas's commentary on Psalm 42, where the saint distinguishes harsh judgments from merciful ones. Aquinas claims that harsh judgments focus on abstract notions of the human while mercy looks at the concrete condition of a specific person and wants to do that person justice.[33] Mercy achieves a higher form of justice, a more profound compliance with the law.

At one point in his *Summa Theologiae*, Aquinas considers "Whether the Natural Law Is the Same in All Men?"[34] He answers that, when dealing with speculative reason, we treat universal principles, which are the same for all people, but the moral actor also needs to attend to the practical reason, which deals with contingent matters, particular facts that vary from circumstance to circumstance. For example, a person ought to return property borrowed from its rightful owner. That general principle communicates something essential about everyone's moral rectitude. It applies to everyone universally. However, when the issue is whether a particular borrower needs to return an item to a

32. See AL 305n351.

33. Kasper, *Message of* Amoris Laetitia, 16.

34. ST I-II, q. 94, a. 4.

particular lender, the universal principle may well fail. Circumstances are not always the same. "[C]onsequently, although there is necessity in the general principles, the more we descend into matters of detail, the more frequently we encounter defects [in the general principles]." Aquinas borrows an example from Plato. Everyone understands that "goods entrusted to another should be restored to their owner. Now it is true for a majority of cases." But what if the rightful owner has become a traitor and intends to use the knife to fight against one's country? Must the knife still be returned? The general principle directing the person to return the knife has failed. "And this principle will be found to fail the more, according as we descend further into detail . . . because the greater the number of conditions added, the greater the number of ways in which the principle may fail . . ."[35]

Aquinas rejects any cookbook approach to the application of rules to complex circumstances. AL cites Thomas' observation that might be summed up in the common adage that principles are one thing while the application of those principles to concrete circumstances is quite another. AL notes that various factors might inhibit one's ability to follow a rule precisely. One might be in the state of grace even though external acts make it appear that one is in the state of mortal sin. This can be due to mitigating factors and situations. For example, aside from ignorance, a person may "have great difficulty in understanding '[a rule's] inherent values,' or be in a concrete situation which does not allow him or her to act differently and decide otherwise without further sin" (AL 301). AL then cites Aquinas to point out that even a saint may have the habits of all the virtues and yet experience great difficulty in bringing a particular virtue to action because of circumstances.[36] A person may have charity, which includes all the virtues, but may find it difficult to exercise a virtue (say, honesty) because of the circumstances. Aquinas states that just as a person who has acquired the habit of science (whereby science comes easily to the person) may find it difficult to understand scientific theories when he is sleepy; so, too, the exercise of a habit of moral virtue may be rendered difficult by an inhibiting circumstance. Thus a charitable person may feel sleepy and may not

35. See *Republic*, 331c. ST I-II, q. 94, a. 4.
36. ST I-II, q. 65, a. 3, ad. 2 and 3.

be quick-witted enough to avoid a lie. Those circumstances reduce the person's moral culpability.

What might constitute those inhibiting circumstances in irregular marriages? Such partners may find themselves in a dilemma. They may have been married for some time before they raise the issue of their invalid marriage in confession, only recently aware of the significance of what they have done. Their invalid marriage may have produced several children. Furthermore, the marriage may have withstood the test of time. It may have even flourished by its "proven fidelity, generous self-giving, and Christian commitment" (AL 298). They may feel that they cannot satisfy the obligation to separate without causing new damage, falling into new sins, such as the neglect of their children. In suing for divorce of the irregular marriage, one might also be acting unjustly to one's partner. Bonds have developed not only with the children but also between mother and father. Psychological, emotional, and financial dependencies may have developed that cannot be set aside easily. It may well be cruel to expect one to simply divorce and leave a family structure that has proven successful. We will have the opportunity to bring this into focus by considering real cases in chapter 4 below.

Pope Francis recognizes that any person's culpability for mortal sin may also be "diminished or even nullified by ignorance, inadvertence, duress, fear, habit, inordinate attachments, and other psychological or social factors" (AL 302, citing CCC 1735). Once again, outward appearances alone do not suffice to make a valid judgment on one's state of sin. Moreover, "affective immaturity, force of acquired habit, conditions of anxiety or other psychological or social factors" may also "lessen or extenuate moral culpability" (AL 302, citing CCC 2352). The pope and synod fathers have no intention of altering the general rule against divorce, but they realize "that responsibility with respect to certain actions or decisions is not the same in all cases" (AL 302).

Once again, a principle is one thing; its application is quite another. A person may live in a state of objective sin according to all outward appearances but may actually live in God's grace and receive the church's help to advance in that state of grace (AL 305). At this point, footnote 351 asserts that, in proper cases, this assistance includes the help of the sacraments, especially confession and Eucharist. Those in distress must desire to change the situation but lack the power to act on that desire. This involves a more informed interpretation of Scripture than has usually been the case when Catholics consider who may receive

Communion "worthily." The Scriptural justification for sharing the sacraments with properly disposed couples in irregular unions will be taken up in detail in chapter 7 below.

Those who consider this line of thinking to be an innovation have to contend with the fact that not only Thomistic scholars have cited these mitigating factors but also that the manualists taught the same thing. Moral acts never occur in a vacuum; only universal principles do. Circumstances always accompany real actions in the real world. The theological manuals of the 1930s through the mid-1960s typically included sections on the significance of circumstances. For example, the manual by Hieronymus Noldin, published in 1960, enumerated seven circumstances that may affect the moral quality of an act: who, what, by what aids, why, how, [and] when. The author has lifted these factors straight out of Thomas Aquinas's *Summa*.[37] The manuals taught that concrete circumstances can be determinative of the moral quality of the act, as did Thomas.[38] The more astute priests of those days understood the implications of such texts for irregular marriages and applied them as necessary when appropriate cases arose. They did not hesitate to apply the virtue of prudence, which Aquinas described as the virtue of discerning what is to be done in the particular concerns of life.[39]

The virtue of prudence takes into account the concrete circumstances and fashions a plan of action designed to produce concretely whatever good can be realized from a given situation. Prudence operates in a world of complex contingencies where things can go wrong. Prudence sees what is possible. It assesses a particular situation, decides on a course of action that may or may not work, and then takes the risk. A giant step removed from the logical assurances of abstract prin-

---

37. Hieronymus Noldin, *Summa Theologiae Moralis*, I: *De Principiis*, 33rd ed. (Innsbruck: Felizian Rauch, 1957), 73ff., citing ST, I-II, q. 7, a. 3.: *"quis, quid, ubi, quibus auxiliis, cur, quomodo, quando."*

38. Noldin, *Summa Theologiae Moralis*, I, 74: "Actus humanus *moralitatem accipit* etiam a circumstantiis, quae in concreto determinant: nam circumstantiae efficere possunt, tum ut actus sit vel non sit naturae rationali conveniens, tum ut magis vel minus conveniens sit" (emphasis in the original). "A human act receives its *moral quality* also from circumstances, which determine [morality] in the concrete: for circumstances are able to effect not only whether the act comports with natural reason or not, but also whether it agrees with natural reason more or less."

39. ST I-II, q. 57, a. 4, ad. 3.

ciples, prudence depends on knowledge gained by experience—what typically happens in the real world. Hence, prudence cannot be reduced to a principle. Jean-Pierre Torrell, OP, notes that prudence "closes the deliberative processes by daring to prescribe action in a specific situation, singular each time, that will never repeat itself as such."[40]

In a 2016 interview on AL, Cardinal Christoph Schönborn, the general editor of the *Catechism of the Catholic Church*, called attention to the fact that St. John Paul II wrote in his apostolic exhortation *Familiaris Consortio* (n. 79) that "pastors must know that, for the sake of truth, they are obliged to exercise careful discernment of situations." This discernment, the cardinal said, especially pertains to those who are "subjectively certain in their consciences that the first marriage, now irreparably destroyed, was never valid."[41] The cardinal further recalled a comment by Cardinal Ratzinger offered in response to a question posed to him by Schönborn in 1994 concerning internal forum solutions. The future Pope Benedict XVI said, "There is no general norm that can cover all particular cases. The general norm is very clear, and it is equally clear that it cannot cover all the cases exhaustively."[42] This is precisely the approach taken by AL.

Perhaps the only innovation by Pope Francis in this regard is that he chose to acknowledge those real possibilities for irregular marriage cases in the context of an apostolic exhortation. AL requires a sense for the proper functions and necessary limitations of rules. Francis simply discusses openly what more pastorally effective priests have been practicing for years without making a spectacle of themselves or their parishioners. Indeed, they knew intuitively how to apply the International Theological Commission's insight that "natural law . . . is a source of objective inspiration for the deeply personal process of making decisions."[43] The apostolic exhortation now gives those astute priests added confidence to continue their ministry of mercy.

40. Jean-Pierre Torrell, *St. Thomas Aquinas*, vol. 2: *Spiritual Master*, trans. Robert Royal (Washington, DC: The Catholic University of America Press, 2003), 270.

41. Antonio Spadaro, "The Demands of Love: A Conversation with Cardinal Schönborn," *America* (August 15–22, 2016): 25.

42. Spadaro, "The Demands of Love," 26.

43. International Theological Commission, *In Search of a Universal Ethic*, 59, cited in AL 305.

When Pope Francis deals with irregular marriages, he is aware that varying circumstances attend each couple. Not all couples face the same circumstances. Each case must be assessed taking into account the circumstances that may well alter one's conclusion if only general principles were applied. The dilemmas encountered by couples offer no easy, universal solutions.

Those who would apply the law to any situation need to enter into the type of discernment described in AL. They cannot presume that Christ's graceful response comes automatically, as if no human touch were required.

CHAPTER THREE
Mercy and Chapter 8

A lthough aware of abstract principles, mercy attends primarily to concrete circumstances. There is no law of mercy in the statutory sense of the term. No recipe exists for when and how it should be applied. Mercy subsists in a different realm. It pertains to concrete circumstances that need individual assessment. Mercy resists legal formulation. Nor is mercy an alternative to law. *Mercy is rather a way of applying rules and laws.* Jurisprudence that attends only to abstract principles or rules, therefore, can result in a mean-spirited application of the law.

In his novel *Crime and Punishment*, Fyodor Dostoevsky described the villain Raskolnikov as "young, abstract, and therefore cruel."[1] Those who do not sufficiently value experience grow too confident in abstract principles. They simply do not appreciate the concrete dilemmas that people can face. When this happens, the application of abstract principles regardless of circumstances tends to cruelty.[2] Mercy, on the other hand, listens for the voice of Jesus in the particular circumstances it faces.

Mercy is so central to the Gospel that St. Paul at times seems to doubt that law retained any relevance at all (see, e.g., Rom 10:4 and Gal 2:16). Francis understands that in certain circumstances people can paint themselves into a corner. The response that "sin has unfortunate consequences" pays too little attention to the power of mercy.

1. Fyodor Dostoevsky, *Crime and Punishment*, trans. Constance Garnett (New York: Modern Library, 1994), 374.

2. As Bernard Häring put it, "Mere legalism strengthens hard heartedness" (*No Way Out? Pastoral Care of the Divorced and Remarried* [Middlegreen: St. Paul Publications, 1990], 27).

Francis proposes that in appropriate cases, partners in a second marriage may enter a period of discernment, accompanied by an experienced priest, so they can reflect on relevant issues. After a suitable period of time, they may celebrate a sacramental confession in which they accept an appropriate penance and receive absolution. Communion may follow that discernment and penance (see AL 305). Such a case may involve, for example, a man who selfishly leaves his wife early in a valid marriage. He obtains a civil divorce and marries another. Years go by. Eventually, after the second marriage produces four children, the man comes to his senses about the first marriage. He admits his earlier, selfish ways and seeks pardon and forgiveness. What does conversion require of him? Is he supposed to leave his second wife and their children to return to his first wife? That may constitute a sinful refusal of his duties to the four children. What if his first wife will not have him back? What if she has remarried? Is there no way for the repentant husband to stay in the second "marriage" and still receive Communion? Time does not nullify the sin, but it can and does change what can be done about it. Chapter 7 below will treat this issue in some detail.

Understanding that such a man cannot simply divorce his present spouse and return to his original marriage, the traditional response to this unfortunate circumstance requires such a man and his second wife to live in a "brother-sister" relationship—denying to each other normal conjugal relations. Some circumstances may indeed call for such an arrangement. Some may not. Can nothing else be done?

1. The Unity of Mercy and Law

Is it possible to bring together the concerns of both mercy and law? Are the two necessarily at loggerheads with each other?

The problem may not be as difficult as it sounds. In the Christian dispensation, law and mercy belong together. One need only perceive the two correctly to discover their unity. Again, the Christian never needs to choose between mercy and the law. Rather mercy constitutes *a way of interpreting and applying the law*. One can enforce the law with mercy or with harshness. Mercy is the sensibility with which Christians interpret the sense of the law. Sometimes mercy will produce a hug and sometimes a kick in the pants. It depends on the circumstances.

Some people treat the pope's apostolic exhortation on marriage and the family as if he were trying to fashion a new doctrine. He is not. He is trying to elucidate the correct way of interpreting and applying the law, and *that* cannot itself become a rule. It is not as if the pope were making a new law, but refusing to say clearly what it is. The part of AL that looks like new doctrine is really the application of mercy, which cannot be "doctrinized."

The Gospel of Matthew consistently features Jesus as applying the law, but with nuance. Mercy informs his use of the law. Matthew guards against legalism and authoritarianism by insisting that the voice of Jesus be heard in the application of any law.[3] Matthew consistently reports Jesus mercifully relaxing the application of the law in appropriate circumstances. For example, he will not allow a strict observance of the Sabbath laws to prevent a simple act of mercy that dispels the hunger of his disciples (see Matt 12:1-12). Moreover, mercy sometimes demands more than the law. So Jesus will not allow the son to bypass his obligation to his parents by declaring certain property as dedicated to the Lord (Matt 15:3-6; Mark 7:11). *Mercy in both of these circumstances overrides the law without overturning it.* Pope Francis seeks to do the same in the context of the law regarding some second marriages.

Francis agrees with the prohibition against divorce, but thinks that mercy must be added to avoid one-sided misapplications of the law. The result looks confusing because opponents try to force the sensibility of mercy into a rule that seems incompatible with the rest of the rules. They assume that Francis is trying to formulate a new law or a new principle when in fact he is only trying to incorporate compassion into the application of the old rules. The pope's position should not be viewed as a softening of the law, as if permission for divorce were being granted. AL does not treat divorce as any more virtuous or permissible than present laws allow. It does not declare some divorces as "tragic but good" and others as evil. It acknowledges the mess caused by the sin and suggests that mercy to contrite parties might make reconciliation and Communion possible again. It tries to help couples pick up the pieces and resume the Christian journey. Divorce is not only tragic, it is wrong; and mercy shown to those guilty of divorce does not make it right.

3. Raymond E. Brown, *The Churches the Apostles Left Behind* (New York: Paulist Press, 1984), 136.

Sinners sometimes have no choice but to live with the consequences of their actions. Where it is within the power of those who care, relief ought to be given simply because Christians strive to imitate their merciful forgiving God. Both sacred tradition and Scripture appear to give the church such power, as we will see in chapter 5 below.

Both the sense of the law and the sensibility of Jesus must be preserved and unified. Jesus does not abrogate the law, but neither does he use it simply to condemn those who run afoul of its requirements. The church must hear the voice of Jesus within the application of its laws, as Matthew insists. It must strive for the unity of *Christ's* sense and sensibility so that both may not only avoid disagreement, but also support one another—with mercy informing the application of the law. Only then will marital realities come closer to reflecting the kingdom of God.

By the very nature of laws, even good and necessary rules simply cannot address adequately every situation that might arise in life. When rules falter, when they lead to untoward results, the church can and must apply mercy, even if mercy takes it beyond the letter of the law. Pope Francis has allowed for that possibility in his apostolic exhortation.

2. A Pagan Sensibility

Rigorists insist on a strict application of the law. They fail to mention the proper place of mercy in Christian life, and, at best, would reserve mercy only for the worthy poor and others who deserve it.

Such a position resonates with the values of pagan Greece and Rome. Pagan philosophers viewed mercy as a violation of justice. It ignored the rational observance of the golden mean by granting relief that was unearned. Rather than give in to leniency on the one side or to cruelty on the other, the moral person should seek the middle ground of justice. Mercy counted as so much nonsense, embraced only by the immature and fools.[4]

---

4. Edwin Judge, "The Quest for Mercy in Late Antiquity," in Peter T. O'Brien and David G. Peterson, eds., *God Who Is Rich in Mercy: Essays Presented to Dr. D. B. Knox* (Homebush West, Australia: Anzea Publishers, 1986), 107. See, for example, Plato, *Laws* 936c. At times compassion was viewed positively, but only for those who

When plagues struck throughout the empire in the fourth century, pagans ran out of town, abandoning even family members. Adherence to the golden mean saved the lives of those who fled. Mercy would only imperil their health. On the other hand, Christians, motivated by mercy, stayed and ministered to the sick whether they were family members or not.[5] To the irritation of Emperor Julian, Christians mercifully created "a miniature welfare state in an empire which for the most part lacked social services."[6] Indeed, the church counts among her martyrs those who died while ministering to people inflicted with the empire-wide plague that struck Alexandria in 261 AD.[7]

Even when pagans sought a greater place for mercy, it fell short of the Christian ideal. For example, the first-century Roman poet Statius favored "justice which mercy may accompany but never overturn."[8] The statement of Statius summarizes the sentiment of those who oppose Pope Francis. Reason alone was clearly in the driver's seat in the pagan world. For them, mercy could never overrule just laws. They would struggle with Jesus's preference for mercy over justice and with his preference for generosity over fairness.

In 1 Corinthians, Paul noted that some of his correspondents appear to be guided by a way of thinking based on their culture and not on the shocking novelty of the paschal mystery. Paul invokes the center of Christian faith, the cross, opposing it to a "human wisdom" (1 Cor 1:25). In Paul's view, such worldly wisdom denies the specifics of the Christian faith. It seems wise, but it amounts to folly as the cross is the true wisdom brought into the world by Christ (1 Cor 1:18, 21, 23). God's love for sinful humanity (see Rom 5:5-8), displayed in the cross of Christ, goes beyond human reason and, because of that, such human wisdom may be considered as nonsense (1 Cor 3:18-19; 1 Cor 2:14).

---

deserved it. In similar fashion, Malcolm Bull has noted that, to many of the thinkers of the Enlightenment, such as David Hume and the legal theorist Casare Beccaria, mercy appeared superfluous or even harmful. See Bull, *On Mercy*, 14.

5. Rodney Stark, *The Rise of Christianity: How the Obscure, Marginal Jesus Movement Became the Dominant Religious Force in the Western World in a Few Centuries* (Princeton: Princeton University, 1996), 83.

6. Paul Johnson, *A History of Christianity* (New York: Atheneum, 1976), 75.

7. Their collective memorial is celebrated on February 28.

8. Quoted in Bruce F. Harris, "The Idea of Mercy and Its Graeco-Roman Context," in O'Brien and Peterson, *God Who Is Rich in Mercy*, 102.

The context within which all Christian reasoning must be done is that of faith, centered on the cross as the manifestation of God's mercy.

In Galatians, Paul calls a group of his addressees "foolish" (Gal 3:1) because of their demand from Gentile converts of full obedience to the Jewish law, in particular, circumcision and the celebrations of the Jewish feasts. For Paul, their demand of full adherence to the law clashes with and empties the revelation of God's mercy in Christ. That is why in Galatians 2:4 he can refer to "the freedom we have in Christ Jesus," which enabled him to avoid imposing circumcision on Titus. *The law finds its fulfillment, that is, its goal and climax, in love* (Gal 5:14; Rom 13:9).

Ironically, some of today's Catholic critics adopt the pagan position that mercy is fulfilled in the law, whereas the church teaches the opposite: the law is fulfilled in mercy. Justice and rationality must be viewed in the greater context of faith and mercy, not the other way around.

3. The Pastoral Application of Mercy and the Law

Again, the choice is never between mercy and law. The choice is whether a law will be applied mercifully or harshly. Mercy does not present itself as an alternative to the law; rather mercy is the Christian way of applying the law and can even lead a person beyond the law. Some critics think that the mercy of the pope would overturn longstanding laws against polygamy and adultery, for example. Let's take this a step at a time.

A simple analogy might help. A while ago, I was stopped by a police officer for exceeding the speed limit by a good fifteen miles per hour. He informed me of the infraction and asked for my license. I explained that I did not see the speed limit sign. He asked, "How good is your driving record?" I responded, "Pretty good" (since I had not received a ticket in more than ten years). He returned to his squad car. When he came back, he handed my license to me, and said, "Please watch your speed." No ticket! Am I to conclude from this that the speed limit laws have been revoked? Quite the opposite. I am now much more aware of the allowable speed on any street I travel. Did the officer "apply the law"? Yes, he did. He stopped me, questioned me, and made me aware of my failure. Yet his application of the law did not require him to write a ticket. He applied the law with mercy. Not only does the law still stand; it is even more emphatic in my mind. The police officer did not apply mercy instead of the law. He applied the law mercifully.[9]

How can a Christian know when mercy will allow such an action? What rules govern mercy? Only love governs mercy, which also cannot be reduced to a rule. Mercy is acquired with faith. Its content is partially communicated by the law, partially by parables, and fully by Jesus. The merciful actions of the saints continue to teach disciples.[10] Believers develop a finer sense of mercy as they become more mature in the faith.[11]

An analogous application of the law should be possible in the marital arena—obviously making allowances for the differences in subject matter. Of course, marriage laws differ from the laws against speeding in many ways, but the principle stands that just because the rule was not applied to the letter does not mean that the law has been abrogated. Polygamy and adultery remain wrong. Mercy can act so as to take the situation out of the realm of the judgment of general laws. It can recognize special circumstances in which there is no need to write a ticket. Indeed, it might even create more harm than good.

When a couple in an irregular marriage comes to a priest for pastoral counseling, if mercy does not hold them to the letter of the law, it does not mean that the law has been revoked. It means that the merciful application of the law in their circumstances may not require them to break up the second marriage. What circumstances could possibly justify that? None whatsoever because the situation has gone beyond what

---

9. "In this way, mercy does not rescind the general law; rather, it is the higher realization of law, which sees that justice is done to the concrete, always unique person" (Walter Kasper, *The Message of* Amoris Laetitia: *Finding Common Ground* [New York: Paulist Press, 2019], 16).

10. See, for example, Mother Teresa, *A Simple Path*, Lucinda Vardey, ed. (New York: Ballantine Books, 1995), 122–24, where she described her ministry to the destitute on their deathbeds. She honored the burial rites of the faith of the decedent, and, if she did not know his or her faith, she buried them according to the Hindu rites, since most of those she accommodated were Hindi.

11. Once again, mercy shows itself as a "thick" concept that inevitably requires the Christian to grapple with "two features of the equitable: its attentiveness to particularity and its capacity for sympathetic understanding" (Martha C. Nussbaum, "Equity and Mercy," *Philosophy and Public Affairs* 22 [1993]: 105). As Walter Kasper notes, behind such a perspective "stands the change from an abstract anthropology, which speaks generally of the human being, to a concrete anthropology" (*Message of* Amoris Laetitia, 12).

justice can properly handle. *The claim is not that the irregular marriage is "justified" (a term that relies on legal jargon), but that the merciful application of the law can tolerate what the law does not permit. It can thereby ironically fulfill the law.* Mercy can achieve more than the law. Law is always shaped by mercy, not mercy by the law. Mercy can find a way forward when the law appears to offer only roadblocks.

The standard position of the church requires remarried couples to avoid sin by living in "brother-sister" relationships when a seriously unjust situation might otherwise result.[12] This remedy has been widely accepted by church leaders for a long time. Some people think that the "brother-sister" relationship avoids objective sin under the law. That opinion deserves a closer look.

4. The "Brother-Sister" Relationship

Many couples who have experienced marital dilemmas have had recourse to the solution known as the "brother-sister" relationship. The church recognizes that, for those couples, it is the closest they can come to fulfilling difficult obligations (such as the raising of children) while maintaining the semblance of propriety. It means that the invalidly married couple must live in continence and abstain from sexual intercourse with their partner.[13] They must maintain the "brother-sister" relationship for as long as the prior valid marriage bonds exist.

The arrangement proceeds with the good graces of the official church. Such couples often expend enormous effort to comply with those rules and rightfully can take full advantage of the sacraments of reconciliation and the Eucharist. Their invalid marriage is not thereby validated, nor is their living situation considered to be normal. Their marital status and living situation are not held against them.[14]

Any prior valid marriage remains in force in these circumstances. The church disregards the continuing infidelity against the original

---

12. John Paul II, *Familiaris Consortio* 84.

13. See Matthew Levering, *The Indissolubility of Marriage:* Amoris Laetitia *in Context* (San Francisco: Ignatius Press, 2019), 78.

14. Walter Kasper properly calls attention to the fact that the "brother-sister" relationship "is not a doctrine, and definitely not a dogma, but an ecclesial (!) discipline, which has been derived from the doctrine of the indissolubility of marriage" (*Message of* Amoris Laetitia, 49n12).

marriage because of the dire circumstances the new marriage has created. Of course, infidelity means more than simply a sexual union in violation of one's marital commitment. The *Catechism of the Catholic Church* notes, "Christ condemns even adultery of mere desire" (2380). When a husband flirts with someone else's wife, romantically caresses her, becomes "emotionally involved" with her, or dates her on the side, everyone would agree that those constitute acts of infidelity. They adulterate the marriage. No one would consider those acts to be chaste. Yet in the "brother-sister" relationship, might the "brother" become emotionally involved with the "sister"? Might they emotionally caress one another, and "date" each other? It would seem almost inevitable. In other words, the "brother-sister" relationship already adulterates a marriage in the day-to-day inclinations and bonds that naturally arise. After all, the Lord said, "Whoever divorces his wife and *marries* another commits adultery against her" (Mark 10:11, emphasis mine). The marriage itself, not merely sexual union within the marriage, constitutes adultery. Continence in a brother-sister relationship does not remedy that fundamental defect.

Consider this situation: What if a man were to separate from his wife and move in with another woman. They marry civilly and hold themselves out as husband and wife but do not have sexual relations. Certainly such an arrangement would constitute a colossal act of infidelity against the wife—indeed, it would form grave matter by anyone's standard. Yet that so-called "brother-sister" arrangement is allowed by the church where a second marriage cannot simply be broken up without causing serious harm. Catholics rightly seem unfazed by the arrangement in view of the fact that children need to be brought up in something resembling normal family life. Yet *this merciful answer to such a dilemma does not nullify the fact that a prior marital bond is violated in that relationship*, which continues even after the children have grown.[15]

The solution is imperfect at best. In the objective order, even the "brother-sister" relationship would constitute grave matter. Even in this seemingly pure subjective relationship, objective sin abounds. The partners falsely hold themselves out as a married couple in various social contexts. Even though they forego sexual intercourse, the living

15. See Ladislas Örsy, SJ, *Marriage in Canon Law: Texts and Comments, Reflections and Questions* (Wilmington: Michael Glazier, 1986), 288–94, for further reflections.

situation itself adulterates the original marriage bond. In holding themselves out as husband and wife and living in the same quarters, they also simulate a sacrament, violating canon 1379.[16] Moreover, people living in a "brother-sister" relationship constantly place themselves in the near occasion of the sin of non-marital intercourse. In the final analysis, try as they might, they simply are not brother and sister—especially when they look with parental concern upon their common offspring. When an irregular couple in a "brother-sister" relationship obeys the rules and refrains from sexual relations, St. John Paul II knows very well that he cannot call their relationship "chaste." When he writes, "they take on themselves the duty to live in complete continence," he refers to them as living in "abstinence from acts proper to married couples."[17] He does not mention chastity.

Those who claim that the church cannot allow an irregular marriage to remain as it is because of its objective sinfulness have not considered the "brother-sister" relationship itself as an arrangement that already adulterates the original marriage in the objective order. Nevertheless, the church's action constitutes a legitimate exercise of the power of the keys as given in Matthew 16:19 and 18:18-19, where Jesus gave Peter and the church the power to decide such individual cases. Generally Catholics easily accept that others may need to live in "brother-sister" relationships. They rightfully have a sense for its propriety. People who now live in "brother-sister" relationships legitimately take part in the full life of the church. No one would take that act of mercy away from them.

How can mercy permit a sinful action? The question is poorly phrased. One must acknowledge that the church has not *permitted* such actions, but it has *tolerated* them in appropriate cases for a long time. Even though the couple follows the lesser of two evils, it nonetheless remains evil, which ironically also constitutes God's will for that couple. Pastoral circumstances may require it, as we will see below.

---

16. Canon 1379 states that "a person who simulates the administration of a sacrament is to be punished with a just penalty" (John Beal, James Coriden, and Thomas Green, *New Commentary on the Code of Common Law* [New York: Paulist Press, 2000], 1587). All subsequent quotations of canon law are taken from this source. Marital partners administer the sacrament to each other. In the case of the "brother-sister" relationship, they only simulate such a sacramental relationship.

17. Pope John Paul II, *Familiaris Consortio* 84.

A better phrasing of the question would be whether the church has the power to manage marital dilemmas in a way that can reach for mercy beyond the law. It can, and it does.

Obviously, adultery, divorce, and the fornication involved in couples who live together without the benefit of marriage are all gravely sinful, and they remain so in Pope Francis's view. The focus of the pope's attention concerning difficult second marriages is conversion. What does conversion require in each circumstance? After remarried couples have expressed contrition, church leaders have a delicate pastoral situation on their hands. How best to allow life to go forward after people have worked themselves into impossible circumstances? Each dilemma needs to be assessed with love and understanding. That is mercy's task.

5. What Cases Are Affected?

Many critics seem to have only the most inappropriate cases in mind when they reject mercy as grounds for letting a couple remain in their irregular union. Comments that entertain the possibility of whether AL would condone unmarried couples sleeping together or whether marriage has any purpose anymore seriously distort AL. They constitute signs of impatience and arrogance in the consideration of these issues, and a lack of appreciation of the rule of law.

Many people who disagree with Francis seem to hold predominantly one scenario in mind: the man who has grown tired of his marriage and leaves his wife without much regard for the trail of heartache and tears he leaves behind. Freshly back from his second honeymoon, he expects an easy absolution along with his new "wife." But if no dilemma exists in his case, how could he be allowed to Communion? He may disagree with the church's teaching, but that will not suffice to gain him a place in the Communion line. Conversion requires him to put an end to his second marriage. Obviously the previous valid marriage bond must be honored, and the second invalid marriage must be declared null. This man needs a wake-up call, which in the long run would be the most merciful thing that could happen to him. The same goes for his second wife. Conversion in these circumstances will not permit even a "brother-sister" relationship.

Some couples live in invalid marriages and file for a declaration of nullity, but are denied because of insufficient evidence. What if the marriage has been abusive? Some couples enter matrimony in a strange way, producing not a true husband-wife relationship but something different—as when a woman wants to escape her father, but ends by marrying, against all her wishes, a man who relates to her as a father figure but not as a husband. What if only the spouses can testify about the ensuing difficulties, but they offer conflicting testimony? Outside witnesses may be few in number, and they may have died. If the petition for annulment is denied for lack of sufficient evidence, the marriage stands as a valid marriage on the books. In these circumstances, would the opponents of AL instruct the couple to live the rest of their lives as celibates? Or worse yet, would they encourage the couple to set aside their divorce and reunite because canon law has declined to judge their marriage as invalid? Is mercy powerless in such a case?

Or consider the case of a refugee who, in the process of flight from a country, becomes separated from her husband. She needs to support her children and herself. If she lacks adequate skills to become readily employed in a foreign land, she might enter a civil marriage. When she "remarries," she cannot certify that her first husband is dead. He may be dead, or in prison, or hopelessly trapped in a country from which he cannot escape. Is mercy powerless in this circumstance?

People can make a horrible mess of their lives and the lives of those around them. Unjust regimes can impose terrible conditions that give rise to decisions that people would never otherwise choose for themselves. When couples in irregular relationships want to reconcile with the church, it makes sense for the church to assess the particular situation to see what conversion demands. The pope has wisely refused to prejudge those sorts of cases.

6. The Language of Indissolubility

While Pope Francis fully supports the church's position on indissolubility, a review of the imprecise language of indissolubility should help to alleviate fears that Francis is treading on forbidden ground.

All Catholics know and admire the devotion of husbands and wives in successful marriages. This often inspires rhetorical loftiness at weddings, anniversaries, and funerals with the result that sometimes people grant marriage a life of its own. Sometimes spouses and their admiring friends romanticize marriage. They become so enthusiastic about a marriage that they feel it should survive the death of both spouses.

Jesus actually considered the possibility of whether marriages continue after death, and he rejected it. A group of Sadducees tried to illustrate the absurdity of the notion of resurrection by posing the problem of a woman who had married legitimately seven times. Each of her seven husbands died. At the resurrection, whose wife will she be? The Lord answers that in heaven people "neither marry nor are given in marriage, but are like angels" (Matt 22:30). The question of marriage simply no longer pertains to eternal life. The production of offspring has already occurred. People will at that point enjoy a radically different stage of life and have no need of any of the sacraments. Indeed, Walter Kasper calls attention to the fact that the term "indissolubility" comes from contract law, not from Christ. Hence, Pope Francis prefers to use the more Scripturally based term, *fidelity*.[18]

Even though marriage ceases to exist in heaven, many spouses rightly look forward to enjoying a new relationship with their earthly spouses after they have passed from this life. Any human bond of love and fidelity can last forever. There is no reason to suppose that the special relationship between a husband and wife will not endure in heaven, but it will not be a "marriage" as we know it. Their relationship will be transformed into something new. Although it will no longer be the sacrament of marriage, spouses can anticipate a happy reunion of some sort that the Lord will provide—although *the* happy indissoluble reunion is with the Lord himself in whom all will be united.

Certainly, then, marriage is not *absolutely* indissoluble. All marriages dissolve at the death of one or both spouses. In fact, it is more accurate to say that *every marriage is dissoluble*. Marriage has been recognized as the sacrament of Christ's union with his church. That union is unique. Earthly marriage is only a sign of that union. It only reflects the greater reality; it is not its equal.[19] Eventually the complete union between Christ and his church will take place. Only *that* union is absolutely indissoluble in the permanent sense. When earthly marriage attains the same status as Christ's union with his church, it illegitimately acquires properties that do not belong to it.

18. Kasper, *Message of* Amoris Laetitia, 27.

19. See Thomas Aquinas, *Summa Contra Gentiles*, bk. 3, ch. 123.6 and bk. 4, ch. 78, where Aquinas claims that marriage only *figuratively* represents the union of Christ and his church.

All marriages dissolve sooner or later. Modern Catholic theology holds that any marriage dissolves at the death of either spouse. People forget this unremarkable fact perhaps because they have heard the phrase "the absolute indissolubility of marriage" so often they figure it must adequately describe the teaching. It does not. The wording of canon 1141 contributes to the confusion. It declares, "A marriage that is ratum et consummatum can be dissolved by no human power and by no cause, except death." One should note that death is not an "exceptional" circumstance. It is an inevitable part of the very makeup of human marriage, part of the rule, not merely an accidental exception. What good is achieved by declaring that marriages are indissoluble except in every case? When an exception applies to every case, it is no longer an exception. It belongs to the very reality of the thing itself.

A more candid approach would admit that when the church uses the term "indissoluble," it really means that the parties to a marriage need the intervention of the church to obtain a dissolution prior to death.[20] Positively stated, it means that the spouses remain committed in marital love until death and thereby enrich themselves, their children, and their society with the graces that come from such a magnificent sign of Christ's love for his church.

The annulment process can produce ambiguous marital dilemmas of its own. Once a case is submitted, everyone understands that mistakes can be made, even after appellate review. The final decision is not infallible. The church may mistakenly declare a valid marriage to be invalid, allowing parties to enter second marriages, thereby violating an existentially valid marital bond. In those cases, the judicial declaration of nullity seemingly either dissolves an existing bond or tolerates a second marriage. It doesn't make any difference. Unless the case is reopened for reconsideration in view of new evidence, mercy solves the dilemma and overrides any concern over an ambiguous lingering bond.

7. Mercy and the Tolerance of Lesser Evils

In its mercy, the church allows for a lesser degree of certitude when dealing with the bond of matrimony. It tolerates dilemmas, ambigui-

20. See Beal, Coriden, and Green, *New Commentary*, 1362.

ties, and errors mercifully because it answers not to an impersonal law, but to a person, Jesus Christ, who expects disciples to extend mercy to people in difficult circumstances.[21] Only people can extend mercy; laws cannot.

St. Thomas Aquinas taught that mercy constitutes the primary quality of God, stemming directly from his love. "Now the work of divine justice always presupposes the work of mercy and is founded thereupon."[22] Mercy is more basic than justice and is not simply one of God's attributes among several others.[23] Elsewhere, Thomas wrote that "in any divine work, mercy stands above justice as the formal above the material; and this is what is said in Ps. 145: his mercies are above all his works."[24] Mercy comes from the very heart of God who is love. Mercy does not negate justice but fulfills it. This calls into question the inclination of some to place more confidence in law than in mercy.

The choice of a lesser evil presumes that no good alternative exists. In other words, the person is caught in a true dilemma. Sometimes one hears of a person who feels mildly proud that he has taken the "lesser evil," even though plenty of good alternatives exist. So a young man may go out on a date and feel good about having "protected sex" with his girlfriend. To him, it was a lesser evil than having sex without a prophylactic condom. That young man simply chose evil over good. The young man had plenty of good alternatives in spending time with his date. After seeing a decent movie, they might go out for dessert and conversation. They might get to know one another at a deeper level, exploring each other's spiritual values and the like.

---

21. See John 12:47; Luke 15:2-32; 10:25-37; Mark 6:34; etc.

22. ST I, q. 22, a. 4.

23. See Walter Kasper, *Mercy: The Essence of the Gospel and the Key to Christian Life* (New York: Paulist Press, 2014), 88.

24. "However, in any action, what exists on the side of the agent is formal, as it were; but what is on the part of the patient or receiver is like the matter. . . . [M]ercy in every divine work results from the side of God himself, . . . but justice from the side of the receiver, who receives according to his own proportion; and therefore in any divine work mercy stands above justice as the formal above the material. . . ." (Thomas Aquinas, *Commentary on the Sentences*, bk. IV, d. 46, q. 2, a. 2, ad. 3, trans. Beth Mortensen, Peter Kwasniewski, and Dylan Schrader [Green Bay: Aquinas Institute, 2018], 258).

In a true dilemma, one is caught in circumstances that admit of no good way out. If a woman's husband has divorced her and left her with three young children, she may indeed have the resources to pull herself together and raise the children on her own. These women often come from backgrounds where their parents raised them with care and attention. They may benefit from not only good college educations, but also professional degrees. Their upbringing in the faith may have instilled in them the fortitude to pick up the pieces and move forward. Their families may offer them continued support, not only morally but also financially. Such a person has a viable way forward. And she must take that challenging path. Such single mothers have the admiration of all who know them.

Not all divorced women have those resources. Some have not been raised in healthy families and did not have any good model to show them how to rally in such difficult circumstances. They lack adequate emotional resources and cannot cope with childrearing while working at some gainful employment. Some divorced fathers simply ignore alimony and child support payments. Although a divorced woman may want to both raise her children and provide for them financially, her education may not permit her anything but the most menial of jobs. Family and close relatives may live far away or simply not be interested in helping. They may have problems of their own. As her children begin to fall apart emotionally as their development falters, she may look for male companionship and support. If someone is willing to take on the role of husband and father, one can understand how a woman could entertain such a proposal.[25]

St. Paul VI succinctly noted in *Humanae Vitae* that, while it is never permissible to do an evil act so that good can come of it, "sometimes it is lawful to tolerate a lesser moral evil in order to avoid a greater evil or in order to promote a greater good."[26] Paul VI did not apply that

25. An example of a dilemma from another area might help. During the 2016 presidential election in the United States, both of the main candidates showed that they had serious faults that sent many voters looking for another alternative, but no other viable alternative existed. Many had to choose what they considered to be the lesser of two evils. Life indeed presents dilemmas.

26. Paul VI, encyclical letter, *Humanae Vitae* (July 25, 1968) 14. See also the analysis given in James Bretzke, *A Morally Complex World: Engaging Contemporary Moral Theology* (Collegeville, MN: Liturgical Press, 2004), 59–66.

principle to the use of artificial methods of birth control, since natural family planning is available in dire circumstances. He nonetheless acknowledges the legitimacy of the toleration of the lesser evil in other cases that do not admit of any clean resolution involving no evils. Hence, church leaders may well tolerate the evil of a second marriage to avoid the greater evil of child neglect. Whenever other good alternatives exist, couples in irregular situations must pursue them. However, it happens at times that no purely innocent alternatives present themselves, as chapter 4 will illustrate. Sometimes, one needs to take the least offensive alternative as the only reasonable thing one can do. Indeed, philosopher Eleonore Stump points out that God does not necessarily will only the intrinsically good. God can will the lesser evil as the best available option in given circumstances.[27] Indeed, Aquinas admits that circumstances might arise "when some evil is tolerated lest something worse happen."[28] Pope Francis thus counsels that parties to a broken marriage must discern God's will carefully as they attempt to respond to his will as best they can (AL 300).

Of course, this does not mean that whatever happens is God's will. Obviously God does not desire any dilemmas that require the selection of the lesser evil. At times circumstances dictate the tolerance of a lesser evil, such as can happen when the marital bond breaks down with unresolved responsibilities lurking on the horizon.

8. Marital Bonds

More analysis of the bonds established in fruitful marriages would help. Those bonds reflect the bond of Christ and his church. Just as the church is still on its way to becoming what it ought to be,[29] married

27. Eleonore Stump, *Wandering in Darkness: Narrative and the Problem of Suffering* (Oxford: Clarendon Press, 2010), 428: "But God does not will as intrinsically good everything he wills; what he wills in his consequent will, what is the best available in the circumstance, might be only the lesser of evils, not the intrinsically good." The consequent will of God refers to God's will exercised after the commission of sin. Aquinas says the same thing: "Therefore God knows all truth; but does not will all good, except in so far as He wills Himself, in Whom all good virtually exists" (ST I, q. 19, a. 7, ad. 3).

28. Thomas Aquinas, *Commentary on the Gospel of St. Matthew*, trans. Jeremy Holmes and Beth Mortensen (Lander, WY: Aquinas Institute, 2013), ch. 5, lect. 9 (p. 174).

29. Precisely in his discussion of Eucharist as Communion, Kevin Irwin writes, "The pilgrim church on earth is not the fully united and perfectly sinless bride of Christ.

couples are also on the way to becoming what they ought to be. As Aquinas contended, marriage only figuratively represents the union of Christ and his church.[30] It would be a mistake to consider the marital bond as if it possessed all the qualities of the bond between Christ and his church.

Nevertheless, sacramental marriages affect the church. When marriages flourish, the church flourishes. When marriages falter, the church falters. Its ministers need to come to the assistance of struggling husbands and wives and buoy them up. When that intervention fails, marriages can break down, sadly. When separations happen in contradiction to the Lord's mandate in Matthew 19:9, the church insists that such couples honor their commitments to the extent they can. Even when broken marriages strive to salvage those commitments in very imperfect and limited ways (such as the "brother-sister" relationship), this does not constitute a moment of rejoicing. Broken families cause sorrow, not joy. A church filled with broken families and unfulfilled commitments does not flourish. Already in such circumstances, the unity is broken and contradicted, yet the church finds a way forward and admits those spouses to penance and the Eucharist.

One cannot describe the truth of the "brother-sister" relationship as simply expressing the truth of the unity of Christ and his church—as if failed marriages were no different ontologically than joyful marriages. The church does the best it can in the circumstances. Partners to such a relationship, no longer capable of true chastity, settle for abstinence as the closest they can come to the ideal. Many couples comply and cope as best they can. Any couple that strives to avoid greater evils when only evil alternatives exist, any couple in a dilemma, should have access to the sacraments—as do those in "brother-sister" relationships, even though their objective living situations fall short of the ontological ideal.

Much has been made of the church needing to honor the truth of the marital bond. But the situation affecting only the husband and wife does not always adequately describe the truth of the ontological state of a marriage. The children of broken marriages suffer the most. As described in chapter 4 below, children face unspeakable turmoil at a

---

We are always on the way toward fulfillment and perfection" (*Models of the Eucharist* [New York: Paulist Press, 2005], 86).

30. *Summa Contra Gentiles*, bk. 3, ch. 123.6; bk. 4, ch. 78.

time when they are least equipped to handle it. Children also partake in the bond formed by the husband and wife, and their participation is not of their choosing. They were born into the bond. When their situation becomes intolerable, the church is not reduced to simply sitting on its hands and watching the tragedy unfold. Cold declarations of confidence in a couple's "real, essential, and intrinsic relationship with the mystery of the union of Christ with the Church" tend to fall flat.[31] Some thinkers obsess over the divorced who face dilemmas because they introduce a state of "objective contradiction . . . between their state of life and the Christ-Church union" even though the couple can do nothing about it.[32] The concerns of those thinkers come too late and consider too little. The observation comes too late because the separation of the spouses already contradicts the union; and it considers too little because the observation ignores the plight of the children. This truncated approach to the marital bond reflects an equally truncated approach to the Eucharist. The Eucharist does not simply constitute a prize for those fortunate couples who enjoy good marriages; it also forms food for the journey and nourishment for the weak.[33]

Fruitful marriages produce two fundamental types of bonds that find their roots in the unitive and procreative dimensions of marriage. The unitive dimension gives rise to the spousal bond between husband and wife; and the procreative dimension gives rise to the parental bond between parents and their children. Francis has noticed in discussions

31. The words come from a 1947 theological manual by Matthias J. Scheeben and are quoted in Carlo Cardinal Caffarra, "Sacramental Ontology and the Indissolubility of Marriage," in Robert Dodaro, *Remaining in the Truth of Christ: Marriage and Communion in the Catholic Church* (San Francisco: Ignatius Press, 2014), 173.

32. Caffarra, "Sacramental Ontology," 174. See also Camillo Cardinal Ruini, "The Gospel of the Family in the Secularized West," in Winfried Aymans, ed., *Eleven Cardinals Speak on Marriage and the Family: Essays from a Pastoral Viewpoint* (San Francisco: Ignatius Press, 2015), 85.

33. See chapter 7 below. Some propose ideas about the Eucharist as "a physical encounter with the Person of Jesus." See Paul Josef Cardinal Cordes, "'Without Rupture or Discontinuity,'" in Aymans, *Eleven Cardinals*, 32. Such notions tend to put the sacramental unity of a marriage on a physical plane as well, which discourages any consideration of what may be possible for a given couple. Physical notions of the Real Presence have long been avoided in church teaching. See Irwin, *Models of the Eucharist*, 248.

concerning irregular marriages that the truth of the spousal bond is only one value that needs attention. The care of children, an obligation stemming from the parental bond, needs much more consideration. In these circumstances, mercy makes its claim (See AL 80-85).

Children naturally depend on parents for nurture and formation, yet the broken spousal bond usually overshadows concern for the broken parental bond, reducing a mother's and father's abilities to care for their children effectively. Although people speak easily of the indissolubility of the spousal bond, few think of the indissolubility of the parental bond, which lasts for the entire life of the child and *never* dissolves. Although spouses can step away from each other in certain circumstances and petition the church to dissolve the spousal bond, they can never dissolve the parental bond.[34] They will always be the parents of their children, regardless of what anyone else says. Canon 1154, in fact, recognizes the needs of children whose parents have separated and calls for their adequate support and education, even though the delineation of those responsibilities remains with the civil courts.

Perhaps some clergy have been blinded to the potential dilemmas that can arise in a marriage because they have been trained to focus only on the spousal bond with its high claims to indissolubility without paying sufficient attention to the parental bond.[35] This second bond addresses the couple not simply as husband and wife, but as father and mother. AL calls attention to that relationship by which children depend on their parents for their growth, guidance, and support, both in their physical and spiritual formation. Although there was a time prior to their marriage when the spouses shared no bond at all, there never was a time when their children were not bonded with their parents. From their perspective, the parental relationship has a foundational quality for their whole lives. Home is wherever mother and father live. Marriage establishes not simply a spousal relationship but also a hearth, a center where the family gathers. This parental bond should receive due recognition as a phenomenon that reaches beyond

34. Examples of the termination of the spousal bond arise in the Pauline privilege as well as in a dissolution of a marriage in favor of the faith.

35. For example, after relating the story of a broken marriage involving four children, Paul Joseph Cardinal Cordes writes that "the marital bond concerns only three persons: . . . [the husband], his wife and God." See "Without Rupture or Discontinuity," in Aymans, *Eleven Cardinals*, 28.

the spousal relationship.[36] Francis calls adults to attend to the special vulnerability of young children (AL 246). Unfortunately, clergy do not always readily perceive the significance of the pain of children in broken families. Some have demanded adherence to the spousal bond without much regard for the significance of the parental bond.

This is not the first time well-meaning clergy have unintentionally failed to regard adequately the pain of children.[37] The sexual abuse crisis of 2002 produced much evidence of young lives that were devastated at the hands of unfaithful priests. Payment to victims to maintain their silence allowed bishops to address the situation as if it were only a clergy personnel problem. Relying on poor psychological advice, leaders did not fully acknowledge the tears left in the wake of interdiocesan transfers until victims began to break their silence.

Nor is the church the only institution to take the interests of children lightly. Family courts have largely ignored the interests of children as well, in spite of well-meaning protections. For example, visitation rights often ignore the needs of the children, but courts will approve them if both parents can reach an agreement.[38] The larger secular culture has also turned a deaf ear to children in broken families. Ingmar Bergman's six-hour drama *Scenes from a Marriage* features a couple in their second marriage. Although the self-absorbed couple spends much time and energy fretting over their own relationship, the impact on the children barely surfaces. The children are practically invisible

36. Of course, as children grow into adulthood, the character of the parental bond changes to the point where the adult children may well need to provide nourishment and security for their elderly parents. Indeed, though adult children may *leave* mother and father to cling to spouses in marriages of their own (see Gen 2:24 and Matt 19:5), they do not *abandon* their parents.

37. Only recently have theologians begun to develop the thought of Karl Rahner on the significance of children expressed in "Ideas for a Theology of Childhood," *Theological Investigations* 8 (New York: Herder & Herder, 1971), 33–50. See, for example, Kasper, *Message of* Amoris Laetitia, 37; Hans Zollner, "The Child at the Center: What Can Theology Say in the Face of the Scandals of Abuse?," *Theological Studies* 80, no. 3 (September 2019): esp. 694, and 703–4; and James Gerard McEvoy, "Towards a Theology of Childhood: Children's Agency and the Reign of God," *Theological Studies* 80, no. 3 (September 2019): 681.

38. See Judith Wallerstein, Julia Lewis, and Sandra Blakeslee, *The Unexpected Legacy of Divorce: The 25 Year Landmark Study* (New York: Hyperion, 2000), 181–84; and Alison Clark-Stewart and Cornelia Brentano, *Divorce: Causes and Consequences* (New Haven: Yale, 2006), 63–65, 180.

during the play. Their lives seem untroubled even though one of them has been sexually active with her father.[39]

In 2016, the Archdiocese of Philadelphia issued an attractively stated yet flawed set of "Pastoral Guidelines for Implementing *Amoris Laetitia*."[40] It insists that any solution for couples living in irregular situations must preserve "chastity." While the "brother-sister" arrangement may be pursued in appropriate cases, it forbids any further pastoral response. As beautiful as such a policy may sound to some, it falters because it has not appreciated the potential dilemmas of some divorced and remarried couples. Why should chastity be the *only* virtue that receives protection? What protection does the parental bond receive? What if a single parent has remarried in order to provide a stable living situation for the children? St. Paul VI's observation that a Christian may tolerate lesser evils to avoid greater ones receives no recognition. Moreover, its insistence that irregular couples must maintain chastity conflicts with its permission to certain couples to live in the "brother-sister" relationship, which upholds abstinence, but not chastity, as explained above.[41]

Once again, some church leaders fail to comprehend the welfare of children in their quest for purity of a more limited sort.

9. The Comforts of Clarity: The Grand Inquisitor

Every so often, one hears, "What the people need is clear, black and white teaching." But what the people really need is the Gospel. Teaching or pastoral practice with no ambiguity, nuance, or attentiveness to individual circumstances would make it easy for the priest, but it can be very difficult, onerous, and sometimes impossible for the one who must follow his black and white guidance. Francis writes, "By thinking that everything is black and white, we sometimes close off the way of grace and of growth, and discourage paths of sanctification which give glory to God" (AL 305).

---

39. Ingmar Bergman, *Scenes from a Marriage*, trans. A. Blair (New York: Bantam Books, 1974), 184, 187.

40. Available at http://archphila.org/wp-content/uploads/2016/06/AOP_AL -guidelines.pdf.

41. See also the further explanation of the virtue of chastity in the discussion on the "Contemporary Situation" in chapter 7 below.

Some complain that the possible confusion and ambiguity that result from mercy pose too great of a problem. They eagerly offer rigid Scriptural interpretations as a failsafe strategy, yet the approach badly betrays Christ's message. The law is not bad; it is simply inadequate. Fidelity to the Gospel never means merely parroting the language and texts of previous generations. If people needed only black and white, God would have given them only a manual, a written word. Instead, he gave them his Son, the incarnate Word.

Nevertheless, people often prefer the disincarnate abstraction of the law to the Word of God, the living Christ. Not a religion of the book, Christianity depends on Christ. Christians revere the Bible as an inspired record of revelation, not revelation itself. Even the divinely inspired written word of God does not interpret itself. Catholics read the Bible within the sacred tradition, guided by the magisterium and animated by the Holy Spirit. As such, Scripture challenges Catholics every day, sometimes in very surprising ways.

The law can give people the illusion that the world will unfold in predictable ways. Consequences seem clear under the law. It imposes an order on the world that is not otherwise present. Although rules promise clarity, they can deliver bitter cruelty. Pope Francis does not expect couples in irregular marriages to navigate these difficult waters alone. He requires them to seek the accompaniment of a priest to help them through this very difficult discernment process. Faith, hope, and love necessarily involve vagueness and ambiguity. So too does mercy.

It does no good to run away from the ambiguities of freedom. Fyodor Dostoevsky described this temptation in a poem, "The Grand Inquisitor," recited by the character Ivan Karamazov in the novel *The Brothers Karamazov*. Ivan claims that the church has given its followers laws and rules. It has taken away freedom, which is only a burden to humanity. Once furnished with bread, people will be happy. The Grand Inquisitor tells Jesus, "There is no need for Thee to come now at all. Thou must not meddle for the time, at least." Freedom causes only suffering. "Thou didst choose all that is exceptional, vague and enigmatic. . . . In place of the rigid ancient law, man must hereafter with free heart decide for himself what is good and what is evil, having only Thy image before him as his guide."[42]

42. Fyodor Dostoevsky, *The Brothers Karamazov*, trans. Constance Garnett (New York: The Modern Library, 1996; orig. ed. 1880) 278, 282–83.

Love, freedom, and mercy make life difficult, burdensome, unclear, vague, and enigmatic, but they also make it authentic, real, human, and worthwhile. That is the challenge Pope Francis lays before Christians: to let the image of Christ guide them. The Grand Inquisitor thought that people needed "black and white," and he was willing to take their freedom away to give it to them. Life seems so much easier that way. Black and white precepts give people false assurance that they are actually doing what Jesus asks. Having lost faith in him, they turn to the abstraction of the law. They look to a text rather than to Christ. The desire for clarity and the wish that every case present only easy decisions can lead to a selective reading of Scripture and history.

A certain cynical mindset interprets the effort to cope with the demands of mercy as "wishy-washy" or as wallowing in a gray area where no rules govern. It suspects that some leaders in the church have begun to incorporate relativism and secularism into their thinking. But the opposite of "black and white" is not "wishy-washy." The opposite of "black and white" is "Mystery." In Dostoevsky's terms, Mystery refers to Christ. As Ivan complains to Christ, when a man seeks to live faithfully, it means "having only Thy image before him as his guide." Only those who deal with Mystery can understand the dynamics involved in these complex situations. When thinkers become enraptured with rules, they unwittingly attempt to domesticate Mystery, as if they could appropriate it and make it fit neatly into this world. As soon as Mystery is domesticated, it is lost. Southern fiction writer Flannery O'Connor observes that any good novelist deals with Mystery in such a manner that "when he finishes there always has to be left over that sense of Mystery which cannot be accounted for by any human formula."[43] When church leaders tolerate a lesser evil to enable a single parent to move to a healthier situation when no good alternatives exist, mercy eliminates the greater evil in a way that extends beyond any system of rules.

Seductive talk of the absolute indissolubility of marriage entices people to enter a romantic world where mercy is not needed. If others suffer under the strictures of the law, so be it. It calls to mind the lawyers of the Gospel whom Jesus criticizes for imposing heavy burdens on people without lifting a finger to help them (Matt 23:4). William Lynch, S.J., called this "the absolutizing instinct." It represents "the instinct

---

43. Flannery O'Connor, *Mystery and Manners: Occasional Prose*, ed. Sally and Robert Fitzgerald (New York: Farrar, Straus & Giroux, 1962), 153.

in human beings that would . . . make an absolute out of everything it touches. . . . [I]t is never subtle but always loud and boisterous, always magnificently present on the scene. It is also a world of false hope which counterfeits the reality of hope."[44] This instinct depends on a world of fantasy. Lynch wrote, "The good becomes tremendously good, the evil becomes the absolutely evil, the grey becomes the black or white, the complicated, because it is difficult to handle, becomes in desperation, the completely simple. The small becomes big. . . . But above all, everything assumes a greater weight than it has, and becomes a greater burden."[45] Unfortunately the absolutizing instinct affects the judgment of not only ordinary people but also the best of theologians.[46]

When spouses encounter challenges, they must face up to them honorably, without walking away from the fidelity they once pledged. When peoples' lives become shattered due to sin, mercy should find a way for them to get on with life. The objective is charity, not legality. Mercy makes life livable, not necessarily regular, by applying the law in ways that recognize that certain exigencies simply exceed the capacity of the law to handle in a loving way. Walter Kasper has noted, "Just as elements of the true Church exist outside the Catholic Church . . . so too elements of Christian marriage can be present in [irregular] partnerships." He cautions readers "not to paint the situation in black and white" as if one could treat irregular situations as if they were all the same.[47]

Mercy troubles the faint-hearted, because it requires mature judgment and discernment. It leads to ambiguity and uncertainty. It treats different people differently according to circumstances that no law can foresee. It respects the sloppiness of conversion and responds not harshly but with love and understanding. Mercy responds to life directly. Most significantly, the Lord calls his people to mercy, and the church must follow.

44. William F. Lynch, *Images of Hope: Imagination as Healer of the Hopeless* (Notre Dame, IN: University of Notre Dame Press, 1965), 105.

45. Lynch, *Images of Hope*, 106.

46. The antidote to the absolutizing instinct is the analogical imagination that allows realities to emerge concretely on their own terms within an enlarged context. See Gerald J. Bednar, *Faith as Imagination: The Contribution of William F. Lynch, SJ* (Kansas City: Sheed & Ward, 1996), especially 65–68.

47. Kasper, *Message of Amoris Laetitia*, 39–40. The cardinal has in mind Vatican II's *Lumen Gentium* 15 and *Unitatis Redintegratio* 3.

CHAPTER FOUR

Entering the Field Hospital

People naturally hesitate to look at horrible pain. In 2003, Susan Sontag wrote a treatise on photography called *Regarding the Pain of Others*. She considers how people both *want* and *do not want* to look at gruesome wartime photographs. She speculates that only people who can do something to alleviate the pain have a right to look, such as doctors working in field hospitals. "The rest of us are voyeurs."[1] A similar situation has developed in the church.

Chapter 8 of AL deals with pain that is difficult to behold. After seven beautiful and inspiring chapters about family life, the document abruptly turns to the breakdown of marriages. Unfortunately, the text offers little preparation to consider families in irregular situations. It does not take a detailed look at the ugly situations that can develop in failed marriages. Nevertheless, those in charge of ecclesiastical hospitals must look closely at the ugly wounds of sin. To understand chapter 8, we need to look at the pain and risk becoming voyeurs.

People often avoid looking by treating the wounded in terms of generalities. There is no such thing as a generic divorce, any more than there is such a thing as generic wartime wounds. Wounds can vary enormously. One soldier's wounded foot differs greatly from another's disfigured face. Both have suffered the wounds of war, but the one is more difficult to regard than the other. So too with divorced and civilly remarried Catholics and their children.

---

1. Susan Sontag, *Regarding the Pain of Others* (New York: Farrar, Straus and Giroux, 2003), 42.

This sort of aversion calls to mind the young German soldier Paul Bäumer in Erich Maria Remarque's novel, *All Quiet on the Western Front*. After going out on a nighttime patrol, Bäumer becomes disoriented. He scrambles to a vacant shell-hole for cover. Soon a French soldier jumps into the same hole, and Bäumer quickly stabs him three times in the throat. As he watches the gurgling man die, he says, "Comrade, I did not want to kill you. . . . But you were only . . . an abstraction that lived in my mind. . . . But now, for the first time, I see you are a man like me."[2]

Detesting the very idea of divorce, good Catholics too easily react against categories of people, without bothering to look at the wounds that lurk behind those categories. Perhaps discomfort comes as they find themselves saying, "But now, for the first time, I see you as a man like me." Those who would impose the letter of the law in every case seem to avoid looking at the pain and thereby miss something essential.

Everyone readily admits that the wounds of divorce present a sad and deplorable picture. No one should have to suffer the evils of divorce. Does that evil constitute only a call to virtuous suffering? Some would say that people caught in these circumstances should stiffen their backbone and accept the grace that God offers.

Certainly many people face these difficulties with virtue and resolve. They bring their strength into play and rise to the occasion.[3] They edify us all. But what about the weak? What about those whose lives, broken by betrayal and abandonment, lay in shambles? What if they give in to weakness and remarry? What would conversion require for them?

Some would say that even if a remarriage gives rise to a stable, loving family after the passage of many years, theoretically a divorce from that second marriage provides the cleanest way to resolve the legal issue. Such a couple would have to break the natural bonds of love and expect the children to understand how their religion requires them to endure the breaking of their family for a second time. The more pastoral alter-

---

2. Erich Maria Remarque, trans. A. W. Wheen, *All Quiet on the Western Front* (New York: Random House, 1928), 223.

3. For example, Rainer Beckmann's account of his unexpected divorce after twenty-five years of marriage and four children offers inspiration for others to find the strength to remain true to their vows. See Paul Josef Cardinal Cordes, "Without Rupture or Discontinuity," in Aymans, *Eleven Cardinals Speak on Marriage and the Family: Essays from a Pastoral Viewpoint* (San Francisco: Ignatius, 2015), 27–28.

native allows the family to stay intact, but only if the husband and wife agree to live as brother and sister, which presents problems of its own.

When remarried couples seek reconciliation after years of absence from the church, pastoral leaders face the unsavory task of sorting out which evil is greater than the other: remarriage-as-adultery or neglected children. Catholics understand adultery. No one recommends it. But when one of these two evils must be tolerated, few have paid sufficient attention to the evil inflicted on the children of divorce.

As noted in chapter 2 above, according to Aquinas, eternal law properly discerned presents the very wisdom of God. Eternal law reflects the product of the divine intellect.[4] It pervades creation. Christians can know it because they live inside it. One finds the law in Christ himself. Catholics discern what comports with a Christian life by referring to the life and teachings of Christ with the aid of the church's teaching office. They do not simply refer to a rulebook. Proper discernment involves an objective order. God has inscribed the law in the very lives of the faithful and in the very reality in which they live. The wisdom of God resides in the natural order of creation as the light of Christ illuminates it. Knowledge of right and wrong flows from such a vision. This natural order, as enlightened by Christ, forms the basis of natural law by which Catholics perceive the objective moral order that should govern moral choices. Aquinas notes that "whatever the practical reason naturally apprehends as man's good (or evil) belongs to the precepts of the natural law as something to be done or avoided."[5]

Unfortunately, people can become so overwhelmed by their passions that they can forget the promptings of practical reason. They can become involved in twisted relationships that put them in difficult positions. Cruelty and self-absorption can inflict intolerable circumstances on some, even to the extent that they can have no alternatives that are right, no decisions that fully comply with the law. For example, a woman may become overwhelmed by the task of raising her children in the face of the abandonment of her husband. Emotionally and financially devastated, she may not have the resources to guide her children through the trauma of divorce. She has a natural obligation to nurture and guide her children in ways that she simply cannot manage. It is

4. ST I-II, q. 106, a. 4.
5. ST I-II, q. 94, a. 2.

"wrong" to raise children that way, in the wake of the abandonment of their father and with a weak mother who cannot cope with her immature children. AL and other official documents have long recognized that children deserve to be raised in family settings with a mother and father.[6] It reflects the natural order. Indeed, even state authorities will intervene if they receive complaints that a parent has become so unfit that his or her children have experienced a "failure to thrive." Such cases pose pathetic circumstances where parents lose custody of their children when the children exhibit a risk of serious emotional damage due to the parent's failures in the upbringing of their children.

If a man proposes marriage to a divorced woman who struggles to raise her children without a father present in the house, she may judge that it would be in the best interests of both her and her children to accept the proposal. She hopes to find some support in meeting her obligation to raise her children. Before she chooses such an option, it occurs to her that a second marriage is also "wrong." Assuming that an annulment is not available to her and that her relatives offer no relief, whatever she does is wrong. Any decision she makes offends the natural order.[7] Such is the nature of a dilemma.

Dilemmas that provoke a merciful response differ from simpler situations in which a person suffers from an immoral decision. Such a person may well have a path to right living, but hesitates to take it because it involves unusual effort or pain. For example, if a person regularly gossips because he enjoys the attention it brings, mercy will not approve his continued indulgence in this weakness. When he confesses the sin, the priest should not make light of it or pass it off as something that everyone does. The confessor should show mercy by giving a penance that addresses the problem at some level. Perhaps the penitent needs a spiritual exercise that tends to convince him that

---

6. See especially AL 55, 88, 165–66, 169, 172–77, 245, 252, and 286. John Paul II, *Familiaris Consortio* 14; *Gaudium et Spes* 52; Pius XI, encyclical letter *Casti Connubii* (December 31, 1930) 113.

7. The situation of a single parent who is a widow differs from single parents who have become divorced. Although both widow and children need unusual attention, their situation lacks the toxic hatred and contempt that can surround divorce. The profound rejection felt even in amiable divorces simply is not part of the experience of the widow and her children.

God shows him the attention he so craves or a penance that enhances his ability to hold his tongue when the temptation arises. Mercy does not content itself with merely providing him with a free pass, as if the sin were not a sin.

If a penitent has willingly become involved in drugs for recreational purposes, more extensive help may be required. Accompaniment will meet him in his weakness and strive to lead him step by step to encourage him to seek the support he needs to become physically, mentally, and spiritually independent. Furthermore, even though his present dependency may actually cause injustice to others, mercy leading to conversion constitutes the most just solution to eliminate the injustice such family members endure. Accommodating oneself to present circumstances, keeping him dependent on drugs, only prolongs the injustice.

The above situations are not dilemmas. Alternative ways of acting exist and can lead to the virtues those penitents need. In a dilemma, no such path is available.

The time has come to enter the field hospital to look at the predicaments of divorced Catholics. We will now consider some instances in which divorced people face a dilemma and must choose the lesser of two evils. Whatever they do is wrong. Dilemmas have no solutions. They can only be managed, not solved. No right solution in which no one is hurt exists. In the course of considering distressed marriages and the annulment process especially in this chapter and in chapter 7, the preponderance of examples will center on the needs of women. This naturally calls for some explanation. Generally women file petitions for a declaration of nullity twice as frequently as men. Women typically retain custody of the children of null marriages. This puts them in a much more difficult position than men. They experience pressures from which men typically can walk away. When men initiate the process, most often they file because they already have a woman in mind to marry. Furthermore, when men are called to respond to petitions, unless their own marriage prospects are affected, they often decline to participate in the proceedings.

Although attention will focus on the "patients," the "doctor" stands as a key person in the hospital. While laws and rules can help, they do not heal the patient. The doctor (*medicus*, in Latin) must apply carefully what is at hand to affect the healing.

The church has long considered Christ as the *medicus* who brings healing or salvation. The image resonated deeply with the early church. Many fathers favored the image of Jesus as doctor or healer who offers the Eucharist as a healing remedy.[8] St. Ignatius of Antioch employed the terminology early in the second century, and others used it extensively from that time on.[9] For example, in his *Confessions*, St. Augustine, soon after lamenting the tardiness of his love for God, declares, "See, I do not hide my wounds; you are the Physician and I am sick; you are merciful, I in need of mercy."[10] During the sixth century, the notion of judgment enters the discussion in the context of penance, but initially it concerns the judgment of a physician, not a legal judge. At the beginning of the eleventh century, St. Gregory of Narek addressed the Lord in these terms: "Be my companion like a physician; / Don't summon me to court like a judge."[11]

Pastoral ministers must immerse themselves in the image of Jesus as *medicus* to apply appropriate cures to particular cases, paying close attention to both the patient and the Divine Physician.

Back to the patients.

8. Isaiah foretold this role when he prophesied the coming of God who would "strengthen the weak hands, / and make firm the feeble knees" (Isa 35:3). Early in his ministry, Jesus takes on the task of the *medicus*, declaring, "Those who are well have no need of a physician, but those who are sick" (Luke 5:31). See Regis Duffy, *A Roman Catholic Theology of Pastoral Care* (Philadelphia: Fortress Press, 1970), 42–43. In the fourth century, the *Epistola Canonica* of Gregory of Nyssa elaborates extensively on the image of sin as sickness of the soul. See Basilio Petrà, *La Penitenza Nelle Chiese Ortodosse: Aspetti Storici e Sacramentali* (Bologna: Dehoniane, 2005), 40. According to the Council of Trent, the confessor serves both as doctor of souls and as judge (see Duffy, 46). Nevertheless, the image of the doctor of souls seems to retain its priority. Well into the twentieth century, Bernard Häring could write, "But in every case the Church's healing mission takes precedence over its judicial function" (*No Way Out? Pastoral Care of the Divorced and Remarried* [Middlegreen: St. Paul Publications, 1990], 85). Analogously, in today's hospitals, the better doctors refer to the "art of diagnosis." They consult the charts and understand the numbers, but they also derive much valuable information from attending to the patient on a personal basis.

9. *Letter to the Ephesians* 7:1-2.

10. Augustine, *The Confessions*, trans. Maria Boulding (New York: Vintage Books, 1997), X:28, 39 (p. 222).

11. Cited in Michael Papazian, *The Doctor of Mercy: The Sacred Treasures of St. Gregory of Narek* (Collegeville, MN: Liturgical Press Academic, 2019), 141.

1. A Viable Family in an Invalid Marriage

The first example is an imaginary one, but the situation it describes is not uncommon. Consider a Catholic woman who years ago married outside the church. Although no one could convince her that she should not marry a divorced man, her passions, her weakness, perhaps her determination to break away from her parents all led her to an invalid union. Six years later, her twins born of this invalid marriage enter their First Communion class. At their first communal celebration of penance, the priest explains the faith in a particularly effective way. The catechists have asked the parents to make a confession as an encouragement for their nervous second grade children. Perhaps the woman's conscience has been troubling her ever since her twins were born. They have a younger brother who will be in the same position soon.

Overcome with a desire to make things right, she seeks reconciliation. After the usual introductory request for a blessing, she confesses that she has been in an invalid marriage for six years and has three lovely children. The marriage is stable. Both partners love each other dearly. Family life flourishes. It would produce nothing but sweetness and light, but for one underlying flaw. Their marriage is invalid. Her husband needs an annulment.

Have they discussed getting an annulment for him? Yes, the topic has been raised. She wants him to apply for a declaration of nullity, but he cannot stand the thought of it. The topic makes him tense and upset. He does not want to revisit the tortuous years of his first marriage, nor does he relish contacting a list of witnesses who would testify to the embarrassing facts underlying his failed marriage. Why can he not do this? He won't say. He simply cannot begin the process.

She has asked her husband if they could refrain from sexual relations so she could go to confession and Communion. She will try her best to do without those relations, but he cannot see the sense of it. He does not consider their relations as adultery. Frankly, she can understand his point of view. After all, he has fathered their children and has contributed to a viable family life. And yet her faith nags at her. What is she supposed to do?

She hardly thinks of his amorous approaches to her as adultery let alone as attempts at rape. She does not simply want to refuse him and wonder what sort of consequences that would entail. She does not want to risk what a cold shoulder would do to the family and frankly to her relationship with a man she loves and who, together with her, supports the family as a loving parent.

She is trapped. Whatever she does is wrong in one way or another. She cannot divorce him and let the children suffer. Nor can she simply refuse her husband. It would jeopardize the whole family. The only alternative is to carry on as if the marriage were normal, doing the best she can to keep the family going. Perhaps she can raise the issue of applying for an annulment from time to time. Perhaps she can bolster his ability to begin to talk about his past marriage. Eventually he might dare to raise the topic, but that possibility lies in the future and may not come at all.

In the meantime, can she not receive penance and Communion in the church? The pope opens a path for ministers to lead such a woman mercifully back to full communion with the church. He enables priests to accompany people in such distressed marriages hopefully in a way that leads to absolution and invites them to share in the eucharistic nourishment offered at Mass. Where there exist an acknowledgment of sin, contrition, and a true desire to convert as best she can, the pope and bishops can offer her the hope of the sacraments.

This act of mercy does not mean that the sin of divorce and remarriage has a limited shelf life, as if the sin expired after so many years. Church leaders can show mercy because, although time does not negate the sin, it can significantly alter what can be done about the sin. What was possible for the couple to do in the early days, months, and perhaps even years of their invalid marriage may no longer exist as viable alternatives. When marriage partners paint themselves into a corner, the sin remains a sin, but confessors can receive an expression of contrition together with a pledge from the penitent to do the best he or she can to practice the faith in the circumstances. They can then assign a penance and offer absolution.

The marriage remains invalid, but the family can practice the faith in those very difficult circumstances. The marriage does not become "right," and it cannot be celebrated in any ceremony in the church. Although it remains the lesser of two evils, the church should not penalize the couple for the dilemma it regrets.

What does conversion require of this couple? Can the church not assist them in this dilemma? Divorce and remarriage can give rise to the unsettling realization that reconciliation with the church is needed even in the best of circumstances.

What about the most difficult circumstances? The time has come to enter the Intensive Care Unit.

2. A Miserable Life after Divorce: The Fort Sheridan Case

In one actual case[12] told from the viewpoint of one of two daughters, a now-adult woman recalls feeling very close to her father. She wanted so much to please both her parents. Her father's work took him away from home to live at Fort Sheridan, where he served in the Army. Her first suspicion of trouble in the family came at her First Communion, when her father did not go to Communion, claiming that he had broken his fast. He visited home now and again. Then his visits became fewer and fewer until they stopped altogether.

Her mother began to act strangely. Her grandmother came to help, but the grandmother and mother argued. The mother cried a lot. The daughters did not learn that their father divorced their mother until seven years later. He had impregnated a woman at the Army base, and she insisted that he divorce and marry her. The divorce had been final for several years before the discussion arose with the daughters. The mother, a recent convert to Catholicism, refused to date. The grandmother thought she would be happier if she remarried. The daughters felt betrayed by their father and blamed their mother. They became unruly. "Mom would go to confession and tell the priest that she didn't know if she could go on, and the priest would tell her that at least she had her children."[13] Dismayed at the hollow consolation, she cried. She spent hours trying to explain her situation to her daughters, pleading with them to behave. "Then she'd cry. I did feel awful for her, and I was convinced that I was

12. This situation and the two that follow were described in a set of letters describing the problems related to divorce, remarriage, and annulment in Catholic life, published in the *National Catholic Reporter* on July 4, 1997. They are reprinted in Pierre Hegy and Joseph Martos, eds., *Catholic Divorce: The Deception of Annulments* (New York: Continuum, 2000), 26–28. See also the series of cases cited in Häring, *No Way Out?*, chap. 1.

13. Hegy and Martos, *Catholic Divorce*, 27.

an awful, even sinful child."[14] Her mother became so depressed that she asked the grandmother to find a mental institution for her.

The mother in this situation did her best to preserve the chastity of her broken spousal bond but could not adequately honor the parental bond with her children. At some point before her steep descent into depression, she might have preferred to offer her daughters a new family structure through a new marriage. If she did so, how should church leaders receive her if she then approached them with sincere contrition? Some commentators suggest that if the divorced spouse simply relies on her God-given strength, all will turn out well. It seems that such a suggestion has its limitations.

3. A Brother-Sister Relationship Leading to Divorce

Do "brother-sister" relationships offer a way out of some dilemmas?

Another actual case[15] shows how precarious "brother-sister" relationships can be. A Catholic woman married a man simply because of his persistence. She intentionally married before a judge so as to make the marriage certainly invalid. She planned to leave him soon after the wedding and then pursue an annulment. In spite of her intentions, he persuaded her to stay in the marriage. So she had the marriage validated instead. The husband went off to war, and when he returned, they divorced.

She married an Anglican man three years later. They started a family and had two children. She met with a priest to start procedures to have the first marriage annulled, but he refused because she did not qualify for an annulment under then-current guidelines. She wanted to receive Communion, so she proposed to her husband that they live in a "brother-sister" relationship so they could continue their cohabitation. "My husband was not happy with that solution. We were separated, got back together, and separated again. He wanted a divorce. Finally, he married another person."[16] Her husband had at first talked about becoming Catholic but became disillusioned.

While "brother-sister" relationships may work in many cases, they do not work in all. The woman in this example faced a dilemma. She

14. Hegy and Martos, 27.
15. Hegy and Martos, 34–35.
16. Hegy and Martos, 35.

could continue her second marriage and raise her children in a stable family while violating her original marital vows, or she could pursue a simulated marriage to the utter frustration of her husband and suffer divorce in the process. Must the honoring of the broken original marital bond be preferred to the parental bond that still requires daily attention?

If the woman chooses to live in her second marriage, can church leaders not tolerate this moral deficiency to prevent a greater evil?

4. A Declaration of Annulment Denied

Although a vast number of annulment applications are granted, some are denied. Sometimes a tribunal cannot grant an annulment simply because it is clear that the marriage was valid. Tragically, at times couples can destroy valid marriages and make them unlivable. At some point, they can become irretrievably ruined. The parties simply walk away from what otherwise could have been a viable marriage. After a spouse has "lost" a marriage in this way, some have the strength to avoid contracting a further (invalid) marriage. They deserve the support of everyone who knows them. They expend much energy in honoring the indissolubility of marriage and in living out the harsh reality life has dealt them while depending on the grace of God. Others may not display the sort of courage and strength that it takes to go it alone. In their weakness, they might contract another marriage and eventually enter the dilemmas described above. A party may also contract an invalid marriage but be unable to prove it before a tribunal.

Consider the following case.[17] A woman married her college sweetheart after he proposed to her in front of a statue of the Blessed Virgin Mary on campus. They married in 1956, and sixteen years later, after fathering four daughters, the husband left his wife for a younger woman.

She fought depression for two years, while she tried desperately to save her marriage. She prayed; she sought the advice of priests; she received counseling from a psychologist. She pleaded with her husband to save the marriage, but he would not return. Finally she filed for divorce. She presented her case to ten priests in hopes of filing an application for a declaration of nullity. None would give her any hope. They all told her that she lacked sufficient grounds.

17. Hegy and Martos, 37–38.

She started to date. She eventually married before a Protestant minister. Wanting to reconcile with the church and to practice her Catholic faith more fully, she consulted with several priests to explore her options. Finally she saw a priest who investigated an internal forum solution[18] with her. The priest accompanied her through the relevant considerations, and she became settled with receiving Communion in the church once again.

If the first marriage was truly invalid, this woman was trapped in paperwork. She had the right to marry but could not legally do so. Whatever she did was wrong. It was wrong not to follow her vocation to enter a valid marriage with the "second" husband, and it was wrong to marry without annulment papers when the first marriage was presumed to be valid. Is the church powerless in such dilemmas? [19]

In 1997, Cardinal Joseph Ratzinger anticipated the day when these sorts of dilemmas might be solved without involving tribunals. He stated, "For example, perhaps in the future there could also be an extrajudicial determination that the first marriage did not exist. This could

18. The notion of the internal forum has undergone some development. Under the 1917 Code of Canon Law, it referred to one's conscience. The category proved unhelpful in more complicated marriage cases. Under the 1983 Code, the internal forum refers not only to conscience but also to the forum where information is not known to the public. If the data are publicly known or publicly available, it belongs to the external forum. A "hardship marriage" (where an invalid marriage follows a valid marriage that has become irretrievably lost) cannot become validated through an "internal forum" solution that appeals to conscience. Pope Francis would agree. Nevertheless, the situation may give rise to a dilemma for an ex-spouse who has no good choices and, with proper accompaniment, may eventually receive penance and Communion. The marriage remains invalid in the external forum, but the person may once again receive the benefit of the sacraments in proper cases. AL uses neither the external nor the internal forum in its analysis. In a "conflict marriage" (where one's previous marriage was invalid but proof sufficient to satisfy a tribunal does not exist), an internal forum solution might indeed be available, making a subsequent marriage valid, although problems linger since what is known publicly about the first marriage may well conflict with the internal validity of the second. See Francisco Javier Urrutia, "Internal Forum—External Forum: The Criterion of Distinction," in René Latourelle, ed., *Vatican II: Assessment and Perspectives: Twenty-Five Years After (1962–1987)*, vol. 1 (New York: Paulist Press, 1988), 639, 651–52. As explained further above, Cardinal Ratzinger thought an extrajudicial solution might be possible.

19. Other cases can arise in more unusual settings, such as families split during immigration or a soldier who goes missing in action.

perhaps be ascertained locally by experienced pastors. Such juridical developments, which can make things less complicated, are conceivable."[20]

Perhaps the day has come to explore how such extrajudicial determinations might be implemented. In AL 300, Pope Francis invites bishops and pastors to develop these sorts of approaches. For him, the problem is not merely academic. People can suffer dreadfully when nothing can be done.

5. A Good Life After Divorce?

Divorced people often want nothing further to do with marriage. To them, the prospect of remarriage simply invites a repetition of the worst experience of their lives. Although single parents suffer much, the children suffer more.[21] The lack of a family structure and the strange experience of honoring the absent parent's visitation rights complicate an already traumatic experience in their lives. Moreover, during this hectic and critical time, single parents have less time and fewer resources to attend to the children as monetary considerations send them looking for better paying jobs.

Other divorced people will attempt remarriage for the sake of the children, and often this solution fails. Some research suggests that a difficult marriage, even one that includes arguing and obvious animosity between husband and wife, is usually less detrimental to children than a divorce.[22] Plenty of second marriages repeat the mistakes of the first marriage and only make matters worse. Second marriages that

20. Cardinal Joseph Ratzinger, *Salt of the Earth: The Church at the End of the Millennium* (San Francisco: Ignatius Press, 1997), 207.

21. Alison Clarke-Stewart and Cornelia Brentano report research that shows that not only older children, but even infants suffer from divorce. See their *Divorce: Causes and Consequences* (New Haven: Yale, 2006), 109.

22. See E. Mavis Hetherington, "Should We Stay Together for the Sake of the Children?," in Hetherington, ed., *Coping with Divorce, Single Parenting, and Remarriage: A Risk and Resiliency Perspective* (Mahwah, NJ: Lawrence Erlbaum Associates, 1999), 101–2, where she observes, "If conflict is going to continue, it is better for children to remain in an acrimonious two-parent household than to divorce. If there is a shift to a more harmonious household, a divorce is advantageous to both boys and girls." See also Judith Wallerstein, Julia Lewis, and Sandra Blakeslee, *The Unexpected Legacy of Divorce: A 25 Year Landmark Study* (New York: Hyperion, 2000), 81–82; and Clark-Stewart and Brentano, *Divorce*, 148–50.

attempt to provide a more stable environment for the children often harm them instead. A host of obstacles needs to be surmounted. How should the child treat the stepparent vis-à-vis the absent biological parent? What if the visitation rights of the absent parent conflict with the extracurricular school activities of the child? Bitter parents may also use the child to retaliate against their former spouses. For example, one ex-wife loved her son's long curly hair. Her ex-husband picked up the child for his weekend visitation with him and returned the boy with his hair closely cropped.

Relationships with stepsiblings can generate rivalries. Will the natural parents unconsciously favor their own children? If the newly formed couple becomes infatuated with their own relationship, they often neglect the emotional needs of the children. Those sorts of re-marriages damage the children severely.

Nevertheless, second marriages work well in some circumstances. Children who see their natural fathers as lacking interest in them, as moral failures, and who reject their natural fathers, "often turn eagerly to their stepfather as a person they can admire and emulate."[23] Psychologist Judith Wallerstein claims that, in the right circumstances, children can benefit from a good second marriage after divorce. She reports her conversations with the adult children of second marriages:

> Many talked of their stepfather with great affection and praise. "I really love him. He's a good, loyal man." Others said, "My stepfather saved my life." One young man explained to me, "I have no respect for my father. He's irresponsible and self-centered. But my stepfather is just the kind of person I want to be. I'm lucky to have him." One young woman, who was rescued from a delinquent life with a motorcycle gang by her stepfather's confidence in her, told me proudly, "He told me that I was smart and that I was too good to waste my time with those losers. He said that I should go to college, and best of all he put his money where his mouth was. He is the father I always wanted."[24]

Wallerstein notes that unfortunately those very positive experiences of children in second marriages represent only a small minority of

---

23. Wallerstein, Lewis, and Blakeslee, *Unexpected Legacy of Divorce*, 245.
24. Wallerstein, Lewis, and Blakeslee, 245–46.

cases. Alison Clarke-Stewart, on the other hand, claims that Waller-stein's data are skewed since the population of children she studied already had significant psychological issues prior to the divorce of their parents.[25] A wider sampling shows more success for children who must deal with divorced parents.[26] Much depends on how both the adults and children adapt to the new circumstances. Too often stepfathers show very little interest in their wives' children. Just as selfish marriages fail, so too do selfish remarriages. People often calculate their chances poorly when considering the promise of second marriages, but one can understand how a divorced person might consider such a solution.

What if a remarried parent desires reconciliation with the church? What does conversion require? Legal rigorists would require another divorce or a "brother-sister" relationship, which itself might lead to divorce. Certainly church ministers can make a more merciful response than abstractly looking only to the spousal bond while largely paying insufficient attention to parental obligations to the children.

Pope Francis understands that divorce concerns not only the integrity of the spousal bond but also the integrity of the parental bond, which needs to protect the children. Pastoral care should not focus on chastity alone but also on the protection of vulnerable children. AL appears to give equal footing to the interests of the children of divorce.

6. The Bestowal of Mercy

One might imagine that these unfortunate single parents play a game of chess with the devil. They have moved some of the chess pieces unwisely themselves. Other pieces have been pushed into place for them. They have come to a position in their lives where the devil is about to proclaim victory: checkmate! No matter where they move, evil triumphs. Has the devil won?

The Lord's mercy is greater than the machinations of the devil. Pope Francis asks priests to accompany single parents and those who have civilly remarried to find ways to most closely follow the life God wants for them in the impossible circumstances that have evolved in their lives (AL 298–300).

25. Clarke-Stewart and Brentano, *Divorce*, 101.
26. Clarke-Stewart and Brentano, 148–50, 235–37.

One never claims mercy for oneself. It is always bestowed by another. AL does not allow divorced and civilly remarried people to claim the mercy of the Lord and to absolve themselves. Marital dilemmas should be raised with a priest or pastoral minister who can assist the couple in sorting out the issues. Accompaniment should proceed carefully, with sensitivity and with encouragement to take up counseling as appropriate.[27]

The Swiss theologian Hans Urs von Balthasar observed that Christians must uphold "the relationship between a justice that puts all things in their place and calls them by their right name and a mercy that takes everything from its place and gives it a radically greater value."[28] In dealing with irregular situations, the magisterium urges church officials to exercise mercy in a way that considers unique elements that defy any sweeping rules. As the devil declares checkmate, the church lifts the pieces from the board and gives them a radically greater value. The two-dimensional game now becomes three-dimensional.

The extra dimension added by mercy frees the afflicted and offers new possibilities. It does not make wrong things right. It does not change doctrine. It does not form any principle at all. It simply declares that the church will not punish a person for being caught in a dilemma, even if that dilemma was partially caused by that person, as long as that person comes as close as he or she can to full conversion and follows the consequent will of God as closely as possible in those impossible circumstances. If so, the church can afford to leave well enough alone.

One of the most preeminent moral theologians of the twentieth century, Bernard Häring, claimed that even the culpable unfaithful spouse of a broken marriage deserves mercy once that person has demonstrated a profound conversion and desires to return to the practice of the faith. Obviously penance and absolution cannot be lightly administered. "But in every case the church's healing mission takes precedence over its judicial function."[29]

---

27. See Bretzke, *A Morally Complex World: Engaging Contemporary Moral Theology* (Collegeville, MN: Liturgical Press, 2004), 187–90, for further guidance.

28. Hans Urs von Balthasar, *The Glory of the Lord: A Theological Aesthetics*, vol. I: *Seeing the Form*, trans. Erasmo Leiva-Merikakis (New York: Crossroad, 1982), 189.

29. Häring, *No Way Out?*, 83–85.

AL does not break from the pastoral practices and doctrinal precepts of the magisterium; it furthers them. The doctrine of the indissolubility of marriage has never meant that competent ecclesiastical ministers could not manage intolerable situations in marriage. More accurately stated, indissolubility means that the individuals in a marriage have no power of their own to dissolve a marriage, whether valid or not.[30] Only the official church, exercising the power of the keys, has the authority to apply mercy as it has already done for virtually its entire existence (Matt 16:19; 18:18-19; 1 Cor 7:12).

Pope Francis has attempted to take into consideration the real needs of broken families in a fallen world. The pope calls us to open our eyes and to look at the real debacle that unfolds in any divorce. AL rejects divorce, as the Lord declared (AL 62). Francis directs ministers to accompany divorced couples so they can reunite where possible (AL 242). He also recognizes dilemmas that need compassionate attention (AL 79).

Mercy is concrete and administered in difficult cases or it is not mercy at all. Remarque's Paul Bäumer came to regret his lethal reaction to an abstraction that hid within the gurgling man he killed. As long as he stayed with the victim, he felt bonded in charity to him. Once he departed from the man he slew, those bonds slowly dissolved, and old habits returned.[31]

Pope Francis calls church leaders to leave old habits behind and to regard the pain of others with mercy. Rules have their place and normally furnish sound guidance, but when dilemmas arise, mercy needs to lead the way, as it has for centuries in the church.

---

30. See John Beal, James Coriden, and Thomas Green, *New Commentary on the Code of Common Law* (New York: Paulist Press, 2000), 1362.

31. Remarque, *All Quiet on the Western Front*, 226.

CHAPTER FIVE

Scripture and History

Having considered the nature of the law and its place in theological discussion, and having reviewed AL at close quarters, together with some of its theological justifications, the time has come to take a closer look at relevant Scriptural passages and to explore the history of the church. This essential step in the process of evaluating doctrinal proposals roots the theologian in the reality of the church as it has developed through her sacred writings and as it has really existed.

The church has a long history of recognizing that mercy can override indissolubility in proper circumstances without overturning the laws concerning indissolubility. It need not always treat the bond in legally strict and demanding ways. Instead, it looks on the total situation in merciful terms. The church has moved a long way from a simple application of the Lord's original dictum, reported in Mark 10:5-12, that forbade divorce because, as Jesus said, it was not that way from the beginning.

Has mercy in fact been deployed in the way Pope Francis suggests in AL that it has? First, we turn to Scripture.

1. Early Scriptural Surprises and Later Developments

One of the most startling verses in the New Testament comes in 1 Corinthians 7 where St. Paul consciously alters the teaching of Christ on divorce. He does it not once but twice.

First, Paul appears to have directly modified the Lord's command itself. At 1 Corinthians 7:10-11, Paul writes, "To the married, I give this command—*not I but the Lord*—that the wife should not separate from her husband (but if she does separate, let her remain unmarried or else be reconciled to her husband), and that the husband should not divorce his wife" (emphasis mine). He is addressing here married Christians who want to separate.[1] He follows Jesus's teaching in declaring that if they do separate, they should not attempt another marriage, a situation that Jesus associates with adultery. Rather, Paul instructs them to reconcile, again in keeping with Jesus's command.

But Paul goes beyond the options offered by Jesus. Paul's rendition of the Lord's original directive has the Lord entertaining separation as a permanent solution.[2] They may "remain unmarried"—an option not mentioned by the Lord. While Paul may reasonably conclude that Jesus would have to agree with him, still Jesus had emphasized that separation itself is unacceptable, not a possible permanent state for Christians who have married.

A review of the earliest form of the Lord's command shows this. Most scholars hold that the original directive from the Lord surfaces in Mark's gospel, where Jesus forbids any separation whatsoever: "[F]rom the beginning of creation, 'God made them male and female.' 'For this reason a man shall leave his father and mother and be joined to his wife, and the two shall become one flesh.' So they are no longer two, but one flesh. Therefore, what God has joined together, let no one separate. . . . Whoever divorces his wife and marries another commits adultery against her; and if she divorces her husband and marries another, she commits adultery" (Mark 10:6-9, 11-12).

Mark reports that Jesus's rejection of divorce is founded upon God's plan "from the beginning." His statement is clear: "Let no one separate."

---

1. It's worth noting that Paul calls the separated Christian "unmarried" (7:11). His language reflects the more normal pastoral usage of common people rather than the precise, hard, technical language that rigorists would employ today.

2. This original privilege explicitly allowed divorce, not remarriage, although it would seem to follow naturally. Paul Mankowski, SJ, suggests that Paul simply re-emphasizes Jesus's teaching on indissolubility. His judgment relies on a very partial reading of Scripture. For example, Mankowski explicitly omits any treatment of 1 Corinthians 7:12, where Paul insists, "I give this command—I and not the Lord." Indeed, consideration of the passage would cause problems for his overall thesis. See Mankowski, "Dominical Teaching on Divorce and Remarriage," in Robert Dodaro, OSA, *Remaining in the Truth of Christ: Marriage and Communion in the Catholic Church* (San Francisco: Ignatius, 2014), 36.

Nevertheless, Paul felt free to insert the clause "but if she does separate, let her remain unmarried."

The point here is not that Paul was wrong. In fact, he was right to offer his expansion of Jesus's thought. The point rather is that the teaching of Jesus begs for development. It cannot rest simply on his words as if they were sufficient without the church's ability to interpret them and expand on them where necessary. In this slight and reasonable addition, we glimpse the authority of the church to manage the marital bond.

But Paul continues, altering the Lord's directive a second time, when he explicitly admits that he "and not the Lord" allows something that the Lord did not, "To the rest I say—*I and not the Lord*—that . . . if the unbelieving partner separates, let it be so; in such a case the brother or sister is not bound. It is to peace that God has called you" (1 Cor 7:12, 15; emphasis mine).[3] Paul asserts that the value of peace can override the prohibition against divorce in a case involving a non-Christian who divorces a Christian spouse—*even though Paul acknowledges that the Lord did not permit any such exception at all*. The Lord had said that there is to be no separation between married couples. Period. Paul makes allowance for the case where a pagan spouse leaves the Christian spouse.

Who is going to stop the pagan from leaving? In that case, the Lord would be understood as commanding the impossible, and Paul knows very well that God does not command the impossible. Paul merely recognizes the reality of the situation and feels comfortable enough to write that "I and not the Lord" declare that "if the unbelieving partner separates . . . ." Paul is not wrong. He merely responds to a marital situation in a pastoral way, again showing that the church has the power to manage the marital bond. Those who opine about the absolute indissolubility of marriage need to consider such dissolutions taken explicitly against a declaration of the Lord. Scripture itself testifies to the need to develop the Lord's sayings.

Furthermore, just prior to the Lord's teaching in Mark on divorce, Jesus acknowledges Moses's toleration of divorce. This needs to be taken into account as another unusual circumstance in which toleration

---

3. See Raymond Collins, *First Corinthians,* Sacra Pagina 7 (Collegeville, MN: Liturgical Press, 1999), 268.

becomes appropriate. Jesus does not condemn Moses but recognizes his departure from the norm as a pastoral accommodation at the time.[4] Clearly Jesus wants all to strive for the way it was from the beginning. Remarriage constitutes adultery, but in the post-lapsarian times of Moses, things were not ideal. For what should we strive? Obviously we strive for the ideal. We do not make the exception the norm. But in the time of Moses, conditions did not favor the ideal. The law of Moses provided for divorce as an accommodation that allowed life to move forward. Thomas Aquinas saw no difficulty in this Mosaic exception because it was "tolerated lest something worse happen."[5]

So Paul reports that Jesus permitted the separation of two married Christians as long as long as there was no remarriage. Paul has altered the words of Christ in a way that recognizes the exigencies of life outside its beginnings, which were very different from the idyllic confines of the Garden of Eden. Beyond that, Paul gives his own counsel regarding the freedom of Christians divorced by their non-Christian spouses—again, a separation not envisioned by the Lord.

Not living in a sinless Garden, Christians must cope with surprisingly complex situations that can destroy the peace that formed the motivation for Paul's relaxation of the norms in 1 Corinthians 7:15. Paul will not hold the Christian partner bound when the non-Christian has won a divorce. Paul understands clearly that Jesus did not have this in mind. Hence, he must add, "I [say] and not the Lord." Paul has the sense that Jesus laid out a general principle that will admit of exceptions. Paul feels free to oversee the marital bond in ways that alter it as the general principle descends into concrete circumstances of daily life.

These Scriptural passages constitute the earliest evidence of the church's ongoing management of the marital bond. It comes with a rec-

---

4. One should not think of the Mosaic accommodation as unique or confined to the earliest days of the Old Testament. Caesarius of Arles (c. 470–542 AD) refers to a remarkably similar circumstance in his day. Even though Caesarius insisted that keeping a concubine before marriage was worse than adultery, he nonetheless commended a group of priests who shared Communion with those men out of pastoral concern. See his Sermon 43 (5). A quotation from the homily appears in chap. 7, section 2, B, below.

5. Thomas Aquinas, *Commentary on the Gospel of St. Matthew*, chaps. 1–12, vol. 33, trans. Jeremy Holmes and Beth Mortensen (Lander, WY: The Aquinas Institute for the Study of Sacred Doctrine, 2013), ch. 5. lect. 9, sec. 514 (p. 631). See also ST Suppl. q. 67, a. 3, ad. 5.

ognition that pre-lapsarian values (the way it was in the beginning) can take on a different light in a post-lapsarian world whose imperfections present intolerable or even impossible situations for broken marriages. Not a desk-theologian but a pastor faced with difficulties stemming from real marriages, Paul saw how some destructive situations can defeat greater values and how the church is empowered to respond.

When Joseph Fitzmyer treats the Matthean version of the Markan text, he agrees that the more primitive form of Matthew 19:8-9 is found in Mark 10:11-12, where the Lord's prohibition against divorce takes an absolute form ("Whoever divorces his wife and marries another commits adultery"). But Fitzmyer observes that Matthew reformulates the question in a way that looks for an exception, "Is it lawful to divorce one's wife *for any cause?*" (Matt 19:3; emphasis mine). When Matthew reports the Lord's reply, he feels free to add the *porneia* exception by reporting Jesus as saying, "And I say to you, whoever divorces his wife, except for unchastity [*porneia*], and marries another commits adultery" (19:9).[6] While the change leaves the prohibition against divorce intact, it renders it more complex and nuanced.[7] Are such changes legitimate?

Fitzmyer raises an important point: "If Matthew under inspiration could have been moved to add an exceptive phrase to the saying of Jesus about divorce that he found in an absolute form in . . . his Marcan source . . . , or if Paul likewise under inspiration could introduce into his writing an exception on his own authority, then why cannot the Spirit-guided institutional Church of a later generation make a similar exception in view of problems confronting Christian married life of its day . . . ?"[8] So Matthew expanded the words of Jesus beyond those

---

6. See Joseph Fitzmyer, "Matthean Divorce Texts and Some New Palestinian Evidence," *Theological Studies*, vol. 37:2 (June 1976): 223.

7. Some scholars think that *porneia* refers to unchastity, while others believe it refers to unlawful marriages. Hans Conzelmann adopts the first position and Francis J. Moloney the second. Also, Aquinas and others would say that the Lord in Matthew 19:9 permits divorce but not remarriage. Furthermore, Matthew offers a surprisingly positive characterization of a divorce involving a non-consummated marriage when he reports Joseph's intentions to divorce Mary in 1:19. See Raymond E. Brown, *The Birth of the Messiah: A Commentary on the Infancy Narratives in Matthew and Luke* (New York: Image Books, 1979), 122, 128.

8. Fitzmyer, "Matthean Divorce Texts," 224. Paul Mankowski seriously misrepresents Fitzmyer's overall thesis when he records Fitzmyer as simply concluding, "the regulation

reported by Mark to include a needed nuance, first by allowing not only divorce but also remarriage in the case of *porneia* (Matt 19:9).

This injunction against divorce along with the *porneia* exception occurs in the Sermon on the Mount as well. It is part of a list of shocking sayings that obviously are hyperboles, such as plucking out one's eye if it causes sin. Jesus has a point to make, but it is not literal compliance to new precepts that need to be imposed regardless of the circumstances.

The six shocking sayings take the following form, "You have heard it said . . . , but I say to you . . ." How does the church apply those sayings? Does anger make one liable for murder in court (5:22)? Will one who calls his brother a fool suffer the fires of hell (5:22)? While acknowledging the point that we need to maintain loving relations with others, the church has shown mercy on those who occasionally display angry outbursts at others. It does not condone anger, but it also does not follow the letter of the Lord's directives. Why? Because the Lord was trying to drive home a point using a type of literary hyperbole.

Throughout the six shocking sayings, Jesus intends to alarm his audience by shaking their confidence in the law. He shakes things up by speaking in a legal format ("You have heard it said . . .") while sending a prophetic message that is intended to be taken seriously but not literally. For example, he says, "You have heard that it was said, 'You shall not commit adultery.' But I tell you that everyone who looks at a woman with lust has already committed adultery with her in his heart" (Matt 5:28). Again, it should be obvious that Jesus considers adultery as a phenomenon that can take different forms. Simple adultery, adultery of the heart, and adultery as remarriage do not simply describe the same thing. Jesus can speak in hyperbolic terms meant to be taken earnestly but not as if nothing could complicate the matter. If one interprets these sayings literally and commits adultery of the heart, the consequences can be severe: "If your right eye causes you to sin, tear it out and throw it away" (Matt 5:29). The point is not to blind oneself, but to gain new insight about what the law has been driving at since the beginning.

[on dissolution] is absolute" in reference to 1 Cor 7:10-11. Indeed, it is absolute. All the more forceful, then, Fitzmyer's further observation that the Spirit-led church of a later age has seen fit to alter such "absolute" teachings. See Mankowski, "Dominical Teaching on Divorce and Remarriage," 41.

Carrying on in this same fashion, the Lord prohibits oaths (5:34). This too has not been taken literally. The church has long permitted oaths for serious reasons.[9] Paul himself swears an oath at least two times in Scripture (see 2 Cor 1:23 and Gal 1:20). Just as the church has justified the dissolution of some marriages through the Pauline privilege, so too it justifies oaths, both in spite of the Lord's explicit admonitions in Matthew 5. Special note needs to be made of the next exhortation, "You have heard that it was said, 'An eye for an eye and a tooth for a tooth.' But I say to you, Do not resist an evildoer. But if anyone strikes you on the right cheek, turn the other also" (5:38-39). Set in the form of a law without any exceptions (such as the *porneia* exception that allows divorce), the prophetic bite of the saying against violence causes all the more discomfort. Yet the church has long recognized the right to self-defense, even claiming it to be a duty for the common good of the family or the state.[10]

Matthew includes Jesus's saying against divorce among the six shocking sayings. As with the other shocking sayings, literal application in all cases risks misinterpretation. Being shocked back to one's senses is the point. He prophetically used the form of law to shock his audience into paying attention to the fundamental concerns of the law. The Lord intends that every marriage in the community should be indissoluble. While individual couples often live their marriages faithfully during their lives, the expectation that an entire community may live that way without any divorces seems ideal, yet it is the goal. What happens to the unfortunate individual whose spouse leaves the marriage? For that person, an indissoluble marriage has indeed become an impossible ideal.

If the church does not in fact consider angry words as murder, if it realizes that a lustful look is not the strict equivalent of adultery, if it can tolerate oaths, and if it can excuse killing in self-defense in the name of mercy, why can't it also tolerate a second marriage when nothing else can be done? Although the church allows merciful accommodations with the Lord's sayings in the Sermon on the Mount, it does not claim that killing, scandal, lust, divorce, and anger have thereby been legitimized. They have not. If a pope can deal mercifully

9. See CCC 2154.
10. See CCC 2265-66.

with tolerating a war, he can deal mercifully with tolerating a divorce in proper circumstances.

The church has not only long recognized the Pauline privilege; it has also acknowledged the legitimacy of the dissolution of a non-sacramental marriage in favor of the faith in particular circumstances. Its Scriptural backing occurs when Christ confers the power of the "keys of the kingdom" on Peter. After Peter declares Jesus to be "the Messiah, the Son of the living God" (Matt 16:16), Jesus bestows on Simon the name Peter and assures him that the gates of hell will not prevail over the church. Jesus immediately declares, "I will give you the keys of the kingdom of heaven; and whatever you bind on earth will be bound in heaven, and whatever you loose on earth will be loosed in heaven" (16:19).[11]

In a 1991 work, then-Cardinal Ratzinger called attention to the fact that "the reference to the keys clearly approximates the meaning of binding and loosing." In rabbinic literature, such action stood "for the authority to make doctrinal decisions and . . . denotes a further disciplinary power." Moreover, Jesus gives Peter a role far beyond that of a prophet like Jeremiah. Whereas the Lord made Jeremiah merely "a fortified city" (Jer 1:18) who would oppose the powers of flesh and blood, Peter must stand against the very powers of hell. In spite of the apparent mismatch, the Lord gives assurance that the gates of hell shall not prevail against this Rock (Matt 16:18). Ratzinger concludes,

> This seems to me to be a cardinal point: at the inmost core of the new commission, which robs the forces of destruction of their power, is the grace of forgiveness. It constitutes the Church. The Church is founded upon forgiveness. Peter himself is the personal embodiment of this truth. . . . The Church is by nature the home of forgiveness, and it is thus that chaos is banished from within her. She is held together by forgiveness, and Peter is the perpetual living reminder of this reality:

11. This power hearkens back to the eighth century BC in Judah, when the Lord gave authority to Eliakim to act as the master of the royal household. He bestowed on him "the key of the house of David; he shall open, and no one shall shut; he shall shut, and no one shall open" (Isa 22:22). Just as Eliakim became the doorkeeper of the house of David, so too in the New Testament, Peter becomes the doorkeeper of the kingdom of God.

she is not a communion of the perfect but a communion of sinners who need and seek forgiveness.[12]

A similar promise is given to the church at Matthew 18:18-19 where Jesus, having just emphasized the mercy shown in unlimited forgiveness, adds, "[I]f two of you agree on earth about anything you ask, it will be done for you by my Father in heaven" (18:19). This conferral of the keys arises in a judicial context concerning any case, any matter (*pragma* in the Greek), not simply any informal dispute among Christians. Cases concerning marital dilemmas fit this category nicely. In these cases, church leaders must apply mercy and, where appropriate, overrule the law without overturning it, as Christ himself did upon occasion. The power of the keys has nothing to do with the power to change doctrine in an almost arbitrary way, rather, it concerns the application of both doctrine and law to individual cases. Mercy and forgiveness call for a most judicious and discerning application of the power of the keys, especially for people caught in dilemmas.

Both the Pauline privilege and dissolutions in favor of the faith originate in circumstances where pastoral mercy seems to warrant the dissolution of the first non-sacramental (but valid) marriage in favor of a second marriage, which is sacramental. In addition, the church has long recognized that, if a just cause exists, the pope may grant a dispensation even from a valid sacramental marriage if it has been ratified but not consummated (see canons 1142 and 1698). If the dispensation is granted, the partners are free to remarry without fear of committing adultery.

None of those acts is controversial in the least, yet each privilege dissolves a valid existing marital bond in the name of mercy and *each type of marriage falls under the ban against divorce originally pronounced by Jesus.*

---

12. Joseph Ratzinger, *Called to Communion: Understanding the Church Today* (San Francisco: Ignatius, 1996), 63–64. Raymond E. Brown has noted that pronouncements on the relentless nature of forgiveness both precede and follow the granting of the power of the keys in Matthew 18. He claims, "The Matthean Jesus has defined the unforgiveable sin: it is to be unforgiving" (*The Churches the Apostles Left Behind* [New York: Paulist Press, 1984], 145).

Occasionally one encounters anachronistic claims that Jesus's pro-hibition against divorce did not include non-sacramental marriages or sacramental marriages that have not yet been consummated.[13] But Jesus did not limit his prohibition against divorce to sacramental marriages. That category did not even exist in his day. In fact, Paul himself says that Jesus did not have in mind the niceties of the Pauline privilege: "To the rest, I say—*I and not the Lord*—that if any believer has a wife who is an unbeliever. . ." (1 Cor 7:12; emphasis mine). Jesus referred to *all marriages from the beginning.* Otherwise marriages and divorces in the days of Moses would not even pertain to his debate with the Pharisees (Matt 19:3-9). The church carved out exceptions and rea-sonable accommodations as it judged appropriate in the Spirit at the time it made its decisions.

This should not be considered as a radical disjunction from the Lord's will. Peter of Tarentaise (the future Pope Innocent V and a colleague of Thomas Aquinas), wrote commentaries on the Pauline epistles in the mindset of Aquinas. His commentary concerning 1 Co-rinthians is often included in collections of Aquinas's Scriptural com-mentaries. His entry for 1 Corinthians 7:12 helpfully suggests that Paul did not intend to speak *in opposition to the Lord.* He imagines Paul as silently adding, "I say this from the Lord, although he does not say it with his own lips."[14] Even though Paul could say, "I speak, not the Lord," this does not imply that Paul's pronouncement contradicts the Lord. He views himself as furthering the Lord's mission. This indicates that the Lord's sayings have a certain "play in the joints," that they need to be understood in the spirit in which Jesus spoke. In other words, Peter of Tarentaise assures us that, if the Lord had considered the situation facing Paul, he would have said what Paul said. The proper interpre-tation of Scriptures in the light of Christ requires accommodations such as this.

---

13. See Matthew Levering, *The Indissolubility of Marriage: Amoris Laetitia in Context* (San Francisco: Ignatius Press, 2019), 170. Chapters 6 and 7 below will deal more thoroughly with other claims made by Levering.

14. Thomas Aquinas and Peter of Tarentaise, *Commentary on the Letters of Saint Paul to the Corinthians*, trans. Fabian R. Larcher, Beth Mortensen, and Daniel Keating (Lander, WY: The Aquinas Institute, 2012), ch. 7, lect. 2, sec. 342 (p. 129).

To emphasize the difference between the starting point of Christ's prohibition and where the church has legitimately come after two millennia of experience, Theodore Mackin recasts the foundational text on which Jesus relied: "What God has joined God can separate through his vicar on earth."[15] That fictional reconstruction has more theological validity to it than a reconstruction that would have Jesus referring to unconsummated sacramental marriages. In fact, Aquinas said practically the same thing as Mackin.[16]

In view of the above discussion, we need not be startled when we read Paul's admission that "I [say] and not the Lord . . .," nor need we become alarmed when we hear the pope's offer of mercy to couples who have become trapped in second marriages. They also need to remember that if a person simply divorces his or her spouse and seeks remarriage to someone else, a Catholic priest will invariably deny the remarriage because the indissoluble bond of the previous marriage forbids it. This situation has not changed in the least. That case differs from the one in which a person has already remarried and has a viable family of some years standing. Seeking conversion, he or she may come for counseling and eventually to confession in hopes that the church can give a penance that will not damage the upbringing of the children and destroy the good that has already developed in the new family. Here accompaniment becomes pertinent. Mercy should treat each case according to its own specific facts as the Lord would treat it.

2. Dilemmas, Ambiguity, and History

The church has a long history of managing the marital bond starting right from the beginning, as is evident in Paul's alterations in 1 Corinthians 7. Church leaders continued this management of extraordinary marital

---

15. Theodore Mackin, *Divorce and Remarriage: Marriage in the Catholic Church* (New York: Paulist Press, 1984), 401.

16. Thomas Aquinas, *Commentary on the Gospel of St. Matthew*, ch. 19, lect. 1 (p. 162): *"Vel propter consensum mutuum, ut Deo liberius serviat, et sic est a Deo"* ("Or it [separation] can come about by mutual consent, that one may serve God more freely, and in this way it is from God").

circumstances in the years after Paul's ministry.[17] These types of dilemmas are handled on a case-by-case basis and do not involve the alteration of old principles, nor the development of new ones. Nevertheless, significant evidence of mercy extended to couples caught in dilemmas does exist in the historical record. A brief review of some cases will shed further light on chapter 8 of AL.

Among the earliest witnesses, Origen (c. 185–c. 254) testifies to a situation in which "some leaders of the Church recently permitted a certain woman to remarry while her husband was still living. By doing so, they acted in a way that was not in accordance with the Scriptures." Nevertheless, he grants that the decision "was not entirely unreasonable . . . . Although this concession is not in accordance with what has been ordained and written from the beginning, it is very likely that they made it in view of worse things that might happen."[18] The significance of the citation from Origen lies not in his opinion about the favor granted to a couple, but in the fact that he testifies to the early practice of several leaders showing mercy to a couple who could not reasonably leave an invalid marriage. Regardless of whether Origen agrees or not (I think he does agree), he plainly offers evidence of this merciful practice in his day.

These types of decisions involved a departure from a restrictive reading of Scripture and the application of mercy to prevent a greater evil from happening. The leaders did not attempt to formulate a new principle; they simply responded to a particular situation in a merciful

---

17. David Bentley Hart, "Divorce, Annulment & Communion," *Commonweal* (September 2019): 24–26, provides a very useful summary of historical points of interest for a different purpose.

18. See Philip Lyndon Reynolds, *Marriage in the Western Church: The Christianization of Marriage during the Patristic and Early Medieval Periods* (New York: E. J. Brill, 1994), 179. Origen has 1 Corinthians 7:39 and Romans 7:3 in mind. Much has been made of the fact that Origen typically gives far more weight to Scripture than to reason. See John Rist, "Divorce and Remarriage in the Early Church: Some Historical and Cultural Reflections," in Dodaro, *Remaining in the Truth of Christ*, 84. His concern badly distorts Origen's stance on reason. See Henri Crouzel, "Origen," in René Latourelle and Rino Fisichella, *Dictionary of Fundamental Theology* (New York: Herder & Herder, 1994), 748–49. In the case under consideration, Origen understands the contribution of reason as avoiding "worse things that might happen." It does not sound as if Origen advocated the occurrence of the "worse things."

way. The pastoral position Pope Francis has outlined in AL reflects the same sort of thinking.[19]

Although at times the evidence is only indirect, at other times evidence of extraordinary measures taken in the name of mercy assume the most public and direct form.

The Synod of Arles in 314, for example, produced twenty-two canons dealing with various ecclesiastical abuses. Canon 11 states that when young Christian men divorce their wives for committing adultery, they "as far as possible should be counseled not to marry again as long as their wives are alive, even though the latter are adulteresses."[20] If synod fathers were trying to formulate a rule that automatically incorporated mercy, it comes across as confusing and imprecise. What did they mean by "as far as possible"? How much effort in counseling qualifies as enough under that standard? Popes in later years wisely will not attempt to make rules from the very difficult individual cases presented to them. Acts of mercy belong to a different category. In any event, the synod's canon 11 testifies to the fact that the church continued to manage the marital bond well into the patristic era.[21] It happened on a case-by-case basis, even in contravention of existing marital bonds, as envisioned in the power of the keys (Matt 16:19; 18:18-19).

Soon after the Synod of Arles, the issue of the toleration of second marriages arose in one of the greatest councils ever convened in the church, the Council of Nicaea (325). Canon 8 explicitly requires all the faithful, including the so-called Cathars[22] ("pure ones" who followed a

19. The often cited position of St. Basil the Great (330–79) in his Letter 188 concerns divorce and remarriage after an incident involving the *porneia* clause of Matthew 5:31. The position is irrelevant. Pope Francis does not propose any such accommodation.

20. The synod dealt mainly with the Donatist heresy. Evidently, the young men justified themselves using the *porneia* clause of Matthew 19:8. The synod fathers permitted them to separate, but would not allow them to remarry. What is of interest is the qualification that pastoral counseling should urge them "as far as possible" not to remarry. This resonates with the Lord's Mosaic exception in Matthew 19:8 and seems to concede the inability of some men to remain continent. See Reynolds, *Marriage in the Western Church*, 181.

21. Curiously, John Rist cites canon 10, forbidding husbands who divorce adulterous wives from marrying again. He ignores canon 11. He seems content to argue against those who would simply permit all the divorced to remarry, a position that AL does not propose. See Rist, "Divorce and Remarriage," 85.

22. Certain moral rigorists (Cathars), under the leadership of Novatian, had been expelled from the church at a synod in Rome, in part because they refused to accept

rigorist priest, Novatian), to "be in communion with those who have entered into a second marriage."[23] The term "second marriage" (*digamos*) referred both to situations of adulterous marriages and to marriages contracted after the death of a spouse. Nicaea did not limit the term *digamos* to one or the other situation. It seems to refer to both. The first situation recalls the state of affairs of the young men referenced at the Synod of Arles just eleven years previously. What if the recommended counseling did not have its intended effect? What if they entered second marriages that they could not simply terminate?

The council determined that the Cathars who wished to be received back into communion with the church must "accept and follow the decrees of the catholic church, namely that they will be in communion with those who have entered into a second marriage and with those who have lapsed in time of persecution."[24] Although Novatianists held that God alone has the power to forgive and rectify sins that tend to death (apostasy, murder and adultery), the fathers at Nicaea claimed that those powers had been given to the church. It could therefore judge that at least some of those in second marriages can live in communion with the church.[25]

How do we know that the Council had in mind adulterers whose spouses were still alive, in addition to widows?[26]

---

into communion with the church those in second marriages and those who had been guilty of apostasy during the persecutions under Decius (249–50 AD). They denied the church's authority to absolve the mortal sins of adultery and apostasy. Excommunicated, the Novatian sect survived on its own. The Novatian Bishop Acesius, although accepting the Nicene positions concerning Arianism, remained in schism because he would not accept the church's absolution of those who committed adultery or apostasy.

23. Norman Tanner, *Decrees of the Ecumenical Councils*, 2 vols. (Washington, DC: Georgetown University Press, 1990), 1:10.

24. Tanner, *Decrees of the Ecumenical Councils*, 1:9–10.

25. See Giovanni Cereti, "Reconciliation of Remarried Divorcees according to Canon 8 of the Council of Nicaea," in J. Provost and K. Walf, eds., *Ius Sequitur Vitam: Law Follows Life: Studies in Canon Law presented to P. J. M. Huizing* (Leuven: University Press, 1991), 198–200.

26. Paul's explicit statement in Romans 7:1-3 (that death frees one from the law and therefore frees a surviving spouse to remarry) may have given Novatianists some hesitation in withholding communion from widows who remarried. It seems that the Novatianist church gave special tribute to widows who refused to remarry, which indicates that the practice of remarriage may have been the more common practice. See Cereti, "Reconciliation of Remarried Divorcees," 201n23.

Giovanni Cereti notes that "Novatians excluded from penance and reconciliation those Christians who had been guilty of sins leading to death. These sins are apostasy or idolatry . . . and adultery or fornication."[27] Cereti further observes that remarried widowers were never considered as *mortal* sinners by anyone in the church. It would seem, therefore, that the Cathars had in mind those in second marriages while their original spouses lived. Those sinned mortally, not widows whose sins counted as much less serious.

Cereti explains that in those early days, the church had no law of marriage of its own. It followed the civil laws. Once a divorce and remarriage occurred, the church, relying on its Scriptures, recognized that the sin of adultery was committed. Nevertheless, exigent circumstances could dictate the bestowal of mercy. The formation of a new civil marital union signaled that "a new situation had developed, which to the church of the time appeared almost irreversible."[28] So church leaders argued that at least some of those in second marriages can be reconciled to the church, as is witnessed by canon 8 of the Council of Nicaea.

Although Cereti incorrectly argues that the early church permitted divorce and remarriage in the normal course of affairs, his observation that people did not consider the remarriage of a widow as a sin leading to death has merit. The Nicaean reference to the twice-married in canon 8 refers both to widows and remarried divorcees who happen to enjoy communion with the church. The church can forgive both sins.[29] The Novatianists resisted communion with both remarried

27. Cereti, "Reconciliation of Remarried Divorcees," 198. Cereti claims, ". . . [I]t follows that 'those who live in a second marriage' are not 'remarried widowers' (as was maintained traditionally), because never in the history of the Church was marriage after the spouse's death considered to be 'a sin leading to death' or made equal to apostasy. In fact, [those referenced in Canon 8] are remarried divorcees; i.e., those adulterers of whom we have been constantly reminded in the texts of the Novatian controversy, those who, as a matter of fact, have remarried after leaving their spouses or having been left by them" (200–201). For example, the *Shepherd* of Hermas did not think a remarried widow committed any sin at all (*Mandates*, 4, 3, 1).

28. Cereti, "Reconciliation of Remarried Divorcees," 204.

29. Certainly the "twice-married" include widows. Henri Crouzel, SJ, has observed that some twenty-five years after the Council of Nicaea, Epiphanius (290–?) refers to how unfairly the Novatians treat the twice-married, since the Novatians hold the laity to the same standard as Scripture holds clergy—that they may marry only once (1 Tim 3:2, 12; Titus 1:6). Henri Crouzel, "Les digamoi visés par le Concile de Nicée dans son canon 8," *Augustinianum* 18 (1978): 541. But the language used in Nicaea's canon 8

widows and divorced and remarried Catholics, which, as we saw above, were occasionally present in the church. Indeed, the famed patristic scholar Henri Crouzel recognized "a desirable evolution of the Church's practice showing to the divorced and remarried a certain indulgence, without keeping them perpetually away from the sacraments."[30] He freely acknowledges and approves of the church's tolerance of certain distressed marriages. His disagreement with Cereti and others centers on a common error: "Frequently, tolerance is mistaken for permission," a blunder frequently made by the pope's critics.[31]

All this pertains to the resolution of concrete cases of hardship, not the revision of the Lord's call to fidelity to one's marital bond. It is supported by the power of the keys given to Peter and the church. One issue settled in Nicaea, therefore, is this: "Has the Church the power to forgive any sin or has it not?"[32] Nicaea answered yes, it does. Pope Francis continues to exercise that power today for appropriate divorced and remarried couples, without even implicitly validating the resulting union. He can do that because a couple's circumstances may allow for no other way.

The church gradually became more conscious of its power to manage the marital bond.[33]

---

would seem to include also some of those caught in adulterous marriages. If not, it would be remarkable for a council that was so focused on precise language concerning the divinity of Christ to fall into inaccurate and broad generalities concerning "second marriages." If the council fathers meant that the Cathars had to be in communion with only "remarried widows," they could have said so.

30. Henri Crouzel, "Un nouvel essai pour prouver l'acceptance des secondes noces après divorce dans l'Église primitive," *Augustinianum* 17 (1977): 566: (". . . une évolution de la pratique de l'Église qui serait souhaitable, témoigner envers les divorcés remarriés d'une certaine indulgence et ne pas les maintenir perpétuellement à l'écart des sacrements"). In similar fashion, Crouzel refers to the understandable indulgence allowing wives to remarry when their husbands have gone missing in combat ("Les digamoi," 537).

31. Henri Crouzel, "Divorce and Remarriage in the Early Church: Some Reflections on Historical Methodology," *Communio* 41 (Summer 2014): 499.

32. Cereti, "Reconciliation of Remarried Divorcees," 205.

33. By later patristic times, the church, following the work of Ambrosiaster (writing in about 384 AD), solidified the Pauline privilege by explicitly allowing not only the divorce but also the remarriage of a newly baptized person whose unbelieving spouse ends the marriage. This clarification of 1 Corinthians 7 consolidated the church's practice of granting the Pauline privilege and made it more widely available.

In the fifth century, Pope Innocent I indicated his willingness to allow a second marriage to stand in the face of an existing marital bond. During the barbarian invasions, a woman named Ursa, married to a man named Fortunius, was captured by the Visigoths. After some time, Fortunius married another woman. Ursa subsequently returned from captivity and asked Pope Innocent I to reinstate her marriage to Fortunius.[34] The pope ruled that the first marriage stood, unless the husband chose to divorce his first wife. In the eyes of Innocent I, in those circumstances, mercy can give the husband his choice to resume his first marriage or not. Mercy can override indissolubility without overturning the law. One can see the sense of possibly upholding the second marriage especially if, for example, it has produced several children while the original marriage may have lasted only months without having produced any offspring.

In any event, one must note that this same Pope Innocent I in 405 issued a letter in which he asserted that "any man who hastens to marry again while his wife is alive, even though his marriage seems to have been broken up, cannot but be considered an adulterer."[35] The pope can maintain *both* his position on Fortunius *and* his position on the law of indissolubility because the first is a merciful pastoral response to a dilemma and the second is a statement of a general principle by which he expected all Christians to abide. As that principle descends into the concrete facts of a given case, like that of Fortunius, it can look very different. Pope Francis follows the same path in AL.

Pope Leo I handled similar cases in 458 AD. Bishop Nicetas from northern Italy wrote to him that, due to foreign attacks (probably led by Attila the Hun), some men were taken captive. Their wives remarried, presuming that their husbands had either died or would not return from captivity. When some of the captives did return, the bishop asked Pope Leo what could be done. The pope responded that although the second husbands were blameless, the original husbands could claim their wives back. Their marriages had not ceased to exist merely

34. Reynolds, *Marriage in the Western Church*, 133–34. In a letter to Probius (probably a civic official), Innocent declares that the "alliance with the second woman, as long as the first wife survives *and has not been dismissed in a divorce*, cannot by any means be legitimate" (emphasis mine).

35. See Reynolds, *Marriage in the Western Church*, 214.

because of the lengthy separation. *Must* they return to their original marriages? Pope Leo claimed that if the returning captives did not want to go back to their remarried wives, their marriages need not be reinstated.[36] Like his predecessor, St. Innocent I, St. Leo the Great did not feel constrained to make his solution consistent with the rules. He did not explicitly sort out the issue of whether he considered the first marriage as dissolved or whether he tolerated a second marriage. The life situation had changed for both the first husband and his wife, possibly making a return to the original marriage quite artificial.

Although church law would require the restoration of the original marriage today (see canon 1707), Pope Leo explored such cases in a way that did not prejudge them. Each marital situation that faces such a difficulty needs individual attention. Both St. Innocent I and St. Leo the Great seem to have handled these cases in a more enlightened way than the modern canons allow. In fact, the issue deserves a brief excursus at this point.

Church leaders have not treated existing valid marital bonds as if they were so sacrosanct as to be untouchable. For those who consider bonds as absolutely indissoluble, one would expect the utmost care in the observance of existing bonds. Such is not always the case. Under today's canons, when a soldier goes off to war and fails to return, what can his wife do? Before she can remarry, canon 1707 expects her bishop to investigate the case, looking for evidence that the husband might have died in battle. The bishop needs to arrive at a "moral certitude" that the husband has died. Then he can issue a declaration of presumed death, which allows a new marriage to go forward.[37] Even though the declaration of presumed death requires "moral certitude," the evidence that supports that standard can be mercifully low. Obviously a bishop will look for solid evidence, eyewitness testimony, if possible. However, he may rely on hearsay evidence, if necessary. These standards fall far below what federal courts require in the U.S.

---

36. Leo states, "*if men* who have returned after long captivity so persevere in the love of their wives that they *want them to come back* to their partnership, then that which misfortune brought about should be set aside and what fidelity demands should be restored" (emphasis mine; cited in Reynolds, *Marriage in the Western Church*, 136–37).

37. The original marriage is treated as dissolved, although it is not really dissolved. If the original husband returns, he may claim his wife without any need for a new wedding to reinstate the supposedly dissolved union.

In the United States, civil courts generally require a preponderance of evidence to prove a case. This means that the party bearing the burden of proof must submit evidence that substantially outweighs opposing evidence. The evidence must overbear the weight of the evidence given by the other side and must be reliable, probative, and substantial. But bishops can reach "moral certitude" and issue a declaration of presumed death even if the evidence of the death of the first husband is based on a reputable rumor.[38] A "reputable rumor" sinks well below even the lowest standard in U. S. criminal law, which allows certain actions to take place on the showing of "probable cause." When the church does not know for sure whether a bond exists, it may allow the wife to enter a second marriage.[39] Under such lax rules of evidence, everyone understands that the original husband may still be living in a prison or trapped in a foreign land without the means to return home. Yet his wife can remarry. The canons allow such a merciful practice even though they may well violate the bond of the first marriage—even if it is sacramental and consummated.

This situation does not indicate that the church considers the marital bond lightly. It does not. Rather, the church considers the practice of mercy to be more important than the possibility of trespassing on an existing marital bond. The marital bond is not absolutely inviolable when mercy makes its claim. If it were, the standards of proof would be much more stringent.

Medieval popes seemed to understand this. They even recognized that certain other exigent circumstances required a merciful application of the law as well. In 726 AD, Pope Gregory II sent an official reply to St. Boniface, responding to a question regarding a marriage where the wife became mentally ill and of unsound mind. Could the husband take another wife if complete abstinence seemed impossible to him? Pope Gregory allowed the man to take a second wife on condition that he look after the needs of his first wife.[40] Although details are sketchy, the pertinent facts clearly affirm the possibility of a remarriage for the

---

38. John Beal, James Coriden, and Thomas Green, *New Commentary on the Code of Common Law* (New York: Paulist Press, 2000), 1799.

39. Today, if the husband returns, the wife must give up the second marriage and return to her original husband (under canon 1707).

40. Bernard Häring, *No Way Out? Pastoral Care of the Divorced and Remarried* (Middlegreen: St. Paul Publications, 1990), 47. See also Reynolds, *Marriage in the*

husband while his first wife was still living, not as a rule, but as a merciful response that met a pastoral need in a particular circumstance. While modern popes would probably not treat this case the same way today, it nevertheless demonstrates the degree of authority the pope felt he had in managing the marital bond.

Medieval popes took care to preserve the sense of the faith and to protect the marital bond. Nevertheless, they understood the primacy of mercy. For example, Pope Stephen II (752–757) upheld the marital bond in cases of the illness of one of the parties, even if one of them became incapable of fulfilling the marital obligation. But even that principle had its limits. He held that the complaining party is not allowed to marry another "unless demonic possession or leprosy has arisen," although they should continue to care for each other.[41] Although Pope Stephen holds firm to the general rule that remarriage is forbidden even in cases where one spouse becomes severely ill and incapable of marital intercourse, he nonetheless acknowledges that he would tolerate irregular situations as extraordinary circumstances arise. This constitutes another papal witness to mercy rather than the letter of the law.

Medieval bishops recognized that a new situation could obtain after an initial divorce and remarriage. It could call for absolution and penance without prohibiting the second marriage. Interestingly, an episcopal handbook of canons dating to around 1000 AD seems to recognize Pope Gregory II's line of thinking as controlling authority. It states that "a man whose wife has left him and refuses to go back to him may remarry after five or seven years with the consent of a bishop if he is unable to remain continent. He should then do penance for at least another three years after remarrying, and perhaps even for the rest of his life, since 'in the Lord's judgment' his second marriage makes him an adulterer."[42] Although the canonist tries to fashion a general principle from an instance of mercy, it does seem to indicate that medieval jurists did not feel totally constrained by the notion of absolute

---

Western Church, 346, which does not specify the malady of the wife and notes that the circumstances of the case are vague.

41. Cited in Reynolds, *Marriage in the Western Church,* 347.

42. This is taken from the *Excerptiones Egberti* (an early-eleventh-century English canon law collection), 108, and is cited in Reynolds, *Marriage in the Western Church,* 149.

indissolubility. This handbook version of mercy explicitly takes into account the Lord's pronouncement on divorce, but it also makes room for a second marriage in exigent circumstances.

The practice of mercy helps to explain the existence of divorce laws in officially Christian states. John T. Noonan has observed that after Christianity became the official religion of the empire, marriage laws curiously retained provisions for divorce. As a Christian empire, the realm's laws were supposed to reflect Christian values. Even the laws of Emperor Justinian, who was a devout and skilled theologian, included provision for divorce in 559 AD. Although bishops vigorously contested other anti-Christian provisions from 331 to 566 AD, they did not enter into any debates with Christian state officials concerning divorce.[43] Nor were divorce laws restricted so as to apply only to cases that sought the Pauline privilege. Even though the likes of Augustine and Jerome developed robust theologies supporting the indissolubility of marriage, the bishops seemed to have accepted the divorce laws with equanimity. This does not prove that the bishops approved of divorce. They did not. Evidently, they found divorce laws as useful enough in the pastoral realm to allow their provisions to remain in force.

All those decisions by bishops involve cases that touch on valid, consummated marriages. All of those divorces fall within the purview of Jesus's original wish for a world without divorce (Mark 10:6). Nevertheless, "the Spirit-guided Church of later days" exercised power to make the exceptions it did.[44] The power of the keys grants the successor of Peter and the church authority to issue such directives (see Matt 16:19 and 18:18-19).

Church leaders have also not shied away from occasionally changing the rules concerning marriage within one's own family. Certainly marriage between first cousins seems too close, but how far across the branches of the family tree does one need to go before the church

---

43. John T. Noonan, "Novel 22," *Ius Sequitur Vitam* (Leuven: University Press, 1991), 54ff. Perhaps bishops and others kept the divorce laws because they recognized the need for mercy. My conclusion from these historical facts differs from Noonan's conclusion. He thinks the evidence shows that Christians could accept that marriage was dissoluble without anyone charging them with heresy. See Noonan, 87.

44. Fitzmyer, "Matthean Divorce Texts," 223–24.

permits a marriage?[45] The management of the marital bond is not a precise science, and at times it seems that the temporal interests of the church may have determined its rules. Scripture provided some guidance (see Leviticus 18:16-18), as did Roman law. Sometime between the sixth and tenth centuries, "the Church shifted the method of computing degrees of consanguinity from the Roman practice . . . to the Germanic practice."[46] The Fourth Lateran Council reduced the scope of the impediment in 1215. The 1917 Code of Canon Law further reduced the impediment to the third generation in the collateral line. The 1983 Code returned to the Roman system of computing degrees of consanguinity.

To some extent the dividing lines are arbitrary, but whatever the basis of the decision, the result determines whether a marital bond exists or not. If a couple violates those sometimes-shifting rules, no marital bond exists. Not only that, but today "the local ordinary can dispense from the impediment in the third (uncle-niece) and fourth degrees (first cousins) of the collateral line."[47] Although bishops rarely employ it, the power exists.

Bishops throughout the ages have dealt with those matters as part of their responsibilities in managing the marital bond. They did not gaze into a crystal ball, trying to discern where an objective marital bond did or did not exist. They actively and consciously determined it through a fluid set of rules that shifted from time to time. Some

---

45. The church has varied its treatment of the indissolubility of the marital bond when it perceived that the greater societal good required it. Thus, it fought during the Middle Ages to end endogamous marriage (marriages permitted only within one's caste or class). By the eleventh and twelfth centuries, royalty and nobility had insisted on consolidating their power through marrying only within royal or noble families. This inbreeding could give rise to a level of consanguinity and affinity that threatened to produce null marriages. Occasionally the church would ignore the indissolubility of a marriage bond to ensure that endogamous marriages would not continue (see James A. Brundage, *Law, Sex, and Christian Society in Medieval Europe* [Chicago: University of Chicago Press, 1987], 199). Some claim that the Lord's directives on indissolubility took a back seat to the bishops' interests in freeing the church from the influence "of the grand noble clans whose power rested squarely on the control of extensive landed estates" (Brundage, *Law, Sex, and Christian Society*, 193).

46. Beal, Coriden, and Green, *New Commentary*, 1292–93.

47. Beal, Coriden, and Green, 1293.

bonds obviously call for recognition and other bonds do not. Yet an ambiguous area exists and testifies to the fact that marital situations admit of some flexibility when church leaders perceive the need to make adjustments. Once again, history illustrates that the church manages the marital bond; it does not simply take its marching orders from Christ's prohibition in Mark 10:5-12.

The church has also claimed the power to dissolve the bond of a sacramental marriage as long as it was not consummated and sufficient reason exists. For example, Thomas Aquinas thought that what God has joined together God could separate. He wrote that if a couple wants to enter consecrated religious life and they have not consummated their sacramental marriage, it may be dissolved in favor of the faith.[48] The same holds today for any reason that a pope deems sufficient. Although many people value outward compliance with marriage laws as necessary because of the public nature of marriage, here dissolution of a valid sacramental marriage hinges on the most private and intimate detail of a marriage: whether the couple has consummated the marriage. At times, scrupulous application of this rule has led to outrageous legal practices.[49]

In 1537, Pope Paul III issued his apostolic constitution *Altitudo* whereby he dissolved a good number of marriages. During this time of growing missionary activity, priests encountered natives who wanted baptism but were already married to several wives. The pope declared that if the convert could remember which wife he married first, he was bound to her and must dismiss the others. If he could not remember, he could keep whichever wife he chose and could contract a valid Christian marriage with her. The pope considered the marriages dissoluble because they were not sacraments. How far this decision is from the absolute prohibition found in Mark 10:5-12! At the time, the pope claimed that he merely extended the Pauline Privilege, but he actually developed a new ground for dissolution because it lacked an essential element of the privilege: there was no unbaptized spouse

48. Thomas Aquinas, *Commentary on the Gospel of St. Matthew*, ch. 19, lect. 1, sect. 514 (p. 162).

49. Bernard Häring tells of a horrendous case in which a woman was subjected to four physical inspections to assure the tribunal that she was still a virgin (*No Way Out?*, 16–17).

who refused to live in peace with the convert.[50] Again the church managed the marital bond, acting mercifully in very trying circumstances.

The Council of Trent followed suit. It recognized the need for leeway so the church could respond to the wide variety of challenges marriages could pose. Canon 3 refers to the grades of consanguinity and affinity described in Leviticus 18:6-18 and asserts that no one can say "that the Church can neither dispense from any of them nor enact others that prevent marriage or make it null." Canon 4 asserts the church's "power to establish diriment impediments to marriage." Canon 8 claims that the church may impose a separation between spouses "for a variety of reasons." Once again, the church claims the power to manage the marital bond, not just to recognize bonds as if they had an obvious existence in and of themselves.[51]

In 1571, Pope Pius V faced a missionary situation in which a convert who had many wives honestly admitted that his first wife wanted to remain a pagan. He wanted a sacramental marriage, but could not have one if he had to take the pagan as his wife and reject a later potential wife who wanted baptism. In *Romani Pontificis*, Pius determined that such a convert may dismiss his pagan wife and declare as his Christian wife the one who has received baptism with him "because it is a cruel thing to separate such a man from the woman with whom he received baptism . . . and We declare that such marriages between them are legitimate."[52] Again the papacy demonstrates its merciful power to manage the marital bond to avoid cruelty in difficult circumstances.

Fourteen years later, Gregory XIII confronted the marital problems produced by the then-burgeoning slave trade that regularly separated families. For example, a husband may have been moved against his will from Africa across the Atlantic to the West Indies while his wife had to stay behind. If the newly baptized slave in the West Indies wanted to marry, he could not vouch that his pagan spouse back in Africa would reject the marriage as required by the Pauline privilege. If she agrees to live peacefully in the marriage, the marriage stands. But what if he has no way to determine her wishes? In his constitution *Populis ac*

50. Mackin, *Divorce and Remarriage*, 396.

51. The "Canons on the Sacrament of Marriage" from the Council of Trent (1545–63). See Council of Trent, Session 24, in Norman P. Tanner, *Decrees*, 754–55.

52. Mackin, *Divorce and Remarriage*, 397–98.

Nationibus (1585), Gregory showed mercy in that, if it was impossible for the slave in the West Indies to communicate with his pagan wife, the requirement to determine if she would live peacefully with the Christian husband could be dispensed. In making this sensible accommodation in the name of mercy, Gregory went beyond the Pauline privilege. As Theodore Mackin states, Gregory dispensed "the newly baptized Catholics from what was in fact impossible to them."[53] There was no way that a slave in the West Indies could communicate with his original wife to see if she would repudiate the marriage or not. Gregory refused to hold a spouse to an impossible standard.

Pope Francis acts on a similar concern: that couples should not be held to standards that are impossible for them to satisfy. Francis differs only in the fact that he does not issue a dispensation but tolerates the new union while allowing the merciful administration of penance and the Eucharist.

Gregory treated an even thornier issue in *Populis ac Nationibus*. If the originally pagan wife was later baptized after being separated from her husband, the Pauline privilege technically did not apply at all because both parties received baptism and both parties had consummated the marriage. According to then-prevailing law and theology, it was a sacramental marriage that was consummated and was no longer susceptible to dissolution under the Pauline privilege. This did not stop Gregory XIII from holding that even though a baptized slave was in a consummated marriage with a recently baptized wife, a second marriage would be allowed to stand because Gregory reasoned that only consummation *after* the baptism counts as making the marriage a consummated sacramental marriage.[54] Otherwise the marriage would not be consummated *as sacramental*.

What set of statutes could possibly anticipate the scenarios that Gregory faced? These cases could have gone either way. Gregory did not follow a pre-determined path. He certainly did not follow a system of rules that would produce unlivable results. He responded as a merciful pastor, managing marital bonds for his flock as best he could in a merciful way.

---

53. Mackin, 399.
54. Mackin, 399–401.

These sorts of instances of mercy and tolerance do not arise only in medieval and Counter-Reformation contexts. Popes in modern times have also applied merciful solutions as the need arose. In 1947, Pope Pius XII dissolved a marriage between an unbaptized woman and a Roman Catholic man even though the church had issued a dispensation allowing the marriage. After the wife won a civil divorce, she wished to become Catholic and marry a Catholic man. The pope dissolved the marriage in favor of the faith. In 1959, Pope John XXIII dissolved a non-sacramental marriage for an unbaptized man who wished to marry a Catholic woman but without any intention of becoming Catholic himself. According to Theodore Mackin, under then-current rules, the justification for this dissolution did not rest on a privilege given in favor of the faith in the sense that it did not result in a sacramental marriage. The pope seems to have issued the dissolution simply on the basis of mercy.[55]

What motivated those acts of mercy throughout two millennia? To paraphrase Oliver Wendell Holmes, the life of the law of Christ has not been logic; it has been the lived experience of the Christian mystery of love and mercy in the power of the Spirit. An abstract reflection on the nature of the marital bond did not give rise to those cases, but a view of Christ gazing upon the concrete dilemmas and horrific predicaments of some married couples did.

* * *

To further illustrate the difficulty of discerning the existence of the marital bond and the importance of mercy, one need only recall that the church has long involved itself in the nearly impossible task of judging which marriages, in spite of all appearances, might not actually have been marriages at all. Although annulment procedures require evidence from those familiar with the couple prior to the marriage,

55. One further case shows that the author of *Casti Connubii*, Pope Pius XI, in 1924 dissolved a marriage of an unbaptized man who was married to an Episcopalian woman so that he could receive baptism in the Catholic Church and marry a Catholic woman. This reinvigorated an old category of valid but dissoluble marriages in favor of the faith. All three cases in the above paragraph are reported in Mackin, *Divorce and Remarriage*, 14–15.

and in spite of an appellate process designed to ensure the integrity of any previous marital bond, nevertheless, mistakes can happen. Even though cases can be reopened and reversed when necessary, the church lives with the ambiguity because mercy demands it. Judicial procedures can accomplish only so much.

Truth be told, the Pauline privilege, decisions that grant dissolutions in favor of the faith, and decisions that grant a dispensation in sacramental marriages that have been ratified but not consummated, as well as the occasional toleration of marital dilemmas, constitute exceptions and instances of tolerance that arise from the "Spirit-guided institutional Church of a later generation," as Fitzmyer claimed.[56]

In these cases, the instances of tolerance of irregular marriages and exceptions to otherwise valid marriages are not so much a commentary on the indissolubility of marriage as they are affirmations of the centrality of mercy and the church's right to manage the marital bond accordingly.

56. Fitzmyer, "Matthean Divorce Texts," 224.

CHAPTER SIX

Other Viewpoints

I t might be productive at this point to consider some of the positions taken by those who question AL or who interpret it in overly restrictive ways. They take these positions because they love the church. They offer many good and well-researched opinions that actually do shed light on parts of Catholic teaching.

Unfortunately, their passionate love occasionally distorts their ability to read chapter 8 with a calm heart that discerns correctly its message. Most of those who pose challenging questions and present restrictive interpretations fail to appreciate that AL addresses not only normal divorce and remarriage situations, but also marital dilemmas that could otherwise paralyze couples who need to act in ways that protect valid interests, often the upbringing of children. Furthermore, when these thinkers linger at the level of abstract doctrine, they miss the issues that are brought on by concrete circumstances. These commentators, therefore, also have a propensity to pay insufficient attention to the events of history and their implications.

Sometimes faithfulness means enduring great struggles. In the context of marriage, some faithful couples must fight for their marriages. Some may be tempted to look back and wonder if they could have done better, but they accept and nurture the bond they have made. They stay in their marriages and make the best of it. They indeed live up to the Gospel ideal of love and mercy and incur some suffering in the process. Everyone needs to come to the support of such couples.

Some other marriages, on the other hand, consist of at least one spouse who does not endure. The marriage is lost. This also causes great suffering and can give rise to predicaments that have no ethical solution. Most of the critics of AL recite all the correct sections of the *Catechism*, and they call upon Scripture as it supports their case. They are not wrong. They simply argue against a position no one holds.

We will now consider some of these other viewpoints concerning AL, along with some observations about why I believe their positions to be inadequate.[1]

1. The *Dubia*

On September 19, 2016, four cardinals—Walter Brandmüller, Raymond Burke, Carlo Caffarra, and Joachim Meisner—privately sent Pope Francis a set of five *dubia*—that is, questions or requests for clarification that are written in such a way that they call for "yes" or "no" answers—on issues raised in AL. After receiving no reply from the pope, the cardinals made their letter public and disclosed the five *dubia*, together with an explanatory note.[2] Each of the *dubia* submitted by the cardinals revolves around the notion that second invalid marriages always constitute adultery and are, therefore, intrinsically evil. Such unions, they argue, cannot therefore remain in place. Let's explore that notion.

The first *dubium* (singular of *dubia*) asks how the document can be squared with St. John Paul II's *Familiaris Consortio* 84, which imposes three conditions on couples living in an invalid second marriage. The couple may live together if: (1) the persons concerned cannot separate without committing new injustices; (2) they abstain from acts that are proper to spouses; and (3) they avoid giving scandal. The teaching is based on Matthew 19:3-9, where the Lord proclaims, "And I say to you, whoever divorces his wife, except for unchastity [*porneia*], and marries another commits adultery."

---

1. Much of the literature published prior to the issuance of AL is treated in the footnotes that appear in relevant sections above. This chapter deals with major works that have appeared after the promulgation of AL.

2. Card. Walter Brandmüller, Card. Raymond Burke, Card. Carlo Caffarra, Card. Joachim Meisner, "Seeking Clarity: A Plea to Untie the Knots in 'Amoris Laetitia,'" available at https://aleteia.org/2016/11/14/full-text-seeking-clarity-a-plea-to-untie -the-knots-in-amoris-laetitia/.

The second *dubium* asks whether "the teaching . . . on the existence of absolute moral norms that prohibit intrinsically evil acts and that are binding without exceptions" is still to be considered valid. Does AL now claim there are no intrinsically evil acts?

The third *dubium* asks, "[I]s it still possible to affirm that a person who habitually lives in contradiction to a commandment of God's law . . . finds him or herself in an objective situation of grave habitual sin?" In other words, AL seems to allow for mitigating circumstances for at least some couples living in irregular marriages. Their objective circumstances seem no longer to count. According to AL, such couples may still enjoy sanctifying grace, with the right to receive Communion. The cardinals rely here on, inter alia, canon 915, which states that people who "obstinately persist in manifest grave sin are not to be admitted to Holy Communion."

The fourth *dubium* asks whether the church is still to hold that (quoting John Paul II's encyclical *Veritatis Splendor*) "circumstances or intentions can never transform an act intrinsically evil by virtue of its object into an act 'subjectively' good or defensible as a choice." Similar to the second *dubium*, this question asks whether circumstances can transform an intrinsically evil act into something that is "commendable or at least excusable."

The fifth *dubium* asks whether one's conscience can assume the role of granting "exceptions to absolute moral norms that prohibit intrinsically evil acts?" It makes reference to some who have fashioned creative pastoral solutions based on the supremacy of conscience, suggesting that, in their view, a person may know very well that he is engaged in adultery on the objective level, but it is possible that God may really be calling him to commit adultery. Of course, the role of conscience is never to remake the moral law, but only to judge the morality of a particular concrete act in light of existing ethical norms.

The *dubia* seem to make a lot of sense as far as they go. The obviously preferred answer to each of the *dubia* does point in the direction of some of the church's teachings and practices over the ages. Nevertheless, church leaders may want to reassess some of those practices.

For example, the concern to avoid scandal mentioned in the first *dubium* sometimes has caused problems. A major element of the shock waves emanating from the sexual abuse scandal of 2002 is that many bishops covered up misdeeds of the clergy and sought protection in nondisclosure agreements with affected parties. As those contracts unraveled, the scandals came to light with much more force than they would have otherwise. Bishops and their advisors overestimated their ability to manipulate scandals. As applied to couples in irregular unions, perhaps the greater scandal today would come from the church's overt shunning of couples who are doing the best they can in impossible circumstances. Many of the Catholic laity have already come to accept the "brother-sister" relationship without needing a full recounting of the facts in each case. It seems likely that they would also give the benefit of the doubt to those irregular families being accompanied through a very difficult time in their lives. Perhaps such a situation can evolve naturally, with the pastor attending to the distressed couple but also keeping an eye out for potential scandal in the parish. This approach would still leave in place the possibility of a pastor withholding the Eucharist from couples in irregular marriages who simply think they have a right to the Eucharist, regardless of the status of their marriage.

Although the *dubia* rely on various Catholic teachings, they frequently address positions that no one proposes. Walter Kasper has perceptively commented, "None of the seven implicated sentences is contained in *Amoris laetitia* or in any other document of the pope. At root, it has to do with misrepresentations that no theologian that I know holds."[3] Nevertheless, the *dubia* deserve a closer examination.

A. Intrinsic Evil and Exceptions

As several of the *dubia* emphasize, an intrinsic evil allows for no exceptions. And yet in the only passage of Scripture cited in the *dubia*, Matthew 19:3-9, the Lord seems to offer *two* exceptions to the prohibition on divorce and remarriage. First, Jesus comments that Moses allowed divorce because of the stubbornness of his people (19:8). Jesus does not criticize Moses as having done something wrong; rather he criticizes the hardheartedness of the people. To him, Moses's action is understandable as an exercise of pastoral mercy. Although scholars typically refer to this as the Mosaic exception, technically it describes the application of toleration to a difficult situation, not an exception. Although the cardinals do not explain it, they are justified in holding

3. Walter Kasper, *The Message of* Amoris Laetitia: *Finding Common Ground* (New York: Paulist Press, 2019), xi n3.

that it does not form an exception to indissolubility. Nevertheless, they fail to grasp that the pope bases his merciful position in chapter 8 also on toleration, not on the fabrication of a new exception.

Second, Jesus himself grants an exception in the case of *porneia*, thereby permitting separation (19:9). The cardinals' position that considers divorce and remarriage as an intrinsic evil seems to be subverted by the very passage they cite. To what does the *porneia* exception refer? Most likely, *porneia* refers to unlawful marriages, analogous to today's canonically invalid marriages.[4] If so, the cardinals can also defend themselves by claiming that the *porneia* exception is not really an exception, but a reference to what we today would consider as a null marriage.

But here the issue becomes murky. Consider a couple who marries in good faith, but whose relationship in fact fails to satisfy the requirements for a valid marriage. Years later, the marriage falls apart. A tribunal issues a declaration of nullity, indicating that the marriage was not really a marriage right from the beginning. Null marriages are not really marriages. Well, then, what are they? No one would say that such couples lived in sin before the annulment. Those marriages certainly looked valid at the time they were contracted. They are certainly treated as valid marriages until a final declaration of nullity is issued. Oddly, the canonical validity of a marriage can coincide with its existential nullity.

Perhaps one key to a better understanding of the implications of Jesus's prohibition can be found in the obvious but often-ignored fact that the Lord was not considering the ordinary case of simple adultery (uncomplicated by an attempted second marriage) when he spoke of the Mosaic and *porneia* exceptions. He did not have in mind the simple situation of lusty husbands wandering from their wives for a secretive one-night stand. Obviously such acts of adultery are evil, but they do not necessarily result in divorce. Thus they do not directly pertain to the topic Jesus addresses: that although divorce and remarriage is one way to commit adultery, exceptional circumstances might arise in complicated cases that give rise to tolerance, such as in the indulgence

---

4. The opinion that *porneia* refers to unlawful marriages has not been universally held. For example, Aquinas believed that *porneia* refers to fornication, and that it allows for divorce in certain circumstances. See his *Commentary on the Sentences*, bk. IV, d. 35, q.1, art. 1, ad.

granted by Moses (who was certainly not giving permission to commit adultery) and the *porneia* clause (in which Jesus permits a divorce).

Jesus did not draw a simple equivalence between second marriages and adultery, even though adultery is committed in such situations. Second marriages complicate matters enormously, and Jesus knew it. The fact that second marriages produce families makes the situation much more complex than the adultery that one spouse tries to hide from another. In the latter case, the cheating spouse wants to keep his spouse and family. In the former case, the spouse has already publicly given up on the marriage as a whole. The intentions and circumstances involved in remarriage differ greatly from simple adultery. That's why Jesus talked about the two exceptions and why Paul could add other exceptions. If a second invalid marriage were equivalent to simple adultery, critics of AL would have to ignore the Mosaic and the *porneia* exceptions, and they have.

The point is that *some critics take Jesus's words as if he said that an irregular marriage "is" adultery, as if they were equivalent concepts.* He didn't say that. Jesus said that one way to commit adultery is to enter into a second (invalid) marriage. True, but that is a far cry from considering an irregular marriage to be nothing more than an adultery, no more complex or nuanced than a one-time-only adultery that leads to nothing further. People who treat an irregular marriage as nothing more than adultery unduly simplify their task. They fail to consider the children who arise from the invalid union and the financial and emotional hardships that may have led to that union. They fail to consider any other bind into which the couple has entered. It's simply, they insist, adultery. That's all they need to know. Case closed. Such thinking makes invisible an array of issues that need careful consideration.

The cardinals seem unaware of such predicaments and unacquainted with Joseph Fitzmyer's observation that Matthew himself attached an exception to the marital bond that Mark does not mention in his earlier rendition of the Lord's prohibition. Further, the cardinals' position seems not to take sufficient account of the fact that Paul had also altered the sayings of Jesus regarding indissolubility. Nor do they demonstrate how the "brother-sister" relationship, which violates a valid marital bond, can receive official church approval while withholding mercy from other couples who are also in dire straits but who cannot manage such an artificial relationship.

B. Circumstances and Intentions in Intrinsically Evil Acts

The cardinals claim that irregular second marriages constitute evil, even intrinsic evil. That is, they can see no circumstances or intentions that would justify a second marriage while one's spouse by a valid marriage is still living. This claim needs closer scrutiny.[5]

The notion of intrinsic evil has come to mean different things to different people. For some, an act being recognized as intrinsically evil is an indicator of how deeply offensive it is to the moral order. Such an act is so bad, it carries such moral turpitude, that it holds a special place in the list of sins. No serious thinker subscribes to this version of intrinsic evil. The term "intrinsic evil" designates *not how evil an act is* but that *it is always evil.*

Others consider the term "intrinsic evil" as a rallying cry against relativism. It becomes a shibboleth, a password that reliably identifies a person as a member of a group that takes morality seriously. The term contains an implicit critique of others who choose to equivocate about an issue and search for excuses to allow immoral actions. Those who understand that an act represents an "intrinsic evil" reject all equivocation. Although relativism and the search for weak excuses deserve condemnation, the term "intrinsic evil" serves a greater purpose than merely as a rallying cry against relativism.

Many others hold to the curbstone opinion that intrinsic evil refers to an act that so severely offends the moral order that no good intention and no circumstances can possibly exculpate the person. One need not consider the intention or circumstances of the moral actor at all. They feel that any such consideration invites equivocation. They would view questions about intention and circumstances as a softheaded and cheap imitation of compassion that has lost sight of its moral compass. In its search for clarity and simplicity, this understanding takes the intrinsically evil act out of the moral realm altogether. The mere physical act itself always results in culpability.

Such an understanding cannot withstand analysis. Circumstances and intention can never be omitted from the moral evaluation of an event, even for intrinsically evil actions. For example, under this

---

5. See James Bretzke, "*Responsum ad Dubia*: Harmonizing *Veritatis Splendor* and *Amoris Laetitia* through a Conscience-Informed Casuistry," *Journal of Catholic Social Thought*, 15:1 (2018): 211–22.

thinking, if a woman goes to a hospital and has an abortion, she is guilty of grave sin, no matter what else she may claim. What intentions or circumstances could possibly establish her innocence? How could they exculpate her from the intrinsically evil act of abortion? Consider this improbable scenario: Two pregnant women enter a hospital. One comes to have an abortion, and the other is having another unrelated surgical procedure. Both require anesthesia that will render them unconscious. Unfortunately, hospital orderlies negligently confuse the two gurneys. They take the wrong woman into the operating room where she has an abortion. Of course, abortion still gravely offends against the moral order. The circumstances surrounding this tragedy and the innocent intent of the woman do not render the abortion as good or even as indifferent. Abortion is still evil, but the woman who had the abortion is not guilty of any sin at all under these circumstances. She lacked the intention that the term "abortion" assumes. The circumstances prevented her from stopping the abortion. In this case, intention and circumstances determined the morality of the action of the woman. Although she underwent an intrinsically evil operation, she was innocent.

When an act is called "intrinsically evil," it presumes within its very definition that sufficient intentions and circumstances are already in place to make the actor morally culpable. Just as the very definition of murder includes a consideration of intent and circumstances that distinguish it from negligent homicide, so too any intrinsically evil act includes consideration of intent and circumstances.[6]

An intrinsically evil act requires that the moral agent do the act freely before it even qualifies *as sin*. The end of the physical act constitutes evil, but the moral quality of any concrete act still depends on it being a voluntary act that takes into account the intention of the moral actor, what he or she meant in doing the particular action in its particular circumstances. The sin has not only a material meaning (how it impacts the world in a negative way) but also a formal meaning (the freely formed intent of the actor).[7] Although Aquinas never

6. St. John Henry Newman, in defending himself against the attacks of Charles Kingsley, made the same distinction. See his *Apologia pro Vita Sua* (New York: E. P. Dutton, 1949), 308.

7. See James Bretzke, *A Morally Complex World: Engaging Contemporary Moral Theology* (Collegeville, MN: Liturgical Press, 2004), 72–73. Aquinas supports this position. See ST I-II, q. 18, a. 6.

used the term "intrinsic evil," *Veritatis Splendor* uses the term in its full sense, describing an act as "*intrinsice malum in se*," that is, "intrinsically evil in itself,"[8] meaning that the requisite circumstances and intention are assumed already to be in place as part of the act itself.[9] John Paul II writes that such acts are evil "on account of their very object, and quite apart from the ulterior intentions of the one acting and the circumstances."[10] The "ulterior intentions" of the actor refer to intentions *beyond those* that the definition already assumes present in the actor that make him or her culpable of the sin. "Ulterior circumstances" refer to circumstances *in addition to* a circumstance that would keep the definition of the sin in place. No exceptions allow intrinsically evil acts—assuming the requisite moral intention remains part of the act.

The argument in AL does not claim that an evil act has been rendered good, excusable, or commendable. Insofar as the irregular second marriage is evil, AL would agree with the *dubia*. The irregular marriage that violates an existing marital bond remains evil. The couple caught in an irregular marriage cannot have their marriage "blessed" by the church in any sort of second marriage ceremony. But the *dubia* fail to appreciate that a dilemma can exist for some couples. It fails to appreciate that parties may not be at liberty to act differently. One essential element of moral action—freedom—has been rendered null. Walter Kasper is correct when he writes, "The weakness of many criticisms of *Amoris laetitia* is that they represent a one-sided moral objectivism and do not consider the subjective dimension, which is an essential element of moral action."[11]

In a dilemma, a divorced parent has options that promote only one evil or another. A distressed single mother may insist on clinging to the remnants of her chastity while witnessing the continued deterioration of her children, or she may surrender her chastity in the hopes of providing a more adequate family structure for her children. Whatever she does is evil. The woman must discern and choose the lesser of the evil

---

8. Pope John Paul II, *Veritatis Splendor* 80.

9. See James Bretzke, Dana Dillon, and Michael P. Jaycox, "Debating 'Intrinsic Evil,'" *Horizons* 41:1 (June 2014): 120–65, for a more thorough discussion. Although Aquinas uses the term "*malum in se*" ("evil in itself"), Bretzke and Dillon note that he never uses the term "intrinsic evil" (120, 134).

10. Pope John Paul II, *Veritatis Splendor* 80.

11. Kasper, *Message of* Amoris Laetitia, 41.

alternatives that present themselves in her situation—a situation that requires discernment and accompaniment. The decision should not be considered as obvious, as if the divorced mother were expected to remarry. It may well be that her suitor would make a terrible husband and stepfather. Such a single parent needs to read the future in making a decision. Hope does not necessarily suggest another marriage.

C. Obstinate Persistence in Grave Sin

The cardinals' reliance on canon 915 also falters in view of the dilemma faced by couples in irregular marriages. Under that canon, Catholics who "obstinately persist in manifest grave sin are not to be admitted to Holy Communion." But couples caught in a dilemma are not being "obstinate"—as if they had another reasonable choice and refuse to act rightly out of mere stubbornness. They have only choices that pose one evil or another. An obstinate person acts out of laziness, vainglory, rivalry, or self-satisfaction. He shuns the work it takes to consider other options. Obstinacy does not describe all couples in irregular marriages.[12] In the situation of the irregular marriage, other more noble concerns may take hold, such as the raising of one's children. Communion under those circumstances offers the contrite couple the strength they need to proceed in a situation they would never wish to encounter—but there they are!

Furthermore, canon 915 requires that the sin be "manifest." If the couple in an irregular marriage has been discrete about their situation, their problematic union may not be manifest in the slightest. The participation in Communion by at least some couples in such marriages seems not to be blocked since their objectively sinful situation is neither obstinate nor manifest.[13] Moreover, following the thinking proposed by the cardinals, those living in "brother-sister" relationships would also have to refrain from Communion since they too persist in an illegitimate relationship in a public and "obstinate" way, as explained in chapter 3 above.

---

12. It helps to consider canon 915 in conjunction with canon 18, which deals with burdens: "Laws which establish a penalty, restrict the free exercise of rights, or contain an exception from the law are subject to strict interpretation." This limits the application of canon 915 to the minimum stated in the law. This means that the words *obstinate* and *manifest* do not apply to the cases of contrite couples in irregular marriages.

13. Walter Kasper agrees. See *Message of* Amoris Laetitia, 42.

The mercy that permits a "brother-sister" couple to receive Communion also permits some other irregular couples to receive. The possibility of Communion in these circumstances will be treated more fully in chapter 7 below.

D. Conscience

The cardinals' reference to a "creative interpretation of the role of conscience" as if it were "authorized to legitimate exceptions to absolute moral norms" in their fifth *dubium* misses the point of AL 303. Conscience, according to *Gaudium et Spes* 16, defines the place in a person where he or she detects a law imposed by God. It holds the person to obedience, always summoning the person to love good and avoid evil. It "speaks to the heart: do this, shun that. For man has in his heart a law written by God; to obey it is the very dignity of man; according to it he will be judged. Conscience is the most secret core and sanctuary of man. There he is alone with God, Whose voice echoes in his depths."

A woman who encounters a dilemma surely wrestles with her conscience. A divorced woman who knows of no "exceptions" to the rules nonetheless looks for the requirements of love in her life. Conscience, according to AL 303, can accomplish more than the simple recognition that a person's present situation violates an ethical norm. As the place where they are alone with God, people caught in a moral quandary certainly raise the relevant issues in deepest prayer: "What am I to do in this mess? How will I carry on? Can I not provide the best situation for my children?" This tangling with conscience involves much more than simply knowing that an objective violation of a moral norm has arisen. It is clear that her irregular situation violates the norm. AL does not fashion an exception for her so she can call the irregular situation "legitimate." It entertains the possibility that church leaders can tolerate some distressed marriages in circumstances that allow them to do nothing else.

When only evil alternatives exist, the moral actor understandably enters into deepest dialogue with God.[14] Conscience "can . . . recognize with sincerity and honesty what for now is the most generous response which can be given to God, and come to see with a certain moral security that it is what God himself is asking amid the concrete complexity

14. CCC 1776.

of one's limits, while yet not fully the objective ideal" (AL 303). In other words, conscience works with the situation that lies before it, not a textbook abstraction of what could happen in ideal circumstances. Conscience always deals with concrete circumstances. Conscience forms the sanctuary where the least evil alternative is identified and subsequently pursued. This extremely difficult situation deserves the accompaniment of good priests and pastoral ministers who can assist the person in sorting out the alternatives. If a good alternative is found, it must be pursued. If no good alternative exists, the moral actor must take the least evil alternative that does exist. This activity does not constitute the search for an exception that would legitimate an intrinsically evil act, as the cardinals suppose in their fifth *dubium*. In fact, AL 300 specifically repudiates the search for exceptions.

In summary, the *dubia* fail to take into account (1) that some couples in irregular marriages live in a dilemma where they have no choice but the least evil alternative that presents itself in their situation (answering *dubia* 1, 3 and 4); (2) that AL does not attempt to identify "exceptions" to intrinsically evil acts nor does it ignore the moral dimensions of freedom and circumstance in intrinsically evil actions (answering *dubia* 2, 4, and 5); and (3) that conscience can serve to bare one's soul before God, imploring mercy for one who has no legitimate choices in the matter (answering *dubium* 5). In addition, the *dubia* ignore the Lord's comments on the Mosaic tolerance of divorce and the *porneia* exception in Matthew 19:3-9, and they do not account for the crucial historical role of mercy in the Christian dispensation.

The *dubia* do not so much fail as they are irrelevant to the question at hand. The same can be said of two similar sets of prominently published objections that are both based on arguments similar to those found in the *dubia*.[15]

---

15. In September 2017, a group of sixty-two Catholic clergy and scholars signed and published online a lengthy "Filial Correction" of the pope, urging him to alter his teaching (see http://www.correctiofilialis.org/). The text suffers from the same deficiencies as the *dubia*. So too with the "Open Letter to the Bishops of the Catholic Church," dated Easter Week 2019 (see https://www.documentcloud.org/documents/5983408-Open -Letter-to-the-Bishops-of-the-Catholic.html), in which nineteen clergy and scholars urge the world's bishops to deal with the pope as a heretic. Both documents fail to consider Scripture in light of the historical dilemmas presented above. See James Heft, SM, "Is Pope Francis a Heretic?," *Origins* 49, no. 12 (August 1, 2019): 183–84.

2. An Ahistorical Analysis

Another notable study of the text of AL is *Accompanying, Discerning, Integrating: A Handbook for the Pastoral Care of the Family According to* Amoris Laetitia, written by José Granados, Stephen Kampowski, and Juan José Pérez-Soba, three professors of the Pontifical Institute of John Paul II.[16] In the authors' view, Francis has offered inspiring support for the indissolubility of marriage. They note, for example, that the pope considers the matrimonial bond to be an expression of true love and not merely the result of a juridical contract. They emphasize that accompaniment should support a person's continuing maturation rather than merely dealing with the paperwork to certify his or her status as "regular" again.[17] They offer their work as a guidebook that will help those who counsel families in distress so they can find their way to renewed holiness and peace.

Granados, Kampowski, and Pérez-Soba raise many admirable points. Nevertheless, their treatment falters in several key respects.

A. Method

First, their theological method deliberately ignores vast segments of church history. To their credit, they state this explicitly when they offer the criteria by which they interpret AL:[18] "When an ambiguous or debatable passage appears in *Amoris laetitia*, the sole valid interpretation is one that reads in continuity with the preceding Magisterium. In no way can the temptation to yield to a hermeneutic . . . based on some alleged return to a patristic tradition be justified. For this would result in a break from subsequent tradition."[19]

---

16. José Granados, Stephen Kampowski, and Juan José Pérez-Soba, *Accompanying, Discerning, Integrating: A Handbook for the Pastoral Care of the Family According to* Amoris Laetitia (Steubenville, OH: Emmaus Road, 2017).

17. Granados, Kampowski, and Pérez-Soba, *Accompanying, Discerning, Integrating*, xiv, 28; AL 211, 315.

18. Their three criteria are: (1) to read AL in the context of its "Synodal itinerary"; (2) to attend to the context of the document as they interpret particular passages; and (3) to interpret the document in continuity with the tradition of the church.

19. Granados, Kampowski, and Pérez-Soba, *Accompanying, Discerning, Integrating*, ix–x.

In fact, the magisterium of the preceding pontificate itself disagrees with the approach of the three professors. In his apostolic exhortation *Verbum Domini*, Pope Benedict XVI repeatedly refers to the importance of the fathers of the church and the complete living tradition.[20] Furthermore, Vatican II's *Dei Verbum* 8 states, "The fathers of the church bear witness to the enlivening presence of this tradition, and show how its riches flow into the practice and life of the believing and praying church." The tradition thrives on the church's ability to tap the thought and experience of former ages. In 1969 then-Fr. Joseph Ratzinger explained, "*The whole spiritual experience of the Church . . . causes our understanding of the original truth to grow and in the today of faith extracts anew from the yesterday* of its historical origin *what was meant for all time.*"[21] Commenting specifically about the fathers of the church, Fr. Ratzinger stated, "Their writings testify to the living presence of tradition and are, as it were, a living expression of the perpetuation of the mystery of Christ in the life of the Church. . . . [The fathers bring] an expression of the act of understanding, which assimilates what has been passed down and holds it for the present."[22]

Finally, not only do the principles that the future Pope Benedict articulated in 1969 contradict the method of the three professors, we also know that following the publication of AL, Pope-emeritus Benedict himself disagreed specifically with the sort of conclusion Granados, Kampowski, and Pérez-Soba have reached about AL. Journalist Austin Ivereigh reports that in July of 2017, the pope-emeritus told Cardinal Christoph Schönborn that "John Paul II's *Familiaris Consortio* and Francis's *Amoris Laetitia* formed a 'diptych.'"[23] Thus the former pope acknowledges the consistency of the teaching of Pope Francis with the teaching of St. John Paul II, for whom he served as the prefect of

20. Pope Benedict XVI, apostolic exhortation *Verbum Domini* (September 30, 2010) 7, 17–18, 29, 37.

21. Joseph Ratzinger, "Dogmatic Constitution on Divine Revelation, Chapter II," in *Commentary on the Documents of Vatican II*, vol. 3, ed. Herbert Vorgrimler (New York: Herder & Herder, 1969), 186 (emphasis mine).

22. Ratzinger, "Dogmatic Constitution on Divine Revelation," 189.

23. Austen Ivereigh, *Wounded Shepherd: Pope Francis and His Struggle to Convert the Catholic Church* (New York: Henry Holt and Company, 2019), 300.

the Congregation for the Doctrine of the Faith. Those who think they perceive a divergence need to reread the documents in light of a more profound theology that considers the real problems some people can face.[24]

In truncating their consideration of the history of the church, the three authors miss the opportunity to consider concrete cases that call for mercy. The dilemmas people can face and the creative responses that popes have applied to those dilemmas become apparent only through historical investigation. Instead, the authors seem to feel much more comfortable with abstract concepts and stereotypical irregular marriages. It distorts their perception.

For example, the authors comment that the religious difficulty of "the lack of full membership in the Church" comes not with the divorce but with the second attempted marriage.[25] In one sense, this is true enough, especially when canonical considerations take center stage. Yet Jesus identifies *divorce* (rather than remarriage) as the more fundamental religious issue because it was not that way from the beginning (Mark 10:6). This tendency to overlook the real life problems of divorce and the impact it has on children, while skipping forward to the problems of full membership in the church (directly affecting only the adults), should not eclipse the obvious difficulties experienced by the children of divorced parents, whether or not there is a remarriage. In fact, the three authors devote only one paragraph to the problem of children. Few other references occur in the text and then only in passing.[26]

Their focus on remarriage reminds one of the proclivities of some church leaders to overlook the pain children experience in divorce while they fixate their attention on adult concerns. Of course, the authors know this. They simply do not let it influence their thinking in a helpful way.

---

24. We might also note that Schönborn himself has commented that AL represents "an 'organic development' of existing teaching based on a 'profoundly Thomistic' theology of grace" (see Ivereigh, *Wounded Shepherd*, 300).

25. Granados, Kampowski, and Pérez-Soba, *Accompanying, Discerning, Integrating*, 65, 71, 76–77.

26. Granados, Kampowski, and Pérez-Soba, 144, and for references in passing, 57, 71, 87, 100, 114, 115, 116.

B. The Law of Rules

Granados, Kampowski, and Pérez-Soba correctly acknowledge the role of the law as a pedagogue that leads the believer towards the fullness of Christ.[27] Indeed, Christ has come not to abolish but to fulfill the law and the prophets (see Matt 5:17). Yet the authors seem to take that statement as an endorsement that the rules always adequately communicate the presence of Christ. At no point do the authors allow the student to let go of the pedagogue to meet the Master. They simply insist that everyone needs to obey the law. Mercy never intrudes.[28]

The three authors properly distinguish the "law of gradualness" (whereby ministers need to take into account the weaknesses and particular circumstances of people and gradually lead them to the fullness of truth and love) from "the gradualness of the law" (whereby some misguided ministers attempt to tailor the law to fit the subjective possibilities of the individual). After much analysis, they conclude, "Under no circumstances can a consideration of . . . mitigating factors adapt the requirements of the law to what the person considers him- or herself able to do, as though sin could be excused because of weakness."[29]

Of course, the pope does not claim in AL that he has developed a new exception to indissolubility. In fact, he endorses the traditional teaching in that regard. Francis does not claim that the law no longer applies to irregular couples, nor does he excuse their sin. He acknowledges that couples in irregular marriages violate the law. They live in a state of objective sin, in violation of the previous marital vows. Therefore, the church cannot allow any sort of second marriage ceremony to take place. It does not recognize the irregular union as a valid marriage. Some of those couples, however, have entered a dilemma that gives them no choice. They face impossible circumstances.

The moral law does not hold people to performing the impossible. Certainly no one can expect a person to perform what is *physically* impossible. For example, a person cannot fulfill both the obligation to

27. Granados, Kampowski, and Pérez-Soba, 18.

28. The authors avoid a discussion on the numerous exceptions that have developed for equally binding laws such as those regarding killing in certain circumstances, or the taking of oaths. See chapter 5 above.

29. Granados, Kampowski, and Pérez-Soba, *Accompanying, Discerning, Integrating*, 25.

attend Sunday Mass and simultaneously the obligation to care for a sick child at home. Nor can one expect a person to perform what is *morally* impossible for that person. For example, no one should expect a father prior to receiving Communion to confess his serious sin to his priest-son, if he is the only priest available.[30] Some people can enter very difficult situations that make it morally impossible for them to leave an irregular marriage. Unfortunately, the three authors fail to treat any of those situations. Much of what they write is true and even inspiring, but irrelevant to the issues faced by distressed marriages that have encountered dilemmas.

Francis refuses to use the law to aggravate an already dire situation. When the law does not accomplish its intended effect in a given case, pastoral necessity takes one beyond the law. Yet the three professors consider only cases that fit neatly within the categories already established by the law. When they abstractly consider other messy cases in general, they simply force them into the mold. For example, they admit that some bishops and theologians question whether the practice of abstinence is practicable for all couples. In rejecting their concern, the professors consider the problem only in global terms, as if all couples in all unions faced exactly the same circumstances and possessed the same resources. In fact, they claim that someone who is separated from a spouse, "whether or not a new union has been established, is in the same situation as someone who is not yet married."[31] The assertion is stunning in its inability to discern a difference between a person who never married and a struggling divorced mother who has remarried in an effort to support her children. When she seeks reconciliation with the church, she may well be trapped in a situation that no unmarried person could fathom. While the moral law applies to both of them, what can be expected of the divorced woman may well be very different from what can be expected of the one who has never married.

30. See James Bretzke, *Handbook of Roman Catholic Moral Terms* (Washington, DC: Georgetown University, 2013), 91, 120. The three authors acknowledge that morally impossible situations can exist. See Granados, Kampowski, and Pérez-Soba, *Accompanying, Discerning, Integrating*, 92n12.

31. Granados, Kampowski, and Pérez-Soba, *Accompanying, Discerning, Integrating*, 118. Once again, even though the single individual and the remarried person both commit adultery, Jesus never claimed that they were in the same situation. See this chapter, section 1 A, above for a discussion of this issue.

At every turn, it appears to the professors that the statement of the law fully conveys the spirit of Christ. The authors seem committed to the law of rules rather than the rule of law. No law or set of laws can ever communicate the fullness of Christ. The three authors fail to recognize that mercy fulfills the law, not the reverse. As Pope Benedict declared, citing St. Bernard of Clairvaux, "The Christian faith is not a 'religion of the book': Christianity is the 'religion of the word of God,' not of 'a written and mute word, but of the incarnate and living Word.'"[32] As explained above in chapter 2, the law is a pedagogue that leads one to Christ. Although generally reliable, at times one needs to let go of the pedagogue to meet the Master (see Gal 3:24). The authors also understand the law as a pedagogue, but they treat the law as if it fulfilled Christ, as if one never needed to let go of the pedagogue, as if a text could replace the Lord of Mercy. It reminds one of the rigorism of seventeenth-century Jansenism. Describing one essential tenet of Jansenism, Bernard Häring wrote, "Behind this [heresy] stood the false conviction that doing good and acting in accordance with the law coincided completely."[33] Clement XI condemned Jansenism in 1713.

According to the authors, a proper marital bond should not be broken, no matter the circumstances. And of course, that's true. A proper marital bond remains in place and invalidates subsequent attempts at marriage. However, valid marriages can be damaged beyond repair. If the authors considered the history of the church, they would find some broken marriages that send a divorced person in pursuit of a lesser evil. When this results in a second marriage, it does not dissolve the prior marriage, nor does it permit bigamy. It simply allows the church to manage marital bonds in a way that does the least harm.

In order to discover this facet of mercy, we again need to refer to church history, a formidable resource for those who choose to use it. St. John Henry Newman wrote, "As the Church is a sacred and divine creation, so in like manner her history . . . recorded on no system,

---

32. Pope Benedict XVI, *Verbum Domini* 7. See also Joseph Ratzinger, *Introduction to Christianity*, trans. J. R. Foster (San Francisco: Ignatius Press, 1969), 203–4.

33. Bernard Häring, *No Way Out? Pastoral Care of the Divorced and Remarried* (Middlegreen: St. Paul Publications, 1990), 60.

and by uninspired authors, still is a sacred work also; and those who make light of it, or distrust its lessons, incur a grave responsibility."[34]

History has plenty to teach, as chapter 5 has illustrated.

C. Dilemmas

Granados, Kampowski, and Pérez-Soba, committed to an abstract analysis, think that dilemmas are impossible.[35] They approach the topic as if some were trying to change the teaching of the church. Mercy does not change any teaching; it addresses itself to concrete dilemmas where the lesser evil needs to be done in order to avoid a greater evil.

Everyone should note that the lesser evil remains an evil. The authors seem to think that providing mercy in a dilemma changes the moral law.[36] It does not. That's one reason a second marriage ceremony is not allowed. Those who have entered the field hospital know that sometimes "leaving well enough alone" is the most charitable response available; at other times it's not. Can dilemmas exist?

Although the Lord never gives anyone a dilemma, people produce them sometimes in the most appalling ways.[37] In his novel *Sophie's Choice*, William Styron presents a scene set during World War II in which a Nazi official at the Auschwitz concentration camp forces a mother to choose which of her two children will be allowed to survive. If she fails to choose, both will be executed.

> "You mean, I have to choose?" . . .
> Her thought processes dwindled, ceased. Then she felt her legs crumple. "I can't choose! I can't choose! . . . *Ich kann nicht wahlen!*" she screamed.[38]

But for one caught in a dilemma, not choosing is never a choice. Any answer given will be wrong. That's the nature of a dilemma.

---

34. John Henry Newman, *Certain Difficulties Felt by Anglicans in Catholic Teaching* II (Westminster, MD: Christian Classics, 1969), 309.

35. Granados, Kampowski, and Pérez-Soba, *Accompanying, Discerning, Integrating*, 61, 87, 97. According to them, a second marriage is "always reversible" (61).

36. See, for example, Granados, Kampowski, and Pérez-Soba, 97, 100–101, 115.

37. See Thomas Aquinas, II *Sent.*, d. 39, q. 3, a. 3, ad 5.

38. William Styron, *Sophie's Choice* (New York: Bantam Books, 1979), 589.

Dilemmas exist not only in novels but in real-life marriages. They need careful discernment to enable a party to a dilemma to choose the lesser of the two evils. Thomas Aquinas identified the first principle of natural law as the obligation to do good and avoid evil.[39] In an effort to capture the true meaning of Aquinas's original Latin—"*bonum est faciendum et prosequendum et malum vitandum*"—James Bretzke offers as a rather free translation: "The nature and meaning of what we term the 'good' is that we are to be engaged in doing, fostering, and supporting it, while the nature and meaning of what we term 'evil' we ought to be seeking to minimize or avoid as much as possible."[40] The Latin word Aquinas used to describe the moral actor's stance vis-à-vis evil, *vitandum* (to be avoided, shunned), connotes a much different tone than other, harsher Latin terms he could have chosen. Thomas did not direct moral actors to destroy evil (*abolere*), annihilate it (*delere*), extinguish it (*exstinguere*), or eradicate it (*eradicare*). Aquinas understood the complexity of a world that sometimes does not offer neat and clean solutions where one might have to live in the presence of evil while being able only to shun it or minimize it.

Many caught in marital dilemmas today would break the vows of their already-failed marriages in order to give their children a more stable home where possible. The decision requires a difficult judgment about the likely effects of the remarriage. Understandably, the divorced agonize over the decision, especially since their first marriages failed and caused such pain. Once they have remarried and seek reconciliation with the church, ministers ought to provide them with compassionate accompaniment in the midst of their trials.

The three professors express confidence that dilemmas cannot exist and cite Trent's 1547 *Decree on Justification* as authority.[41] In chapter 11 of the decree, the council fathers state, "But no one, however much justified, should consider himself exempt from observance of the commandments; no one should use that rash statement . . . that the observance of the commandments of God is impossible for one that is justified. For God does not command impossibilities, but

39. See ST I-II, q. 94, art. 2.

40. Bretzke, *A Morally Complex World*, 61.

41. Granados, Kampowski, and Pérez-Soba, *Accompanying, Discerning, Integrating*, 21.

by commanding admonishes you to do what you can and to pray for what you cannot and aids you that you may be able."[42]

Although on the face of it the statement appears to support the professors' position, the historical context shines a much different light on the topic than the three authors suspect.

The council did not address the issue of whether dilemmas can exist. It formulated its *Decree on Justification* in response to an opinion expressed by Martin Luther in his treatise *The Freedom of a Christian*.[43] The fathers felt that Luther proposed that it is impossible for a justified Christian (or anyone else) to obey the Ten Commandments—even in the best of circumstances.

Against Luther's supposed position that no one could obey the Ten Commandments, Trent simply held the opposite: that everyone can obey the Ten Commandments.[44] The *Decree on Justification* has nothing to do with whether people can encounter moral dilemmas that make the choice of a lesser evil necessary. It certainly does not declare that dilemmas cannot exist.

In fact, Trent's language comes directly from St. Augustine's treatise "On Nature and Grace" (chapter 50) where indeed the saint states that God does not command impossibilities. Augustine knew that original sin weakened human nature to such an extent that human beings cannot simply obey the Commandments. To explicate his thought, he places the discussion in the context of Luke's story of the Good Samaritan (Luke 10:29-37). Augustine maintained *that people can, in fact, find*

---

42. The fathers summarize their concern in canon 18.

43. Martin Luther, *The Freedom of a Christian*, ed. H. Grimm, *Luther's Works*, 31: *Career of the Reformer*: I (Philadelphia: Muhlberg Press, 1957), 348. See also Martin Luther, *The Bondage of the Will*, ed. P. Watson, *Luther's Works*, 33: *Career of the Reformer* III (Philadelphia: Fortress Press, 1972), 128, originally written by Luther in 1526.

44. The church has recognized that the polemical character of its sixteenth-century discussions with Lutherans led to misunderstandings which no longer represent theological positions that merit the mutual condemnations of the past. See *Joint Declaration on the Doctrine of Justification* by the Lutheran World Federation and the Catholic Church, signed at Augsburg on October 31, 1999. The participants agreed that any remaining differences between Lutherans and Catholics concerning justification were insubstantial (para. 40). The *Joint Declaration* does not mention Trent's quotation of Augustine's adage, but it does mention every person's weaknesses and shortcomings in light of the mercy of God (para. 36).

themselves in impossible situations and that God will not hold them to do the impossible. Augustine wrote, "Our present inquiry, however, is about the man whom 'the thieves' left half dead on the road, and who, being disabled and pierced through with heavy wounds, *is not so able to mount up to the heights of righteousness* as he was able to descend therefrom; who, moreover, if he is now in 'the inn' is in process of cure. *God, therefore, does not command impossibilities*; but in his command, he counsels you both to *do what you can for yourself* and to ask his aid in what you cannot do."[45]

St. Augustine saw that sometimes people, like the man who was beaten to a pulp by the thieves, *cannot do* what they must "to mount up to righteousness." They remain "in the process of cure." Sometimes one can expect them only to "do what [they] can." He knows that a merciful God does not command what for them would amount to impossibilities, whether physical or moral.

Augustine's larger anti-Pelagian program runs in the same direction: people cannot simply do everything needed to accomplish their salvation. He insists on the necessity of grace. He knows that sometimes a person can be beaten to a pulp, either by robbers or by spouses who leave them by the roadside. Such people need special attention, special accompaniment. Sometimes they can do nothing. God does not command the impossible, as St. Paul knew.[46] When people find themselves in dilemmas, they can only petition for the mercy of the church.

Frequently in irregular marriages, care for the children presents the major issue that needs attention. At times that consideration will create a dilemma. Yet Granados, Kampowski, and Pérez-Soba only summarily mention parents' natural inclination (and moral obligation) to minimize the damage done to their children. They continually treat failed marriages and reconciliation abstractly, as if no children and no dilemmas ever complicated the matter.[47] They present no extended

---

45. St. Augustine, "On Nature and Grace," trans. P. Holmes and R. Wallis, ed. B. Warfield, in *Nicene and Post-Nicene Fathers of the Christian Church*, First Series, vol. 5 (Grand Rapids: Eerdmans, 1987), 138 (emphasis mine).

46. See the discussion on 1 Corinthians 12–15 in chap. 5, section 1, above.

47. See Granados, Kampowski, and Pérez-Soba, *Accompanying, Discerning, Integrating*, 57, 71, 87, 100, 114, 115, 116, etc. Moreover, they mistakenly claim that AL must officially recognize second marriages when it admits these trapped people to Communion. AL does not make that conclusion, nor must it. See chapter 7 below.

discussion of weak and frail single parents who have become both psychologically and financially desperate and who must undertake grave responsibilities for their children after experiencing the most devastating event of their lives. What if a single mother cannot raise a family on her own and actually remarries? What if that second marriage, against all odds, thrives? Shouldn't mercy allow the lesser evil to prevail? Nor do the professors consider the continuing ill effects of divorce on children, which can last throughout their adult lives. Without looking at those kinds of dilemmas, the authors fail to do justice to AL's depth.

When the authors do consider irregular cases, they call for "particular measures, especially when dealing with persons who have no intention of ending an unjust situation that has become habitual."[48] One wonders what those "particular measures" might include. The section treats prudence only insofar as it concerns setting up well-defined diocesan procedures with professionally trained staff. Yet prudence is at the heart of ethics. It employs right reason about action in order to govern choices to a right end.[49] Prudence is a virtue that can and must be lived not only by diocesan staff, but by a husband and a wife caught in an irregular marriage who face many complex issues.

Moreover, the three authors further avoid the issue by assuming that all couples who stay in invalid unions do so willfully and defiantly, as if circumstances could never create an impossible situation for couples, as if they could just as easily comply with the rules as not. In fact, in their opinion, all irregular marriages are always reversible, a truly astonishing claim.[50]

Indeed, some couples can reverse their invalid marriages through a divorce and a subsequent reconciliation with the church. Some could even win back their original spouses. That sort of activity offers a reversal of an objectively sinful situation and a restoration of the original marital bond.

---

48. Granados, Kampowski, and Pérez-Soba, *Accompanying, Discerning, Integrating*, 45–46.

49. Daniel Mark Nelson, *The Priority of Prudence: Virtue and Natural Law in Thomas Aquinas and the Implications for Modern Ethics* (University Park: Penn State University Press, 1992), 103. See also AL 295.

50. Granados, Kampowski, and Pérez-Soba, *Accompanying, Discerning, Integrating*, 61, 72, 104.

Other couples, however, can find themselves in more difficult circumstances that do not allow for a reversal. Situations that lead couples to live in "brother-sister" relationships, for example, do not constitute simple reversals of invalid marriages. They still live together and hold themselves out in public as husband and wife, with all the difficulties associated with this artificial arrangement noted in chapter 3 above. That simulation of marriage still makes for an objectively sinful situation that has not been reversed. Their recourse to confession after they have fallen while living in the near occasion of sin does not reverse their living status, which still testifies to the broken bonds of the original marriage.

More difficult situations present themselves when a couple cannot manage the "brother-sister" relationship. Recall the real case of the "brother-sister" relationship that was refused by the man in chapter 4 above. A Catholic woman entered an invalid marriage with an Anglican. They had a family together. Later she chose to begin practicing her faith more attentively, but the Anglican husband was unwilling to abide by the requirements of the "brother-sister" relationship. After several attempts at resolving the situation, he finally divorced her, inflicting all the pain and disorientation on the children that usually attends such situations.[51] If she had had children by her first marriage (in the actual case described, she did not), those offspring would suffer a second traumatic jolt to their upbringing. How is this situation "reversible"? Other cases can impose even more intractable dilemmas that call for a merciful response from the church.[52]

Granados, Kampowski, and Pérez-Soba miss the fact that, although Jesus said the one who divorces and remarries another commits adultery, he did not say that the *only* result was adultery. Nor, as we have seen earlier in this chapter, did he intimate that all adulteries yield the same results and offer the same possibilities for recovery. The three professors fail to see that these difficult situations produce not simply an instance of adultery but also a functioning family. The marriage

51. See chap. 4, section 3, "A 'Brother-Sister' Relationship Rejected," above.

52. See Francesco Cardinal Coccopalmerio, *A Commentary on Chapter Eight of Amoris Laetitia* (Mahwah, NJ: Paulist Press, 2017), 17–28, for an example of an irregular marriage that cannot simply be reversed. The case will be discussed in the next section, "A Study of Indissolubility."

may be invalid, but the family is very real and very much in need of protection. The natural family has a claim to make. The damage done to it cannot always be reversed.

Nevertheless, the three authors do mention the possibility that a person may be caught in an objectively sinful situation that is not manifest and without involving any "stubborn insistence" on remaining in the objectively sinful situation.[53] The observation accurately reflects the church's discipline, but it has no impact on their analysis. They ignore it as soon as they mention it. They fail to apply the teaching to any relevant complex marriage situations and revert to cases that are relatively easy to resolve.

D. Adapting the Moral Law

The authors admonish that "*adapting the moral law to what we consider to be our abilities is not a pastoral action.*"[54] Of course, that's true. No one can object. No one is adapting the moral law to anything. What is evil remains evil. A dilemma offers only objectively evil alternatives. Mercy is not part of a system that adapts moral laws to a person's abilities; rather it goes beyond the law in view of circumstances that will not admit of moral action. In fact, in some circumstances, the weakness of a person may be decisive. After all, the Lord himself acknowledged the Mosaic exception due to the hard heartedness of the people (Matt 19:8).

The choice of a lesser evil does not excuse the second marriage, as if it were morally permissible. Some couples caught in irregular circumstances may need to take advantage of unusual accommodations, such as entrance into the "brother-sister" relationship, precisely because they feel concretely the guilt, the unfittingness, of the lesser evil. The official church, too, even when it has tolerated a second marriage, has not permitted any sort of blessing or validation of the second, irregular marriage. The church does not act as if the situation has become completely normal. The objective sinful situation remains in place as the spouses attempt conversion from their subjective involvement in sin.

Mercy comes to the rescue in an *ad hoc* sort of way. Perhaps the cases are rare, but they exist; and history has shown that previous

---

53. Granados, Kampowski, and Pérez-Soba, *Accompanying, Discerning, Integrating*, 78.

54. Granados, Kampowski, and Pérez-Soba, 101 (emphasis in the original).

popes and councils did not feel bound to the letter of the law as they found it. They reached out in love and mercy to offer a way out of the trap some couples had entered.

The three professors complain that "it is necessary to avoid the merely 'tolerant' sense of mercy, which neither eliminates evil nor heals the person, for this only serves to make peace with disorder."[55] They place their confidence in general propositions, basing their opinion on the "truth of love," which includes the condemnation of sin and the invitation to conversion. Normally such a position describes very well Catholic teaching on moral life. The invitation to conversion beckons the sinner to leave the prison of sin and accept the freedom of God's love. Conversion enhances life. Those who truly love others help sinners to convert for their own good. It does no one any good to "make peace with disorder" by allowing wayward sinners to wallow in their sins.

Pope Francis does not propose a "tolerant mercy" in the sense of a laxism that releases all parties from responsible action; rather, he promotes a *Christian* mercy that allows life to move forward as best it can when dilemmas interfere. It does not release a spouse from responsibility but frees her to fulfill her responsibility to provide a bearable home life for her children. What if the sinner has no other viable choices? What if no alternatives exist but dreadful ones? A rejected spouse does not make "peace with disorder," but, in proper circumstances, accepts Christian mercy when there is no other way out. If she cannot pay sufficient attention to her responsibilities to her children, she may well make, not peace with disorder, but *a stressful accommodation with disorder* by tolerating the difficulties of her marriage and family on a daily basis. Often enough, the only one who feels peaceful about these sorts of arrangements is the priest, concerned about upholding the rules. In some households, disorder would exist no matter what the rejected spouse did.

3. A Study of Indissolubility

In his book *The Indissolubility of Marriage:* Amoris Laetitia *in Context*, theologian Matthew Levering explores indissolubility in light of

---

55. Granados, Kampowski, and Pérez-Soba, xiii.

the Pope's apostolic exhortation.[56] To his credit, Levering reviews the history of the doctrine of indissolubility and does consider difficult cases posed by others who think that occasionally mercy can tolerate the continuation of a current invalid marriage. He finds that the church correctly teaches that valid, consummated, sacramental marriages are indissoluble. Much of his heavily footnoted text strives to explain the doctrine of indissolubility in the most definitive terms. Readers can learn much about indissolubility, but Levering's analysis falters when he addresses the more complex issues of AL.

A. History

Levering reviews the early history of the church to demonstrate that it has reiterated its teaching on indissolubility many times. Clearly the church supports the indissolubility of marriage. Here he argues a position that, in my view, few people dispute.[57]

The issue rather centers on whether the church can tolerate a person's second marriage when he or she is trapped. Levering does not recognize the issue of dilemmas in marriage. He neglects the canons of the Council of Nicaea and fails to mention other documents that pose problems for his position. He alludes to the merciful decision of Pope Leo I, but he fails to grasp the significance of it. Early popes did not feel that church teaching prohibited them from applying mercy in certain concrete dilemmas. He cites the letter of Pope Innocent I that maintained the doctrine of indissolubility, but ignores his letter concerning Fortunius's first wife Ursa and the possibility of divorce.

Instead, Levering treats their decisions as ambiguous.[58] Certainly St. Innocent I and St. Leo the Great, a doctor of the church, had a good grasp of church teaching and could write unambiguously about it. But perhaps the real difficulty is that they did not write *about* their actions; they simply took action. They did not produce a treatise on the merciful management of distressed marriages. They simply acted pastorally in

56. Matthew Levering, *The Indissolubility of Marriage: Amoris Laetitia in Context* (San Francisco: Ignatius, 2019).

57. Though one example to the contrary is Kenneth Himes, OFM, and James Coriden, "The Indissolubility of Marriage: Reasons to Reconsider," *Theological Studies* 65 (2004): 453–99.

58. Levering, *Indissolubility of Marriage*, 38.

mercy regardless of whether their action could fit neatly within a system. Those who look for a system in merciful actions will remain puzzled. Even if their actions could not be reduced to a formula that fit within the other rules governing the behavior of spouses, the popes did not consider their actions as outside the teaching of the church, nor should we. Their actions extended beyond the rules, which indicates that both of them could let go of the pedagogue of the law to act in view of the presence of Christ. Those two saintly popes knew what they were doing. They operated beyond the rules but within the teaching of the church, a teaching that gives pride of place to mercy to those caught in dilemmas. Although Levering treats several popes and early church fathers, he omits much of the history that would challenge his theology.

Henri Crouzel, the famed patristics scholar whom Levering admires, provides a much more satisfying interpretation of the actions of the early church. Crouzel summarizes its pastoral practices by stating two contrasting points, both of which make their own proper contributions: "The first point: it does not seem possible to us to see the Church as explicitly accepting remarriage. The second point: *there is however occasionally a desirable evolution of Church practice that shows to the divorced and remarried a certain indulgence, without keeping them perpetually away from the sacraments.*"[59] Pope Francis balances exactly these two points in AL and keeps them in play for divorced and remarried couples who have entered dilemmas.

B. *"Absolute Indissolubility"*

At times Levering forgets that all marriages dissolve at death. He occasionally refers to the "absolute indissolubility" of marriage.[60] He figures that if marriage sacramentally signifies the absolute indissolubility of the union of Christ and his church, marriage must also be absolutely indissoluble. He goes so far as to write, "A dissoluble bond cannot sig-

---

59. Henri Crouzel, "Un nouvel essai pour prouver l'acceptance des secondes noces après divorce dans l'Église primitive," *Augustinianum* 17 (1977): 566 (emphasis mine; my translation). "Premier point: il ne nous paraît pas possible de voir l'Église accepter explicitement le remarriage. Deuxieme point: il y a cependant une evolution de la practique de l'Église qui serait souhaitable, témoigner envers les divorcés remarriés d'une certaine indulgence et ne pas les maintenir perpétuellement à l'écart des sacrements." See also, Crouzel, "Les digamoi," in *Augustinianum: 537*.

60. Levering, *Indissolubility of Marriage*, 64, 90, 161.

nify an indissoluble bond."[61] Why not? A temporary physical washing in baptism symbolizes a spiritual washing away of sin that brings with it a permanent bond to Christ and his church. While human marital bonds dissolve with the death of a spouse, only Jesus's bond with the church endures forever.[62]

Levering does cite a couple of examples of marital difficulties that might give rise to a merciful treatment of a second marriage. One of these is offered by Cardinal Francesco Coccopalmerio in an essay he published on AL. Coccopalmerio refers to a case where a woman lives "with a man who was canonically married but was abandoned by his wife and left him with three young children." The common law wife may have saved the man from deep despair which would have led to suicide. In addition, the woman has given birth to a child by that man.[63] After she realizes the sinfulness of her marital situation, she comes to the church, fully contrite, and seeking reconciliation. But her hands are tied. She would like to change her living situation but cannot act without further sin. The cardinal would allow, after due counseling and accompaniment, the woman to receive reconciliation and Communion, even if she and her partner cannot manage a "brother-sister" relationship.[64] She is in a dilemma. She desires to change her situation and cannot.

Archbishop Victor Manuel Fernandez offers a similar example in which a divorced Catholic woman has taken a non-Catholic civil partner who does not share her convictions about the brother-sister relationship. In his hypothetical, he heightens the lady's predicament. He emphasizes that it is not easy for a woman "to make the decision to leave this man whom she loves, who protects her from a violent spouse and who prevents her from descending into prostitution or suicide."[65] In that case, Fernandez claims that circumstances have

---

61. Levering, 151.

62. He cites Aquinas and Ephesians 5:32. Levering, *Indissolubility of Marriage*, 151. Nevertheless, Aquinas admits that he considers the indissoluble bond of marriage figuratively. See his *Summa Contra Gentiles*, bk. 3, ch. 123.6 and bk. 4, ch. 78, where he considers the indissolubility of marriage as only a type that is derived from the union of Christ and his church.

63. Coccopalmerio, *A Commentary on Chapter Eight*, 20.

64. Coccopalmerio, 23.

65. See Victor Manuel Fernandez, *Chapitre VIII de* Amoris Laetitia: *Le bilan après la tourmente*, trans. H. de Parscau (Paris: Parole et Silence, 2018), 26–27: *"Dans ce cas, il n'est pas facile pour une femme . . . de prendre la décision d'abandonner cet*

142 Mercy and the Rule of Law

trapped the woman. Her objectively sinful situation need not force her to leave her civil partner.

Pointing to this example offered by the archbishop, Levering responds that, while the woman's culpability in extreme situations is certainly reduced, nevertheless, the woman's fidelity to her vows "might also, in God's plan of grace, have powerfully good effects upon her spouse from her indissoluble marriage, upon her civil partner, upon her children (from one or both unions), and upon her community. . . . Choosing to uphold the sacramental sign is a powerful testimony of grace."[66]

Her fidelity to her absent husband might indeed have the effect of a powerful witness, but it might also result in more pain, confusion, and bewilderment. It might lead to the further deterioration of her truncated family life with her children. Even so, Levering continues by asserting that, although "stopping sinning" may cause harm to others, "[n]onetheless, stopping sinning must often be done, for the sake of justice and charity, trusting in the power of Christ and the Spirit."[67] Often, but not always? He seems to admit here that sometimes the appearance of sinning in the external forum cannot be avoided. Perhaps this slip of the pen indicates that he really does sympathize with those in dilemmas but cannot accommodate them into his system.

What if stopping one sin introduces another even worse sin? Will the man descend into suicidal depression? Will their child understand why his parents no longer live together? Levering exhibits little taste for balancing the evils at hand. What can one reasonably expect from the woman whose Army husband chose to divorce her and marry his Fort Sheridan paramour? She did exactly what Levering proposes. She and her children suffered miserably, even to the point where the children felt sinful. This dehumanizing experience left the remnants of her family in shambles.

If this is a witness to justice, one needs no more incentive to look for mercy beyond that sort of justice. When the time comes to cope with dilemmas and to choose a path that best facilitates sociability, peace, and harmony, Levering takes refuge in generalities. Unfortunately, people do not live their lives in generalities.

---

homme qu'elle aime, qui la protégé d'un époux violent et qui l'empêche de sombrer dans la prostitution ou le suicide."

66. Levering, Indissolubility of Marriage, 109.

67. Levering, 110.

C. Mercy as License

Levering reads AL restrictively, as if more expansive interpretations make mercy a part of an organized system of thought that alters current doctrine. He thinks that if mercy were allowed under the terms of AL, it could rearrange the entire system, making a whole category of marriages dissoluble.[68] But the pope's application of mercy in chapter 8 deals in dilemmas. He does not create an extra category of dissoluble marriages. In a dilemma, someone is going to get hurt unjustly whatever decision the divorced spouse makes. A divorced spouse must choose the lesser evil. That situation must be assessed in the concrete. Mercy cannot be applied simply through an objective principle prior to an investigation of the facts.

This fundamental misunderstanding gives rise to Levering's thought that if mercy could change the teaching on marriage, it could change the teaching on anything. He entertains the claim that AL can be extended in ways that clearly violate church doctrine. The argument runs as follows: If a divorced and remarried man can maintain his second wife and family because of a dilemma that forces him to choose a lesser evil, what about a man in a homosexual relationship? Why can't he claim the same merciful treatment and seek the blessing of the church for a marriage with his same-sex partner as a lesser evil? Several reasons come to mind.

First, there appears to be no Scriptural warrant that gives the church the right to manage homosexual marriages in the way it has managed heterosexual marital bonds. It views homosexual conjugal activity as prohibited with no exceptions similar to the *porneia* clause or those that developed with respect to marriage in the subsequent history of the church.

Second, the history of the church does not include any other types of accommodation in the area of homosexual activity. While the historical record does include a line of cases concerning the treatment of second marriages that have encountered dilemmas, it does not include any such recognition for homosexual marriages. Although the pope makes it clear that people with homosexual tendencies need respectful pastoral care, he reaffirmed the position of the church in AL 250–251.

Third, while one may speak of *natural* spousal and *natural* parental bonds that take place in second marriages, there is no natural sexual

68. See, for example, Levering, 166.

144 Mercy and the Rule of Law

bond that obtains in a homosexual union, nor does the union produce
a parental bond.

Fourth, the frustrated desire of one man for another man would
be analogous to the heterosexual situation in which a man desires a
woman whom he cannot marry for various reasons, perhaps because
she is already married or perhaps because she does not want him. In
either event, AL would demand that existing marital bonds be honored
and that any sexual union take place in marriage only. Heterosexual
people regularly have to deal with situations in which they may feel
the urge to become physically involved with a particular member of
the opposite sex but cannot. Such a circumstance is perhaps a pity but
not a tragedy that requires extraordinary resolution.

Fifth, no insurmountable dilemma exists in the case of homosexual
lovers who want to marry. No children of the homosexual union exist.
Where are the conflicting claims of justice analogous to the spousal
and parental bonds of marriage? Although there are none, at the same
time it should be noted that the church needs to redouble its efforts
to respond to the pain felt by those who feel same-sex attraction. If
homosexual marriage is denied to them, what form can their love
legitimately take? Although speculation on this important question
exceeds the scope of this book, those who seek pastoral solutions that
are faithful to the church's teaching deserve everyone's support.

Nevertheless, one cannot legitimately use AL as a springboard for
the adoption of teachings that violate the moral code of the church.

D. Avoiding a Greater Evil

Levering at one point considers Aquinas's position on whether a sacramental marriage can be dissolved to allow a couple to enter consecrated religious life. In the course of his argument, Aquinas refers to
Jesus's acknowledgment that Moses permitted divorce. In Aquinas's
estimation, Jesus was implicitly making the point that "the permission
was not from a precept but rather it was *permitted to avoid a greater
evil*."[69] In other words, Aquinas asserts that not any principle, not any
rule, and not any commandment gives rise to Moses's permission.
Levering acknowledges that it was allowed simply "to ensure that the

---

69. Thomas Aquinas, *Commentary on the Gospel of St. Matthew*, ch. 19, lect. 1, sec.
1557 (my translation; emphasis mine): "*Unde permissio non fuit ex praeceptio, sed ad
vitandum maius malum.*"

people would not create a greater evil."[70] Precisely. That is exactly the issue that the pope develops in chapter 8, and for the same reason as Aquinas gave. Yet Levering manages to mention it and ignore it.

In fact, Aquinas had made exactly the same point in his comment on Matthew 5:31 where he first considered the Mosaic exception to the Lord's prohibition of divorce. Aquinas argues that God tolerates this evil "lest something worse happen."[71] As Eleonore Stump has written, "But God does not will as intrinsically good everything he wills; what he wills in his consequent will, what is the best available in the circumstance, might be only the lesser of evils, not the intrinsically good."[72]

Levering writes, "I note that for persons who seek the aid of Christ, stopping the unjust action always belongs to 'what is possible' by God's grace."[73] Although the statement has validity in garden-variety moral circumstances, it does not pertain to all the situations that AL addresses. In fact, it falls short in at least three ways.

First, Levering confines his comment to a single "unjust action." In a dilemma, at least two unjust actions loom on the horizon. AL deals with much more complex scenarios than Levering has in mind. When an abandoned spouse, faced with a dilemma, limits her options to fixing only one problem, the spousal bond, another major problem, such as her commitment to the children, might well spin out of control. While Levering's thought works in simpler settings, it does not work in all situations.

Second, while Levering confines himself to situations of only one unjust action, he nonetheless agrees with Aquinas's instruction that God can will the lesser evil as he did when Moses gave permission to his people to divorce.[74] Aquinas's observation makes sense only if true dilemmas can occur in the lives of Christians. Sometimes it is impossible to stop the unjust action because those are the only kinds of actions possible in a given situation. No "just actions" present themselves in dilemmas. What if choosing to stop one unjust action gives rise to another even more unjust action? Those who have entered "the field

70. Levering, *Indissolubility of Marriage*, 150.

71. Aquinas, *Commentary on the Gospel of St. Matthew*, ch. 5, lect. 9, sec. 514 (p. 174): "[T]olerantiae, quando aliquid malum toleratur ne peius fiat. . . ."

72. Eleonore Stump, *Wandering in Darkness: Narrative and the Problem of Suffering* (Oxford: Clarendon Press, 2010), 428.

73. Levering, *Indissolubility of Marriage*, 117.

74. Levering, 150.

hospital" in this area of pastoral ministry know this. When Levering writes that stopping the unjust action "always belongs to what is possible," he ignores the possibility of dilemmas (which he had just admitted), as if people never faced such situations.

Third, certainly God can use human weakness to turn defeat into victory, even miraculously at times. Anything is possible. God's grace suffices to defeat sin. That proposition has long been part of standard Catholic theology. However, Levering misapplies that doctrine by presuming that God's grace will always come the way he expects it to come. God's grace may come in very unexpected ways, even by tolerating an objective evil in order to prevent an even greater one. Levering seems to imagine that a divorced person will always be able to gather his or her courage, take a deep breath, and forge headlong into the mess, successfully managing one crisis after another. Some people can manage very well that way. Others cannot. Levering's position provides a neo-Pelagian expectation that often masquerades as faith, as will be shown in the next section below. Sooner or later for many, the effort hits a wall. Levering forgets the considerably more complex and subtle theology that pertains to situations where grace enters a fallen world with weakened moral actors who stumble in darkness and, for various reasons, cannot take full advantage of what would otherwise be theirs.[75]

Not only does Levering's position ignore dilemmas, but it also misunderstands the nature of grace. In 1713, Pope Clement XI rejected a proposition that offered a conception of grace remarkably similar to Levering's: "Grace is the working of the omnipotent hand of God which nothing can hinder or retard."[76] Of course, sin and plenty of other factors can hinder or retard the working of grace, as we will note below in the section on false piety. Interference with grace can happen especially when one falls victim to circumstances beyond his or her control.

Levering also asserts, "God is not yet 'pleased' by the action of a person whose action is objectively gravely wrong."[77] Levering should understand that a person suffering the consequences of rejection by a

---

75. See Rom 7:19-20; CCC 1735.

76. The condemned proposition appears in Clement XI's dogmatic constitution *Unigenitus Dei Filius*, which disapproved of the Jansenist propositions set forth by Pasquier Quesnel. See Josef Neuner and Jacques Dupuis, eds., *The Christian Faith in the Documents of the Catholic Church* (New York: Alba House, 1982), 575.

77. Levering, *Indissolubility of Marriage*, 117.

spouse or of a disastrous marriage are frequently displeased with the choices before them as well. Most would much prefer to be a part of a regular marriage and to have a course of action available that does no further damage or includes no further gravely wrong actions.

No one is pleased with dilemmas. That is not the issue. The issue is whether the church can tolerate an irregular situation in proper circumstances to avoid an even worse situation. Plenty of evidence indicates that it can.

E. False Piety

Levering suggests that the operation of God's grace can immediately fix any situation. "Stopping the unjust action" seems logical as long as stopping is possible, but *even then* it may take considerable time and effort. To draw a parallel with a different difficult situation, one can tell an alcoholic to stop drinking, and eventually, with the grace of God, it can happen, but not always immediately, and, regrettably for some, only with occasional relapses. Levering suggests that irregular couples who have no way out simply do not seek the grace of Christ. Without bothering to pay sufficient attention to examples that challenge his assumptions, he simply posits that no such thing as an impossible situation can exist. It all seems rather simple. Just accept the grace of God, as if an interior personal decision could fix a complex problem that has many exterior interpersonal dimensions.

In his 2018 apostolic exhortation *Gaudete et Exsultate*, Pope Francis identified two modern tendencies that he called neo-Gnosticism and neo-Pelagianism. Neo-Gnosticism promotes an undue confidence in the intellect. Its adherents value doctrines, rules, and abstractions to such an extent that they suffocate the faith that they are supposed to serve. Neo-Gnostics pay outsized attention to subtleties and technicalities and allow them to override more thoughtful responses to real problems people actually encounter in life. They "reduce Jesus' teaching to a cold and harsh logic that seeks to dominate everything." Neo-Gnosticism tends to turn faith into an ideology that has a ready-made clear-cut answer for every question.[78]

---

78. Pope Francis, apostolic exhortation *Gaudete et Exsultate* (March 19, 2018) 36–43 (quotation in 39). This document adopts categories developed more thoroughly in Congregation for the Doctrine of the Faith, letter *Placuit Deo* (February 22, 2018).

As neo-Gnosticism places undue confidence in the intellectual dimension of faith, neo-Pelagianism does the same for the will. Although neo-Pelagians say all the right things, "speaking warmly of grace," in the end, they rely on their own strength to follow the rules come hell or high water.[79] Obedience becomes a matter of personal effort. If people falter, it must mean that they do not trust the grace God sent for their salvation. Grit and determination ultimately answer the call, even though it may mean a ruined household with mothers at their wit's end, chasing after children who cannot understand how to grow up in a broken family. The neo-Pelagian cannot conceive of life outside the rules and simply repeats the tired cant about God's grace. Ironically, that grace might actually come through merciful responses that neo-Pelagians refuse to recognize.

The finest minds in the Christian tradition have perceived much subtler forces at work in the human condition. They all refrain from simple solutions, as if the bestowal of grace sufficed to solve every moral problem. St. Augustine saw that the sin of Adam had insinuated itself into the very conditions that make people human. Hence Augustine could understand St. Paul's agony at not doing what he wanted but doing the very thing he hated (see Gal 5:17 and Rom 7:15). In this complex world, people must cope with both interior and exterior dimensions of their problems, both in their spiritual and physical aspects. Augustine could appreciate the difficulty people have, even with the help of grace, in extricating themselves from lust, deceit, error, fear, desire, wrath, hatred, grief, ingratitude, suspicion, revenge, and the like.[80] Continence did not come easily in Augustine's own life, even though he saw it as a function of grace.[81]

Thomas Aquinas knew that some problems linger even after grace has made its appearance. Even after one has obtained grace, one might still struggle to avoid sin. "But here grace is to some extent imperfect, inasmuch as it does not completely heal man, as stated above."[82] He cites Augustine's analogy that even a healthy eye still needs the assistance of light to see anything.[83] As grace meets the resistance of this

79. Pope Francis, *Gaudete et Exsultate* 48–58 (quotation in 49).

80. Augustine, *City of God*, XXII:23.

81. See Augustine, *The Confessions*, bk. 2.

82. ST I-II, q. 109, a. 9, ad. 1.

83. Augustine, *On Nature and Grace*, 26.

wounded world, as it touches weakened and vulnerable individuals, it cannot simply declare an end to all practical difficulties. A solution may not be within reach. The "healthy eye" may have the grace of a light switch within reach to aid its sight, or it may not. Especially when circumstances depend on the cooperation of other people, grace can do only so much.

Furthermore, Aquinas cautioned that the reduction of the Gospel to a set of rules might have the unintended consequence of draining it of its simplicity and profundity. As the Gospel becomes translated into a code of conduct, it can choke off the free working of grace. While any organization needs a working set of rules, Aquinas urged moderation "lest the conduct of the faithful become burdensome" turning the religion into a form of servitude.[84]

Aquinas's contemporary, St. Bonaventure, even more explicitly rejected the notion that grace simply solves every problem. In his instructions to religious superiors, he acknowledged that "all cannot be equally perfect. . . . [Superiors] do not charge [monks] with excessive burdens, nor do they expect from them anything beyond their strength." Indeed, if they are pushed beyond their strength, "even the little virtue they possess may be extinguished in them by this pressure that is more than they can bear." St. Bonaventure reminds his readers, "I humbly and lovingly took care of you, reaching down to the level of your frailty and imperfection."[85] After all, "Not everyone can do everything."[86]

These profound thinkers show a great deal of compassion to those who labor under various burdens. No one should think that grace simply resolves all situations. Indeed, the *Catechism* declares, "Imputability and responsibility for an action can be diminished or even nullified by ignorance, inadvertence, duress, fear, habit, inordinate attachments, and other psychological and social factors."[87] Pope Francis carries that concern for the frailty of people right into the heart of his deliberations about broken marriages.

84. ST I-II, q. 107, a. 4. See also Pope Francis, *Gaudete et Exsultate*, 59.

85. St. Bonaventure, "The Six Wings of the Seraph: Counsels to Religious Superiors," in *The Works of Bonaventure* III, *Opuscula Second Series*, trans. J. de Vinck (Paterson, NJ: St. Anthony Guild Press, 1966), 3:9.

86. St. Bonaventure, "The Six Wings," 3:8.

87. CCC 1735.

Those who criticize the pope seem far too given to abstract theories and unrealistic expectations for those who suffer devastating losses. Such theologians participate in new forms of old heresies that masquerade as forms of piety that some laity can at times find attractive in the middle-class comfort of their homes.

4. Thomistic Perspectives

The renowned philosopher Serge-Thomas Bonino, OP, has offered a very measured assessment of the use of Thomistic categories in AL. In an article on the "presence" of Aquinas in the text of AL,[88] Bonino gently suggests that the document misinterprets Aquinas on a few occasions. He carefully admits that his observations do not necessarily mean that the theology of AL is wrong. It merely means that it does not reflect fully the thought of St. Thomas.

For example, the pope writes that Aquinas taught that the more one descends from general precepts into concrete circumstances, the less reliable the general rule becomes.[89] Principles are one thing; their application is another. While the statement is true as far as it goes, Bonino notes that Aquinas elsewhere poses the question of whether fraternal correction is a matter of precept. In holding that it is, he notes that "sinful acts are evil in themselves, and cannot become good, no matter how, or when, or where they are done, because of their very nature they are connected with an evil end."[90] Negative precepts oblige on every occasion.

The point may easily be granted. No one claims that those in irregular marriages do not offend the objective moral order. They do. That's why the initial conversations with a priest or pastoral minister most likely eventually will lead to the confessional and why the irregular marriage cannot be blessed in any liturgy of the church. In AL 304–305, Pope Francis is not making a doctrinal point about precepts, but a pastoral point about their use. One must admit that a pastoral counselor can use negative precepts in ways that do more harm than good. The pope is not looking for an exception to any negative precept.

---

88. Serge-Thomas Bonino, OP, "Saint Thomas Aquinas in the Apostolic Exhortation *Amoris Laetitia*," *The Thomist* 80 (2016): 509–19, esp. 513ff.

89. Here he cites ST I-II, q. 94, a. 4.

90. ST I-II, q. 33, a. 2.

He is not making an academic point but a pastoral one. The evil done in an irregular marriage remains evil.

Even though Aquinas noted that negative precepts have no exceptions, the application of a negative precept still needs to take into account the particulars of concrete acts at the subjective level. Consider an example that Bonino offers: "The negative precepts (for example, 'You shall not kill [the innocent]'. . .) oblige always and in all circumstances, without any exception, because the prohibited act is directly opposed to the end."[91] But even that example shows that a negative precept can call for an exception. Bonino adds the exception to the negative precept by parenthetically asserting that it pertains to killing only the innocent. How is it that the church has managed such a limitation if one must always uphold negative precepts? Pastorally the pope sees that the precept concerning indissolubility serves a purpose. It has pointed the way and provided a foundation. It has not necessarily closed all discussion of a pastoral nature. Francis has not fashioned an exception to a negative precept. Abstract analyses must give way to concrete circumstances that demand mercy.

Regardless of the precepts that a sinner may have violated, those rules should not be used as stones to be thrown at sinners, a practice that disregards all mitigating factors (see AL 305). Descent into the particulars of any given situation may well yield a good deal of understanding that would not otherwise be evident. It makes possible a more charitable approach. Furthermore, the pope uses Thomas's insight to dissuade pastoral ministers from turning "what is part of a practical discernment in particular circumstances. . . [into] the level of a rule" (AL 304). People thrive on rules. They easily make them and easily misuse them. Furthermore, when Aquinas treats the Mosaic exception in Matthew 5:31, he does so explicitly in terms of prohibitive (negative) and permissive (positive) precepts. Aquinas nevertheless reaches the conclusion that Moses called for tolerance, as "when some evil is tolerated lest something worse happen, as here."[92]

It would be helpful here to consider concrete material norms, which moral actors produce when they attempt to apply universal norms to particular concrete circumstances. For example, the universal norm

91. Bonino, "Saint Thomas," 516.

92. Aquinas, *Commentary on the Gospel of St. Matthew*, ch. 5, lect. 9, sec. 514 (p. 174).

to drive safely causes no disagreement among reasonable people.[93] When authorities apply that norm to a particular street, it can give rise to disputes. Should the speed limit on this particular road be forty miles per hour or forty-five? Reasonable people can disagree. Other considerations can further complicate the matter. Some may think it advisable to post a "slippery when wet" sign near a curve in the road. Still other situations may arise that affect the speed in unpredictable ways, like a series of potholes that develop late in winter or the need to drive in the opposite lane to avoid an accident. The further one descends into detail, the more universal principles need adaptation. Aquinas knew this and incorporated it into his thinking.

Reflecting on Aquinas's passage concerning the caution needed in applying general principles, the moral theologian Louis Janssens claimed,

> The *concrete material norms* of morality . . . pronounce us guilty of immorality when we bring about or tolerate more ontic evil than is necessary to realize the moral objectives of our human existence. . . .
>
> Insofar as they express *the ideal*, the concrete material norms concern the "desirable degree of humanity" (*le souhaitable humain*). Insofar as they are *norms*, they imply only the obligation to realize that which is possible for man. . . . We must make allowance for our human limitations. That is why Thomas already said that the concrete material norms (*precepta magis propria*) are not applicable in all cases: *valent in pluribus.*[94]

AL quotes the passage from Aquinas accurately and interprets it correctly, albeit not in a strictly academic context. In Janssens's terms, the pope wants pastoral ministers to help those in irregular marriages to assess the amount of ontic evil that a situation will likely produce, and, making allowances for human limitations, to assess what is possible in those particular circumstances.

Bonino further questions whether moral dilemmas actually exist. Aquinas asserted, "Simply, no one is in a dilemma [*perplexus*] ab-

93. See Bretzke, *Handbook of Roman Catholic Moral Terms*, 40–41.

94. Louis Janssens, "Ontic Evil and Moral Evil," *Louvain Studies* 4 (1972): 155 (emphasis in the original).

solutely speaking."[95] The point can readily be granted. Many times, a person who has placed himself or others in a dilemma can just as easily remove the dilemma. For example, the Nazi official in *Sophie's Choice* could easily eliminate the dilemma by rescinding his outlandish command that Sophie choose which of her children to send off to execution. Obviously a person who is able to do it has an obligation to resolve such dilemmas. But the victim of such a dilemma cannot unilaterally resolve the problem. She may find herself in a bind. Bonino contends, "Absolutely speaking, every case of a dilemma is, in the final analysis, the consequence of an earlier action that involves a certain culpability. The Thomist tradition considers therefore that no moral dilemma is legitimately unsolvable, such that a person is never constrained to choose (the lesser) evil."[96]

But then why does Aquinas discuss the Mosaic exception in Matthew 19:7-8 in terms of choosing the lesser evil? It may be that no moral dilemma is legitimately unsolvable, but not by each and every actor that the dilemma affects. Victims of dilemmas may well depend on others who simply will not resolve the predicament. It seems clear that humanly made dilemmas exist today that offer no clean way out. Perhaps the one who created the dilemma can withdraw it, but if that person chooses not to call an end to it, other actors may simply have no choice. Some divorced people can enter such dilemmas through no fault of their own.

Finally, Bonino briefly loses sight of AL 300, where the pope writes of "the immense variety of concrete situations" that characterize irregular marriages. Bonino misrepresents AL when he writes, "Within the context of *Amoris Laetitia* 301, it seems that what is being envisaged is the existence of a moral dilemma that is (objectively?) unsolvable in the case of the 'divorced and remarried.' . . . They would thus be constrained to choose the 'lesser evil.' Among other difficulties, this reasoning seems to hold as certain that it is impossible for the 'divorced and remarried,' even with the grace of God, to live in continence in a humanly balanced way."[97]

95. Thomas Aquinas, II Sent., d. 39, q. 3, a. 3, ad. 5. Cited in Bonino, "Saint Thomas," 510.

96. Bonino, "Saint Thomas," 511n14.

97. Bonino, 511n14.

Bonino seems comfortable with the "divorced and remarried" as a category that describes only one monolithic type of people, as if they all suffered the same condition and, therefore, could all benefit from the same advice. Among the "divorced and remarried," one finds couples in many different and varied situations, as illustrated in chapter 4 above.[98] He forgets that mercy addresses concrete circumstances that vary greatly. It is surely true that some divorced and remarried people ought to divorce each other and seek reconciliation with their true spouses. Others should acknowledge the need simply to divorce, even if reconciliation with their former mates is impossible. Still others should enter the "brother-sister" relationship to tend to difficult situations. Others may not be able to manage such an arrangement. The point here is that AL does not predetermine any of those solutions on the sole basis of their divorced and remarried status.

AL does not hold that it is "impossible for the 'divorced and remarried,' even with the grace of God, to live in continence in a humanly balanced way." Of course, it is possible. What is impossible is for pastoral ministers to effectively address the various situations of divorced couples when they try to pretend as if they were all the same.

5. Slippery Slopes

Some commentators fear that once confessors begin to support a merciful approach to second marriages, they will lose their bearings and begin to encourage people to live as husband and wife even when they should not. This "slippery slope" argument falters in several ways.

First, pastoral ministers and confessors simply need to be self-possessed and pastorally astute enough to avoid such a pitfall. All pastoral ministry, including ministry to divorced people, involves difficult judgments that call for wisdom and prudence. Confessors must make such judgments in the confessional on a regular basis. Some sins are easily recognized as such. Others swim in ambiguity. Priests regularly make such judgments without "going too far." Why should critics assume they will go too far when the issue is an invalid second marriage? Besides, the priest merely counsels the couple and offers absolution where appropriate. He guides their consciences; he does not replace them (AL 37).

98. See Walter Kasper, *The Gospel of the Family* (New York: Paulist Press, 2014), 45.

Second, the slippery slope argument presumes that legal rigidity reflects the Lord's will more faithfully than the application of mercy does. As Paul Mankowski maintains, "[I]t is mistaken . . . to view Jesus as a disputant who championed the rigorist style of legal-moral controversy, and whose appeal was solely to the tough-minded."[99] Confessors who err on the side of rigidity would be mistaken to think that the Lord is pleased with adherence to the abstract law rather than to the law of love. Perhaps it is such rigid priests who have "gone too far" by not letting go of the pedagogue when Christ calls them. Legalistic priests fear that they could be responsible for the sin of a couple while never calculating how they may already sin in their responsibility for the misery of the couple that they keep from Communion and from a normal family life. They have slipped down the other side of the slope. They believe that a sort of legalism will save their own souls even as they burden the souls of others. Those priests may well ruin the lives of those who come to them for counsel, thinking the Lord loves their brand of hard-hearted justice when he really asks them to offer mercy.[100]

Certainly it is possible that lazy confessors might err on the side of excessive leniency. Such priests abdicate their responsibilities and are no more fit to be confessors than the legal rigorists. They need adequate training and spiritual direction before receiving faculties. The application of mercy requires one to grapple with difficult issues in mature discernment, not merely to dismiss them as if they were of no account.[101]

99. Paul Mankowski, "Dominical Teaching on Divorce and Remarriage," in Robert Dodaro, *Remaining in the Truth of Christ: Marriage and Communion in the Catholic Church* (San Francisco: Ignatius, 2014), 63. Mankowski would rely not on a rigid application of the rules, but on the conviction that "no person however fragile should find it impossible to do God's will." He does not elaborate on that thesis and does not consider impossible situations such as those described by the witnesses who report their experiences in chapter 4 above. See also "False Piety," section 3, E, above.

100. Indeed, Pope Alexander VIII condemned rigorism in 1690. See Brian V. Johnstone, CSsR, "Probabilism," in *The New Dictionary of Theology*, ed. Joseph A. Komonchak, Mary Collins, and Dermot Lane (Collegeville, MN: Liturgical Press, 1987), 802.

101. Pope Alexander VII condemned laxism in 1665. See Johnstone, "Probabilism," 802. Pope Innocent XI condemned it in 1679. "Laxism maintains that as long as there is at least some probability [of legitimacy] to the less safe course of action, this could then be followed with a clean conscience" (Bretzke, *Handbook of Roman Catholic Moral Terms*, 136).

By the same token, some fear that the application of mercy to second marriages might duplicate the experience of the granting of declarations of nullity, which some skeptics claim has gone too far. An overwhelming proportion of the marriages scrutinized by tribunals in the United States are granted, rather than denied, declarations of nullity. But that does not indicate that the church has "gone too far." No valid conclusion can be drawn from such a meager observation. Canon lawyers and judges in American tribunals must hold degrees in canon law. That should make a difference, and it does. The competence of American tribunals should not be held against them. The annulment process shows that the church will not shy away from difficult decisions. Church officials should be able to keep their wits about them even in the most delicate cases.

Why deny someone the mercy that is possible in dire circumstances? Even the U. S. justice system imperfectly applies rules that secure important values, even though that might mean that occasionally the guilty go free.[102] The possibility that a priest in good faith might mistakenly guide a couple to remain in an invalid union should remind us of the need for prudence and caution, but it should not discourage us from extending the offer of mercy to those who genuinely need it. Everyone knows that the annulment process can err, yet canonists tolerate those mistakes in the interests of granting annulments to couples in invalid marriages. Nor should the possibility of mistakes deter pastors from applying the mercy of the Lord to those who need it. After all, the Lord himself directed his disciples to allow both the weeds and the wheat to grow undisturbed. His concern centered not on making sure that all the guilty received just punishment but on ensuring that those on watch would not uproot any of the wheat (Matt 13:29-30). If mistakes are to be made, they should favor mercy, not punishment. Both weeds and wheat should be left undisturbed. Nowhere does Jesus ask his disciples to police the faithful. A priest's role is to exhort them, guide them, love them, instruct them, admonish them, accompany them, and forgive them—not catch them, spy on them, or punish them. Even excommunication is medicinal and never final. It is not the priest's job to make sure that people do not cheat.

---

102. For example, the "exclusionary rule" prohibits prosecutors from using evidence that was obtained illegally, in violation of the defendant's constitutional rights. See *Mapp v. Ohio*, 367 U.S. 643 (1961).

Like Christ, priests should come not to condemn, but to save (John 3:17). At times, that requires unusual action in response to dilemmas.

The pastoral objective of AL is not to control people's behavior but to raise awareness of what God asks of people whose only choices involve objective evil. Pope Francis's explicit appeal favoring mercy for those caught in dilemmas ought to encourage couples in irregular marriages to come to the sacrament of reconciliation. At present, many such couples simply keep the irregularity of their marriage secret, ignore the rules, and come to Communion. Others believe that they have no choice but to suffer the continual decline of their children who lack the resources to cope with the jarring consequences of divorce.

Bishops are understandably concerned about how to communicate this pastoral approach without creating false expectations or bitterness. Some of the laity fail to appreciate that not every divorce presents the same problems or potential solutions. Some people have greater resiliency in facing distressing situations than others. Some have opportunities that others simply do not have. Supportive family members may generously help in raising the children and even in offering financial assistance. Not everyone can lay claim to such good fortune. The talents of parents to bring out the best in the children can vary enormously. All these and many other factors will contribute to a decision on whether and how a divorced and remarried couple can stay together to minimize the evil involved. Pastoral ministers should certainly understand this, and most ordinary laity can as well.

The issue is avoiding the greater evil. *That* this should be accomplished does not present any doctrinal problem at all. *How* this can be accomplished will at times constitute a substantial practical and pastoral challenge. Bishops will want to avoid unnecessary misunderstanding and rancor. The pope urges them to implement mercy in these very difficult situations so they can avoid running roughshod over those caught in dilemmas. The bishops can avoid animosity by ensuring that priests and pastoral ministers who have responsibility for marriage issues have a good understanding of the pope's apostolic exhortation. Those who cannot understand AL should not be given responsibilities to implement it. Bishops also will want to avoid giving the impression that the rules have changed or that any divorced and remarried couple can simply return to the sacraments. Above all, they should communicate that couples in irregular marriages need the accompaniment of a competent priest or pastoral minister to help them through their dilemma.

6. Mercy as Weakness?

Some fear that mercy makes things worse. Shakespeare has one of his more unpleasant characters, a senator, observe, "Nothing emboldens sin so much as mercy."[103] Shakespeare thus raised the question of whether Christians of his day appreciated mercy or rather remained in solidarity with their pagan ancestors. Does mercy necessarily embolden sin?

AL does not authorize the nullification of the law, nor does it "embolden sin." St. Paul, who could write so negatively about the law (see Rom 3:28; 4:13-16; 10:4; Gal 2:16, 21, etc.), nevertheless understands the law as a lifeline. The Christian needs to observe both the spirit of mercy behind the law and the law itself. Paul's problem comes when the law is abused by sin. James D. G. Dunne observes that Paul recognized that "*both* the outward norm *and* the inward motivation were essential for ethical living." Without the proper inward motivation in Christ, external laws degenerate into mere legalism, routine and rule. Without the external norms of the laws, the inward spiritual impulses become unmoored from their proper content, in which case Christian conduct would "become antinomian and guru-led." The practice of the law needs to be a "manifestation of love" or else "the Spirit of Christ is not behind it."[104] The law must always operate from within the Spirit. Mercy is not confined to the law but fulfills the law.

Thus, Jesus presents a different picture from the pagans. He observes that the rain falls on the just and unjust alike (Matt 5:45). Even the unrepentant sinner benefits from God's gifts. The prodigal son certainly deserves punishment for his life of profligacy, but the Father welcomes his son's safe return regardless of what the son might have to say (Luke 15:11-32). The tax collector who relied on God's mercy leaves the Temple justified but the Pharisee does not (Luke 18:9-14). Jesus earned the ire of his contemporary religious leaders for showing mercy to tax collectors and other sinners (Luke 7:36-50), but he persists in his

103. *Timon of Athens*, III.v.3.

104. James D. G. Dunn, *The Theology of Paul the Apostle* (Grand Rapids: Eerdmans, 1998), 669.

mercy despite their anger. After all, God desires mercy and not sacrifice (Matt 9:13; 12:7). Jesus commands his followers to be merciful as his heavenly Father is merciful (Luke 6:36). Christians need to apply mercy to those who deserve it and to those who do not. Thus, Jesus defends the woman caught in adultery and protects her despite the laws in both Deuteronomy and Leviticus (John 7:53-8:11; see Lev 20:10 and Deut 22:23-24). He chooses a merciful application of the law and frees the woman from all punishment. Indeed, for such actions, his opponents vilified Jesus as a "friend of sinners" (Matt 11:19; Luke 7:34).

* * *

The issues raised by chapter 8 of AL deal with concrete dilemmas that have no "right" solution. *The critics of AL have missed essential points and therefore oppose a position on indissolubility that no one holds.* Pope Francis understands that divorce concerns not only the integrity of the marital bond but also the welfare of the children. The church's concern should not center on chastity alone. Few would question that Jesus forbids divorce. The issue for chapter 8 of AL concerns what can be done after a divorce and remarriage have already taken place and family relations have solidified over time. In AL, the pope continues the practice of managing the marital bond, a practice that has a solid Biblical basis, as well as a basis in the history of the church.

The pope's plea for priests to accompany couples in second marriages is consistent with decisions made by the bishops of the Council of Nicaea and many popes thereafter, from St. Innocent I and St. Leo the Great in late patristic times all the way to St. John XXIII in modern times. They sought not to punish couples in irregular unions but to help alleviate as best they could extremely difficult marital situations.[105] It is not as if the church has never considered whether it can live in communion with those in second marriages. Historically the church has exercised mercy to help people manage the dilemmas they encounter. Pope Francis follows this tradition in AL.

---

105. Philip Lyndon Reynolds, *Marriage in the Western Church: The Christianization of Marriage During the Patristic and Early Medieval Periods* (New York: E.J. Brill, 1994), 133–34, 136–37.

CHAPTER SEVEN

Penance and Communion

1. The Possibility of Absolution When a Firm Purpose of Amendment Cannot Be Made

C ertainly a good confession involves a firm purpose of amendment. It presumes that the penitent will work deliberately to eliminate the cause of sin, first by performing the penance given by the confessor and then by working to eliminate the root cause of the sin through whatever daily practice might help. That time-honored practice remains in place, as it should.

Nevertheless, the general rule that a Catholic with grave sin must make a good confession prior to receiving Communion, while fully applicable in the vast majority of cases, admits of variances as one encounters the details of particular circumstances. Penitents caught in dilemmas need pastoral treatment that takes into account that they have few alternatives, none of which involves a morally pure course of action.

Pope Francis has devoted a good deal of reflection on these topics in chapter 8 of AL. He has opted for a pastoral practice that reinstates those in irregular situations rather than to cast them off (AL 296). Contrary to approaches that categorically deny that dilemmas can happen or that treat all irregular marriages as if they were the same, Francis calls for pastoral attentiveness to the particulars of each case (AL 298).

Pastoral ministers need to accompany those in irregular marriages to help the couple discern the path forward in as honest and forthright a manner as possible, always remembering that the pastoral minister should help form the conscience of the person and not replace it. Typically, the pastoral minister does not presume to judge the inner strength or weakness of a person and should not lightly challenge a couple on whether a situation constitutes a dilemma (AL 37, 303). It must also be acknowledged that the pastoral minister has a conscience that needs to guide the process in a manner faithful to Christ and appropriate to the circumstances. The bestowal of mercy provides no easy "rubber stamp" decisions. Each case needs individual care and attention. At least three circumstances call for ministers to become more active when listening to an irregular couple's interpretation of events: (1) when they present an objective sin as if it complied with church teaching; (2) when the couple has just formed a "new union arising from a recent divorce"; and (3) when one "has consistently failed in his obligations to the family" (AL 297–98).

Those situations differ greatly from the one in which a couple in an irregular marriage admits to their wrongdoing and expresses a desire to rectify the situation but cannot because of circumstances. Their invalid marriage may have endured for many years. They may have several children to raise. They in fact may have a thriving family. Separation at this point would give rise to grave complications for the children as well as for the couple. They may be able to manage to live in a "brother-sister" relationship which, although the lesser of two evils, nonetheless is still an evil. Nevertheless, the church in its mercy has tolerated this option for many years.[1] A couple who accepts its conditions may be given absolution and receive Communion with a clear conscience, confident that they are doing the best that they can under the circumstances. The laity have accepted such accommodations with ease, as they should.

What if the couple in an irregular situation cannot manage a "brother-sister" relationship? What if simply being in the same house, already having related to each other as husband and wife for many years, makes it impossible to remain continent? Together they look on their children lovingly, not as aunt and uncle, but as mother and father. They see their natural bond alive in their offspring, which understandably should draw them closer together as husband and wife. Both the spousal bond and the parental bond make it difficult to pretend that they can live together as brother and sister. As Vatican II's *Gaudium et Spes* noted concerning the unitive aspect of marriage, "Where the intimacy of married life is broken off, it is not rare for its faithfulness

---

1. See John Paul II, *Familiaris Consortio* 84.

to be imperiled and its quality of fruitfulness ruined. For then the upbringing of children and the courage to accept new ones are both endangered."[2] Indeed, the council fathers noted the very upbringing of children is put at risk when mother and father no longer relate as husband and wife.

Obviously a husband and wife in such an irregular situation must avoid giving scandal even as they are integrated more fully into the life of the church. Certainly they should not publicize their status. If circumstances become sufficiently scandalous in one parish, they might need to move to another. In any event, such a couple should not be made to feel excommunicated (AL 299). Such couples profess to be open to a journey to God in the most difficult of circumstances. As Francis has written in *Evangelii Gaudium*, pastors and lay faithful must accompany such couples "with mercy and patience" as they grow through various "stages of personal growth as these progressively occur."[3]

Those who find themselves in dilemmas need the sacrament of reconciliation to assist them on their way to a life that is more fully integrated with the church and, in fact, consistent with what is possible in their circumstances, giving due regard to both the spousal and parental bonds that have developed in their family. As any confessor knows, the degree of responsibility for an act can vary substantially in any given case. It never suffices to consider only the objective act, since the full consent of the will may be lacking as well as a full appreciation of the nature and quality of the act (see AL 301). Especially with respect to the divorced and remarried, a sin committed in one's young adulthood that has become solidified over the years, making it more and more difficult to reverse until it is virtually irreversible, should receive merciful treatment by a confessor (AL 300).

The modern notion that forgiveness comes only after repentance needs correction. *Fundamentally, forgiveness is God's response to sin. It is not God's response to contrition.*[4] Forgiveness is the work of God's

2. Second Vatican Council, *Gaudium et Spes* 51.

3. Pope Francis, apostolic exhortation *Evangelii Gaudium* (November 24, 2014) 44.

4. Although Catholics tend to forget this principle, it has long been part of standard Catholic theology. See James Bretzke, *Handbook of Roman Catholic Moral Terms* (Washington, DC: Georgetown University, 2013), 91; Joseph Ratzinger, *Introduction to Christianity*, trans. J. R. Foster (San Francisco: Ignatius, 2004), 282-83; Gerhard Lohfink, *Jesus of Nazareth: What He Wanted, Who He Was* (Collegeville, MN: Litur-

grace and patience (see Rom 3:22-25). The repentant sinner has not earned God's love or forgiveness. God does not stand aloof, expecting to be appeased. Through forgiveness, the sinner feels new life, has the power to become truly contrite, and willingly takes on a penance to strengthen his moral life. The sinner receives the forgiveness of God joyfully, precisely because it comes freely, unexpectedly, and with love. God does not forgive grudgingly or expect to be compensated for the trouble, as humans often do. How many times does Jesus encounter a sinner, and offer forgiveness before the sinner could even utter a word? The woman caught in adultery (John 8:11) and the healing of the paralytic (Matt 9:2) are two prominent examples. This is not to say that sinners can presume on the graciousness of God. God's forgiveness does not constitute an invitation to wallow in sin. Forgiveness rather provides the initial remedy by which the sinner begins the conversion process. God forgives the person's sin *even while he is sinning*. Confession and repentance come after God has already forgiven a person. They come as a result of forgiveness, not the other way around.

This does not mean that a person can skip confession. God's forgiveness constitutes the first step to the confessional where the serious business of conversion begins to take place through penance. There is a necessary ecclesial dimension to conversion by which a priest accepts the self-accusation of the sinner in confession and declares a penance appropriate to the sinner's situation as a significant step away from that serious sin and towards solidarity with the body of Christ. In confession, the forgiveness of God gains traction in the life of the sinner through penance. It provides a sort of Velcro by which God's forgiveness can adhere to the penitent's life and can begin to change that person's story. Otherwise that forgiveness can slip by a person's life without sufficient notice. The priest's absolution indicates that in his judgment the penitent accepts God's forgiveness in a way that will help the person to make the necessary changes in his or her life. The sacrament facilitates a more thorough conversion by bringing it to the church's attention. The guilt that drove the person to the confes-

---

gical Press, 2012), 30; and Eleonore Stump, *Atonement* (Oxford: Oxford University Press, 2018), 62–63. Cardinal Caffarra certainly swims against the currents of the tradition when he writes, "God does not forgive the person who does not repent" (Caffarra, "Sacramental Ontology," in Robert Dodaro, *Remaining in the Truth of Christ: Marriage and Communion in the Catholic Church* [San Francisco: Ignatius, 2014], 178).

sional describes the unfittingness of one's sinful action. Penance and absolution make a place in the community so that he or she "fits in" once again. Thus reconciliation happens through the sacrament. The person can also make significant strides in the healing process that further solidifies conversion.

Obviously, one must have faith, a relationship with God, before any of this makes sense. Faith precedes healing and forgiveness in the New Testament. For example, Matthew writes that, as some people carrying a paralytic man lying on a bed came near, "When Jesus saw their faith, he said to the paralytic, 'Take heart, son. Your sins are forgiven'" (Matt 9:2). The scribes who observe the encounter object, but Jesus uses the incident to illustrate his power through a miracle. Faith indeed precedes forgiveness. It describes the relationship that needs mending. Otherwise the person would not even know or care to seek forgiveness. Peter declares at Caesarea, "All the prophets testify about him that everyone who believes in him receives forgiveness of sins through his name" (Acts 10:43). As soon as people realize their relationship to the Lord in faith, they realize God's forgiveness of their sin. Their conversion stories make for powerful testimonies to the faith.

When an irregular couple, caught in a dilemma, approaches a confessor and exhibits "humility, discretion and love for the Church and her teaching, in a sincere search for God's will and a desire to make a more perfect response to it," the couple ought to be offered penance and absolution (AL 300). The couple may wish they could bring their lives into conformity to the rules, but when no way exists to bring themselves to that point, it is simply unchristian to deny them absolution.

When no firm purpose of amendment is possible, when it would involve turning back the clock as if one could relive certain critical moments of one's life, when the concrete decision simply does not allow for the change that would ideally be required without further evil, mercy can take hold and tolerate the illegitimate family's staying together—not because the objective situation is right or is now justified. It is not. The church can allow the situation to move forward because it must allow people to choose the lesser evil when no good option exists. The lesser evil remains an evil, but nothing else can be done short of ruining the fragile lives that come for refuge in the church. Those who glibly maintain that such people should suffer "for justice's sake" are like Dostoevsky's Raskolnikov, who was "young, abstract and, therefore, cruel."

Analogous examples might help to clarify the issue. The firm purpose of amendment expects the sinner to change in ways that avoid the sin in question. Fair enough. What if the sinner has done something irreversible? For example, what if a sinner has received highly offensive tattoos that cannot be removed or hidden? One thinks of the late Charles Manson's swastika tattooed on the bridge of his forehead, right above his nose. How could he stop giving offense? What did amending his life require of him? What if he could not erase the tattoo? Should such a person not receive absolution because he cannot "amend" that part of his life? Mercy would forgive him and let him cope as best he can in the present circumstances.

What if one has received a vasectomy? Current pastoral practice indicates that such a penitent need not suffer the medical risk and expense of reversing the operation. Absolution does not require the reversal of the operation as long as other elements, such as sorrow and contrition, are in place.

Some actions are simply not reversible. If a candidate for the military draft shot off his toe to avoid service, that mutilation remains part of his life that cannot be amended. Amending one's life at times tolerates the defects brought about by the sin. Certain things simply cannot be "undone."

Irregular families, caught in dilemmas, often cannot "undo" their family situation. The firm purpose of amendment for parents of such families might entail simply keeping the family together, which is what they failed to do the first time. Of course, one can think of situations in which that would not be justified. It all depends on the specific facts of the case. No one solution will fit every situation faced by all divorced and remarried couples. Discernment and accompaniment need to take place on an individual basis. When appropriate reflection indicates that an irregular marriage should stay in place, it does not mean that the church is retreating from its teaching on indissolubility. It means that it takes mercy seriously in dire situations where nothing else can be done without inflicting even greater evils (see AL 307).[5]

5. The situation of the person in an invalid marriage who cannot leave the marriage might constitute an example of an "involuntary sin" in the Orthodox tradition. The Orthodox Church expects penitents to confess sins both voluntary and involuntary, both conscious and unconscious, both those done with malice and those done inadvertently. This thinking comports with the notion of sin as sickness. Whether a

The pope has wisely advised confessors to help penitents find "what for now is the most generous response which can be given to God, and come to see with a certain moral security that it is what God himself is asking amid the concrete complexity of one's limits, while yet not fully the objective ideal" (AL 303). In certain circumstances, if confessors do not leave well enough alone, they stand ready to destroy lives. When a firm purpose of amendment cannot fully be made, confessors should not turn away sincere, contrite, humble people caught in objective sin. They should accompany them so they can make meaningful progress in ways that are still possible. Under currently accepted rules and doctrines, people may receive the Eucharist when, fully contrite, they select the least evil option when only evil options exist. They do not exhibit obstinance in impossible cases, but contrition. The church will not expect them to do the impossible.[6] This conclusion requires no change in doctrine at all. Those who are properly disposed and caught in a moral dilemma lack the subjective determination necessary to establish moral fault. They are in the state of grace. Up to this point, Francis has proposed nothing new.

Nevertheless, the pope furnishes an additional reason that such people may receive Communion when he calls attention to the original context of an important teaching of Paul. We now turn to that teaching.

2. The Possibility of Communion for Contrite Serious Sinners

Prior to the issuance of AL, many church officials assumed that anyone conscious of grave sin could not receive the Eucharist, based on Paul's teaching that "whoever . . . eats the bread or drinks the cup of the Lord

---

person became sick willingly or not, the condition still needs treatment. Hence, this situation offers further reason for the importance of accompaniment for those trapped in invalid marriages. See Basilio Petrà, *La Penitenza Nelle Chiese Ortodosse: Aspetti Storici e Sacramentali* (Bologna: Dehoniane, 2005), 11.

6. See Lawrence Feingold, *The Eucharist: Mystery of Presence, Sacrifice, and Communion* (Steubenville, OH: Emmaus Academic, 2018), 551–55, where the author treats AL as properly permitting Communion to those who lack full knowledge or full consent of the will. See also The Canon Law Society of America, *The Code of Canon Law: A Text and Commentary*, ed. James Coriden, Thomas Green, and Donald Heintschel (New York: Paulist Press, 1985), 653, where John Huels asserts, "The minister cannot assume . . . that the sin of public concubinage arising from divorce and remarriage is always grave in the internal forum."

in an unworthy manner will be answerable for the body and blood of
the Lord" (1 Cor 11:27-29). They assumed that the admonition originally directed people to make a good examination of conscience and,
if they become conscious of having committed a serious or grave sin,
to make a good confession prior to going to Communion. While there
always were restrictions concerning those who could rightly receive the
Eucharist, on closer inspection Scripture presumes that the Eucharist would go to all those who needed forgiveness and not merely for
venial sins and the minor peccadilloes that plague any life. Paul wrote
that believers need to receive the Eucharist in a worthy manner (see
1 Cor 11:17-22), but he nowhere prohibits contrite grave sinners from
receiving Communion. Pope Francis has explicitly offered the possibility of eucharistic sharing with some couples in irregular marriages. He
includes in his justification in addition to the usual traditional sources
a much more adequate interpretation of Scripture than many previous
pontiffs (AL 108, 305). Both Scripture and tradition firmly support his
eucharistic discipline in this regard, as explained below.

A. Scriptural Considerations

In Paul's day, Christians celebrated the Eucharist as part of a regular
meal. Some took the occasion to eat with their friends and finished
before the poorer Christians could come from their jobs. Some of the
wealthier ones even took the occasion to become inebriated! The Lord
designed the eucharistic action to express and strengthen the very unity
the Corinthians subverted through their fractious behavior (see 1 Cor
11:18-19). Paul complains that when they gathered for the Lord's Supper, "when time comes to eat, each of you goes ahead with your own
supper, and one goes hungry and another becomes drunk. . . . [D]o
you show contempt for the church of God and humiliate those who
have nothing?" (1 Cor 11:21-22). After recalling the words of institution
pronounced by Christ, Paul lowers the boom: "Whoever, therefore, eats
the bread or drinks the cup of the Lord in an unworthy manner will be
answerable for the body and blood of the Lord. Examine yourselves,
and only then eat of the bread and drink of the cup. For all who eat
and drink without discerning the body, eat and drink judgment against
themselves" (1 Cor 11:27-29). Paul has difficulty with the *manner* in
which certain Christians conduct themselves at the eucharistic meal
inasmuch as they humiliate other less wealthy Christians.

So insistent is Paul on the need to honor all at the eucharistic table, he recommends the exact opposite of a eucharistic fast: "Wait for one another. If you are hungry, eat at home, so that when you come together, it will not be for your condemnation" (1 Cor 11:33-34). If they eat something before they celebrate the Eucharist, they can avoid embarrassing others by waiting patiently for them to arrive before starting the meal without them. Clearly the condemnation Paul has in mind concerns the humiliation imposed upon those who cannot come as early as their wealthier counterparts. They should celebrate the Eucharist in "remembrance" of the Lord. It should be done the way the Lord did it, not in contempt of the lower classes. In that way, they can discern the body, that is, they can perceive Christ's presence, not only in the Eucharist, but also in the assembly.

The Eucharist looks forward to unity and reconciliation. When the Eucharist becomes the private property of the elite moneyed classes, they receive it "in an unworthy manner." Paul's reference to the *unworthiness* of Christians to receive the Eucharist has nothing to do with the types of sins committed by individual recipients, but with the types of communities that gather to celebrate the Eucharist. Those who use the Eucharist to create groups of insiders distort the sacrament, especially when they humiliate a group of "outsiders" in their midst. This is the situation that is created regularly today when a certain group of Catholics cannot join the Communion line based on their sin.

Although the pope unfolds this significant Pauline passage in the context of contrite divorced and remarried Catholics, he nevertheless refrains from pursuing any further implications for other areas of theology. Recent eucharistic practice remains largely in place with the understanding that those trapped in moral dilemmas are not necessarily precluded from the sacraments on a permanent basis. His observations concerning 1 Corinthians 11:27-29 open a way for theological developments that can unlock the potential of the Eucharist to bring mercy to life for those who struggle with conversion from serious sin. For those who remain skeptical, further theological reflection can help.

Some argue that grave sinners must refrain from the Eucharist because their lifestyles do not yet conform to the Christian way of life. This is true for all people who are content to remain in sinful lifestyles and do not wish to change even though they have the power to do so. In one sense, all sin is serious since all sin offends an infinite

God.[7] All sinners who strive for holiness already exemplify the life of the church. They are already integrated into the life of the church in varying degrees. Indeed, Vatican II's *Lumen Gentium* 8 views the church, the body of Christ, as a mother who embraces sinners close to her loving heart. Pope Francis includes within that embrace contrite couples who are caught in impossible circumstances. They lack the subjective dimension of sin.

The Eucharist can encourage the sinner to complete any work of conversion that still remains in his or her life. Francis J. Moloney has demonstrated that the Eucharist constitutes a meal of steadfast forgiveness in the face of the ongoing betrayal by the disciples that plays out over the course of the same evening.[8] Despite the weakness of the disciples, Jesus determines to celebrate the Passover with them (Matt 26:17-19).

Some Catholics might tend to read the Last Supper narratives in a way that preserves modern eucharistic sensibilities so that all the disciples, including Judas, receive only with pure hearts. The texts do not support this understandable anachronism. All the disciples are in the process of betraying Jesus, and he knows it. Obviously Judas's final act of betrayal lies in the future, but he has already set the wheels in motion. Luke explicitly quotes Jesus as saying, "the one who betrays me is with me" (Luke 22:21). The betrayal does not simply lie in the future. What does this mean for Judas? He has chosen a life of woe. It would be better for him had he never been born (Mark

---

7. See Kenan Osborne, *Reconciliation and Justification: The Sacrament and Its Theology* (New York: Paulist Press, 1990), 236–39, on the complexity of making distinctions among categories of sin.

8. Francis J. Moloney, *Eucharist as a Celebration of Forgiveness* (New York: Paulist Press, 2017), chap. 2, esp. 25–43. The story tells a tale of the deepening failure of the disciples: representatives of Israel conspire to arrest and kill Jesus (Matt 26:3-5); Judas joins the plot (Matt 26:14-16); Jesus predicts Judas's betrayal (Matt 26:20-25); he then predicts that all his disciples will that very night desert him (Matt 26:31). He foretells Peter's triple denial, and all the disciples argue that they will remain true (Matt 26:34-35). The disciples sleep while Jesus prays in the garden. He encourages them to stay awake and pray, and, nonetheless, they fall back into their slumber (Matt 26:41-43). As predicted by Jesus, Peter denies Jesus three times (Matt 26:69-74). Though disappointed at all these failures, Jesus is not surprised. He knew all along the weakness and flawed characters of his disciples and nevertheless celebrates the Last Supper with them.

14:21). What does this mean for Jesus? He uses the opportunity to include Judas along with all the other failing disciples in a celebration of his forgiveness. Only after sharing the bread and the cup, does Jesus release Judas so he can complete his betrayal. Jesus maintains this same attitude of forgiveness even as he is nailed to the cross. "Father, forgive them; for they do not know what they are doing" (Luke 23:34).

The failures of the disciples and the faithfulness of Jesus continue throughout the Passion narrative. Matthew in particular emphasizes the Last Supper as a meal of forgiveness by making explicit the import of Jesus's words and actions: ". . . for this is my blood of the covenant, which is poured out for many for the forgiveness of sins" (Matt 26:28). The meal presumes that its participants need the forgiveness for which his blood is poured out.

Francis Moloney concludes, "The meal that Jesus shared was not a meal for 'the worthy.' It was a meal for those who were closest to Jesus but who, faced with the challenge to love him even unto death, betrayed, denied, and forsook their Lord. A new covenant for the forgiveness of sins is established in the gift of his body and blood."[9] Indeed many of his meals were taken with sinners and tax collectors. Why should the Last Supper be any different? In fact, it was not.[10]

Obviously Jesus desires sinners to repent. He tells Peter that Satan has asked to sift him like wheat, but that he will pray for him (Luke 22:31). Perfection is not expected prior to Communion. If perfection is not required prior to Communion, if struggle with grave sin is understandable at the table of the Lord, are there any requirements at all?

Certainly baptism and consciousness of sin are required, as well as a desire for full conversion. If there is no baptism, no consciousness of sin, or no desire for conversion, ministers may deny the Eucharist until the necessary changes take place. So for example, Paul has no difficulty in expelling from the community a member who practices

9. Moloney, *Eucharist as a Celebration of Forgiveness*, 30. Luke takes up this same theme in his own way. He inserts the elements of a farewell discourse in the Last Supper, lending legitimacy to the apostles as the successors of Jesus. But he also shows us Jesus commissioning them in the midst of their failure—instructing them to take a purse, a bag, and even a sword, because Jesus was destined "to be counted among the lawless" (Luke 22:31-38).

10. Moloney, *Eucharist as a Celebration of Forgiveness*, 34-35.

an incestuous relationship with his father's wife (1 Cor 5:1-8). Those who arrogantly posit that their wicked activity constitutes no sin or who refuse to leave sinful situations (where it is possible to do so) have no business participating in Communion. The community should, to borrow Paul's phrase, "hand this man over to Satan" (1 Cor 5:5) to shock him back to his senses. Expulsion from the community looks forward to the day that the complacent sinner becomes contrite and returns to the community founded in Christ.

The measure of worthiness for admission to Communion in the New Testament centers on baptism, adherence to true faith in Christ, the acknowledgment of sin, and the firm determination to conform one's life to whatever repentance requires. One must respect socially undesirable groups and celebrate this Communion of forgiveness in true union with them; otherwise, one receives the Eucharist in an unworthy manner. The celebration presumes that all have work to do in receiving God's grace and deepening their conversion to Christ.

B. The Early Tradition

The pope's directives continue a sensibility that was familiar to the early church. His eucharistic discipline focuses on mercy shown to those caught in dilemmas, those trapped in objectively evil situations but who nonetheless do the best they can to follow God's will in those unfortunate circumstances. Neither the supposed impurity of their souls nor the objective impurity of their circumstances should prevent them from receiving the nourishment of the sacrament.

This approach is witnessed not only by Scripture, which includes a portrayal of the Eucharist as food for the journey for those in need of forgiveness,[11] but also by the writings of the subapostolic age. The basic scriptural understanding of the qualifications for eucharistic participation persisted in the writings of a distinguished line of fathers (including Ignatius of Antioch, Justin Martyr, Tertullian, John Chrysostom and Leo the Great) until about the year 800.[12] This line of thinking constituted one strand of tradition that existed simultaneously with several other approaches to eucharistic discipline. Sometimes different pastoral approaches appear simultaneously within the work of a

---

11. See Jesus's bread of life discourse (esp. John 6:51-59).

12. The reflections in this section come mainly from Moloney, *Eucharist as a Celebration of Forgiveness*, 55–70.

single father, as we shall see. In accord with the biblical witness, these thinkers insisted upon the three conditions that qualified a Catholic to receive Communion: baptism, the consciousness of sin, and the desire for conversion. They knew that when St. Paul mentioned unworthiness in connection with Communion, he referred to the conduct of the eucharistic assembly, not to the interior state of the soul of the recipient.

The *Didache*, written around 100 AD, instructs the community on the procedures to follow in its celebration of the Eucharist. Its author restricts the Eucharist to the baptized: "For let no one eat or drink of your Eucharist except those who have been baptized into the name of the Lord, for the Lord has also spoken concerning this: 'Do not give what is holy to the dogs.'" The author continues, "On the Lord's own day gather together and break bread and give thanks, having first confessed your sins so that your sacrifice may be pure. But let no one who has a quarrel with a companion join you until they have been reconciled, so that your sacrifice may not be defiled."[13] The author keeps in place the three requirements: baptism, consciousness of sin and a desire for conversion.

When the author counsels communicants to first confess their sins, he recommends it as a weekly practice, that is, whenever the Eucharist is received. Modern Catholics might envision those early Christians going to confession as they do today. But the sacrament of penance had not yet evolved that far. In fact, repeated auricular confession was an innovation of the fifth and sixth centuries. The earliest ritual directions for the sacrament of penance come in the middle of the second century. It could be received only once in a person's lifetime since it was offered as a sort of second baptism. The power of the keys justified the action.[14] The instruction could not have referred to sacramental confession.

The practice of "confessing one's sins" in the *Didache* reflects a biblical counsel, "Therefore, confess your sins to one another and pray for one another that you may be healed" (Jas. 5:16), a practice at least as old as Psalm 32 (see v. 5). It was fulfilled by a general acknowledgment of sinfulness, similar to the penitential act in today's Mass. It does not mean confession of individual sins to a priest or anyone else

---

13. *Didache* 9:5 in *The Apostolic Fathers: Greek Texts and English Translations*, 3rd ed., trans. Michael W. Holmes (Grand Rapids: Baker Academic, 2007), 365–67.

14. Carra de Vaux Saint-Cyr, OP, et al., *The Sacrament of Penance* (Paramus: Paulist Press, 1966), 12, 14, 18–22, 30–31; Ladislas Orsy, SJ, *The Evolving Church and the Sacrament of Penance* (Denville: Dimension Books, 1978), 28–51.

but confession as opposed to denial, an attitude of dignified candor rather than a polite cover-up. It emphasized that one should come to the Eucharist with humility, not in a sanctimonious way, as if one had no sin or as if one's sins were of the most inoffensive kind. Furthermore, the *Didache*'s reference to "unreconciled companions" calls to mind the divisions Paul so deplored in Corinth. The directive, aimed at avoiding underlying tensions, should enhance the peace of the community that would gather for the celebration. No other restrictions appear. Of course, baptism presupposes faith in what God has done through Jesus, but the *Didache* makes no reference to excluding those who have committed grave sin. Indeed, theologian James Dallen claims that at the time the *Didache* was written, the Eucharist accomplished the same results that Catholics would later experience in the sacrament of penance.[15]

Modern confessors often hear penitents begin their recitation of sins by saying, "Father, I'm sorry, but it's the same old list." Confession does not certify one's holiness, nor does it guarantee that one's struggles are at an end; rather, in confession the priest judges that penitents have committed themselves sufficiently to continue to strive for conversion so that absolution can be given. Communicants, therefore, do not present themselves as pure but as pilgrims on the way, needing food for the journey. Their imperfect communion with Christ and the church will be completed only in the *eschaton*.

Francis Moloney claims, "Across these earliest written witnesses to the celebration of the Eucharist, the theme of *faith* in the crucified and risen Lord is the only permanent requirement for worthiness. This faith is demonstrated by baptism 'after assenting to the instruction' (see *First Apology* 65). Such assent implies repentance and conversion."[16]

Moloney shows how Tertullian, Origen, Leo the Great, and Cyril of Alexandria are consistent with the *Didache* concerning one's worthiness to receive Communion. At times, they report in their homilies problems reflecting the same situation that prompted St. Paul's

---

15. See James Dallen, *The Reconciling Community: The Rite of Penance*, Studies in the Reformed Rites of the Catholic Church III (New York: Pueblo Publishing Company, 1986), 21.

16. Moloney, *Eucharist as a Celebration of Forgiveness*, 59–60 (emphasis in the original).

admonition on worthiness in 1 Corinthians. For example, St. John Chrysostom claims that groups that came to celebrate the Eucharist at times "pushed and pulled one another in an unruly manner during the services; they gossiped with one another; young people engaged in various kinds of mischief; and pickpockets preyed on the crowd."[17] Faithful to St. Paul, Chrysostom confines his exegesis of 1 Corinthians 11:27-29 to the appalling behavior that could develop in the eucharistic assembly.[18] St. Augustine confessed that he contributed to similar inappropriate activity during the eucharistic celebrations he attended in his younger years, admitting to having engaged in "carnal desires and conduct" during those liturgies.[19]

Bishops responded to this inappropriate conduct in various ways. They ritualized the eucharistic celebration, adding solemnity through ceremonial vesture, processions and sacred music. They emphasized the majesty and transcendence of God and the divinity of Christ.[20] They had altars constructed out of marble and enhanced the physical surroundings, even separating men from the women to discourage the younger congregants from socializing during the celebration.[21]

Toward the beginning of the fifth century, Augustine elaborated on a novel interpretation of 1 Corinthians 11:27. He emphasized that Jesus maintained his goodness to Judas by trying to save him, even as Judas was in the process of betraying him.[22] Augustine's reflections set the stage for an interpretation of the passage that reached far beyond its

---

17. Quoted in Paul F. Bradshaw, *Early Christian Worship: A Basic Introduction to Ideas and Practice*, 2nd ed. (Collegeville, MN: Liturgical Press, 2010), 70.

18. See Chrysostom's *Homily XXVII* on 1 Corinthians, where he gives a thorough exegesis of the circumstances that prompted Paul's comment on worthiness. See also Moloney, *Eucharist as a Celebration of Forgiveness*, 20.

19. Augustine, *The Confessions*, III.iii.5

20. Bradshaw, *Early Christian Worship*, 71.

21. See Paul F. Bradshaw and Maxwell Johnson, *The Eucharistic Liturgies: Their Evolution and Interpretation* (Collegeville, MN: Liturgical Press, 2012), chap. 3, esp. p. 62.

22. St. Augustine, *Tractates on the Gospel of John*, LXII.4 in *The Fathers of the Church, A New Translation*, vol. 90, *Tractates on the Gospel of John 55-111*, trans. John Rettig (Washington, DC: The Catholic University of America Press, 1994), 38-40. Although Augustine elaborates his new interpretation in this Tractate, he refers to it as early as his undated Sermon XXI.

original context in Paul's letter. One's degree of sinfulness now became the focus of concern prior to receiving Communion.

Even though St. Augustine promoted Communion only for the morally pure, he nonetheless also advanced an understanding of the Eucharist as healing remedy. Some people go to Communion every day because of "the wound inflicted by sin and the violence of the soul's distemper." Augustine approves of daily Communion because contrite sinners require a powerful remedy. As long as such a person's sins fall short of bringing him to excommunication, "he ought not to withdraw himself from the daily use of the Lord's body for the healing of his soul."[23] This person feels his unworthiness. He values the Eucharist for its power to heal him from sin. Augustine claims that in this way the man honors the Lord. Indeed, Augustine noted that Christ's remedy could adapt itself to suit any malady, even to the point of saying, "He is both the physician and the medicine."[24] This becomes especially true in the Eucharist at a time when sacramental penance was available only once in a lifetime.

St. John Chrysostom was well aware that St. Paul's comment on worthiness did not refer to the internal state of a communicant's soul. He was also well acquainted with the disorderly conduct that prompted St. Paul's comment in the first place. He and other bishops therefore devised a strategy not only to keep order in the assembly but also to entice people to lead better lives. He decided to use the Eucharist as an incentive. If a congregant leads a moral life, he or she may approach the priest to receive Communion, but not otherwise. Unfortunately, the plan backfired. It had the unintended consequence of keeping people away from Communion. Who could possibly be worthy enough to receive Holy Communion? Neither Augustine's misinterpretation of Paul nor Chrysostom's strategy to encourage the faithful have any

23. Augustine, Letter LIV, *A Select Library of the Nicene and Post-Nicene Fathers of the Christian Church I*, ed. Philip Schaff, trans. G. J. Cunningham (Grand Rapids: Eerdmans, 1988), 301. This may well indicate that Augustine could approve of a serious sinner receiving Communion in the right circumstances. Communion as a remedy for the "violence of the soul's distemper" sounds like serious sin lurks in the background at a time when penance was available only once in a lifetime.

24. Augustine, Christian Instruction 14 in *Writings of Saint Augustine* 4, trans. John Gavigan (New York: CMA Publishing, 1947), 37.

scriptural warrant in 1 Corinthians 11:27-29, although they were later treated as if they did.

Due in part to such decisions, Christians began to understand eucharistic worship less as a meal of unity and forgiveness and more as an expression of personal devotion.[25] Many people came simply to watch the priest transform the bread and wine into the body and blood of Christ.

To further illustrate the flexibility with which some fathers treated the Eucharist, consider St. Caesarius, Archbishop of Arles (c. 470–542 AD). He held that while ordinary works of mercy (giving alms, fasting, visiting the sick, etc.) can redeem one from venial sins, much more is required of those guilty of mortal sin. In addition to tears and weeping, "the sinner will have to separate from communion of the Church, remain in mourning and distress, and do public penance."[26] This puts St. Caesarius squarely in line with other fathers who also followed the lead of St. Augustine.

Nevertheless, St. Caesarius also acknowledged circumstances in which priests might welcome grave sinners to Communion, judging that it was the more pastorally productive approach. In one still-extant homily, he remarks that the practice of keeping a concubine before marriage is worse than adultery. Nevertheless, he acknowledged that some priests did not exclude men who had engaged in the sin from Communion and proceeded to defend such priests' judgments against those who would object. Caesarius preached:

> Perhaps those who are not stained with this sin will say: Why are not those who commit it suspended from communion with the Church?

25. See generally, Bradshaw and Johnson, *The Eucharistic Liturgies*, chap. 3, esp. 61, 63, 64, 66, 67, 70. Among the factors that influenced the shape of eucharistic liturgies in the fourth and fifth centuries, Bradshaw and Johnson note Christianity's acceptance as an officially favored religion, the unacceptable behavior of many worshipers, the desire to include a catechetical element in liturgies, the sense of unworthiness instilled in worshipers, the decline in those receiving Communion leading to a deemphasis on the Eucharist as meal, and the increasing ritualization of the eucharistic celebration.

26. ". . . *le pécheur devra se séparer de la communion de l'Église, demeiurer dans le deuil et l'affliction et faire pénitence publiquement* . . ." St. Caesarius of Arles, Sermon 179 (7) in Cyrille Vogel, ed., *Le Pécheur et la Pénitence dans l'Église Ancienne* (Paris: Editions du Cerf, 1966), 165 (my translation).

This great crime is not so punished by priests because it is committed by so many. If only one or two or four or five presumed to do this evil, they could and should not only be suspended from communion, but even separated from the conversation and banquets of Christian people. . . . However . . . the number of those who commit the sin prevents the priests of the Lord from segregating them. Still, good priests do what they can, striving with perfect charity to pray and sigh continually, together with moans and groans. Thus, by advice and prayer . . . they may sometime be able to recall to repentance those against whom they cannot exercise severity or ecclesiastical discipline because of their large number.[27]

"Good priests doing what they can" was for St. Caesarius a good enough reason to defend those pastorally-minded clerics. In their judgment, they considered the attempt to segregate those men to be counterproductive. Might their segregation introduce into the assembly the very type of judgment and divisions that Paul wanted to avoid? How might their segregation hinder their conversion? We simply do not have enough information to answer those questions. Even if we did have more information, that does not necessarily mean that bishops today would (or should) make the same decision as Caesarius did. Although Caesarius does not elaborate on the details of the situation, he does provide evidence that priests exercised some flexibility in their eucharistic practice out of concern for their flock.

Caesarius is not the only father who at times eased restrictions on eucharistic sharing. When St. John Chrysostom devised his strategy of restricting access to the Eucharist to entice his flock to improve their lives, he had already been teaching the efficacy of individual contrition for the remission of sins. Considering the passage of the woman (thought to be a prostitute) who was forgiven her many sins (Luke 7:36-50), Chrysostom claimed that pure, selfless love can restore any sinner to grace—even one who has committed grave sin.[28] In fact,

27. Sermon 43 (5) in Saint Caesarius of Arles, *Sermons*, I (1–80), *Fathers of the Church* 31, trans. Sr. M. M. Mueller, OSF (New York: Fathers of the Church, 1956), 217.
28. St. John Chrysostom, "An Exhortation to Theodore after His Fall," Letter I, *A Select Library of the Nicene and Post-Nicene Fathers of the Christian Church IX, St Chrysostom: On the Priesthood; Ascetic Treatises; Select Homilies and Letter; Homilies on the Statutes*, ed. Philip Schaff, trans. W. Stephens (Grand Rapids: Eerdmans, 1889), 105–7. Chrysostom, as well as other fathers, bases his reflections largely on Luke 7:47,

Chrysostom's position was already standard teaching among the fathers. Many years later when repeated auricular confessions were made available, this teaching became the basis for the practice of making a "perfect act of contrition," allowing even mortal sinners to receive communion. It would eventually become present everywhere after private confession made its way from Ireland during the fifth and sixth centuries.

In effect, those fathers preserved the traditional requirements for eligibility to receive Communion (baptism, the acknowledgment of sin, and a desire for repentance) but those requirements receded into the background and eventually took the form of the perfect act of contrition, which itself returns a person to the state of grace. Peter Lombard included the teaching on the perfect act of contrition in his *Sentences*, and Aquinas followed with his approval in his *Commentary on the Sentences*.[29] Eventually Trent endorsed the practice, leaving disputed details up to the theologians.[30]

Generally a person who has committed a mortal sin must confess that sin in the sacrament of reconciliation prior to receiving Communion. This expectation should normally prevail. Nevertheless, a person may receive Holy Communion worthily even if that person has not confessed his or her mortal sins as long as the person makes a perfect act of contrition (that is, out of a desire to express perfect charity) prior to receiving the Eucharist and resolves to go to confession as soon as practicable. The manuals of the 1930s contain directives permitting a mortal sinner to receive Communion in a wide variety of circumstances.[31] Authors typically refer to the "urgent need" for Communion but remain rather

---

where the Lord indicates that the woman who greeted him so warmly was forgiven many sins and therefore loves much. See also St. John Chrysostom, *Baptismal Instructions*, trans. Paul Harkins (New York: Newman Press, 1963), 239n49.

29. St. Thomas Aquinas, *Commentary on the Sentences*, bk. IV, d. 14, q. 2, a. 1, quae. 1; and bk. IV, d. 17, q. 2, a. 5, quae. 1-3. Aquinas claims that "any contrition at all is informed by sanctifying grace."

30. See Council of Trent, Session 13, chap. 7 in Tanner, *Decrees of the Ecumenical Councils* II, 696.

31. See, for example, Henry Davis, *Moral and Pastoral Theology*, vol. 3 (London: Sheed & Ward, 1935), 207. If a person is conscious (that is, certain) of having committed a mortal sin and cannot in present circumstances go to confession, he or she may make an act of perfect contrition and receive Communion. The act of contrition includes the resolution to go to confession at the first practicable opportunity to receive penance and absolution.

vague about the nature of such a need, although they always mention circumstances ranging from the danger of death to the possibility of embarrassment.[32]

To appreciate the power of a perfect act of contrition, it helps to distinguish a person who is in a state of mortal sin from a person who has merely committed a grave sin. A person in the state of mortal sin has committed a grave sin with *full knowledge* and *full consent of the will*, with the result that he has ruptured his relationship with God. Indeed, that relationship is dead. The sinful action is completed, and the sinner does not care. He knows very well the seriousness of his sin. It is not a matter of mere intellectual knowledge that his action was bad or prohibited by the authorities; he appreciates the nature and quality of the turpitude of the act. He feels the malice and simply does not care. Furthermore, he wills it deliberately. Under no particular pressure to commit the sin, he views his misdeed as an adventure, a walk on the wild side for the sheer pleasure it affords. He has become complacent and even defiant in sin. He does not particularly care to change. His sin may please him. He enjoys it. He wallows in it and has no desire to leave it. Such a sin is spiritually deadly. It constitutes a definitive rupture of his relationship with the all-loving and merciful God. The sinner has given up on the saving reality offered by God and impatiently leaves God's creation to seek the pleasures of a fantasy world. This person suffers a spiritual death that can be impenetrable, save for the grace of God. Eventually such a person may, through the grace of God, desire to leave that state of sin and experience the conversion offered in reconciliation. The path back to the church may be lengthy and arduous, but such a return will be met with a mother's open arms. A perfect act of contrition returns this sinner to a state of grace. This practice is not an innovation but a development of the common prerequisites in place for Communion in use since the first century, with the addition

---

32. See canon 916 and the commentary by John Huels, OSM, in John Beal, James Coriden, and Thomas Green, *New Commentary on the Code of Common Law* (New York: Paulist Press, 2000), 1111. One mid-twentieth century moral theology text advised that an "urgent need for Communion" can be satisfied if the sinner cannot leave the Communion line without disgrace (John McHugh, OP, and Charles Callan, OP, *Moral Theology: A Complete Course Based on Thomas Aquinas and the Best Modern Authorities*, rev. and enl. Edward Farrell, OP, vol. 2 [New York: James Wagner, 1958], 688).

of the promise to go to confession as soon as practicable. It works not because it borrows from a future confession, but because a baptized person has come to a present acknowledgment of sin together with a deep desire for repentance.

Another person may have committed a grave sin but with less than full knowledge and with less than the full consent of the will. He may not appreciate the seriousness of his actions. He may not fully understand the sin's ill effects on himself and others. He simply does not see the malice involved in the act. In some circumstances, he may also feel unusual pressure to commit the sin. For example, those who suffer addictions (even mild addictions) cannot heal simply through an act of the will. They may want to leave their addictions but need extraordinary support to do so. Others may give in to weakness or a temporary bout with boredom. Once having committed the serious sin, this person deeply regrets it. He suffers from his sin precisely because he has not abandoned his life with God. His sin betrays his living relationship with God and he knows it. Embarrassed by his stupidity and weakness, he longs for reconciliation. Sacramental penance may constitute a challenge for him for either physical or psychological reasons. He may need to work up the courage to admit the sin even to himself, let alone to a priest. He needs strength to return to the confessional. A perfect act of contrition restores also this sinner to a state of grace.

Kevin Irwin has called attention to the polyvalent nature of liturgical theology.[33] A methodology of models illustrates this polyvalent quality well, since one model does not cancel another but makes room for a "both-and" approach.[34] The model of the Eucharist as Holy Communion features the holy union achieved between the Body of Christ (understood as both the Lord and his church) and those who receive the Eucharist. Of course, no one on this earth reaches the highest degree of unity with the risen Lord. The moral purity required for the

---

33. Kevin Irwin, *Models of the Eucharist* (New York: Paulist Press, 1987), 23.

34. Irwin, 46, 32–33. A methodology of models explores theological realities in terms of different types of models that exhibit different aspects of the reality, all of which have a legitimate place. The understanding of the church as institution, for example, does not preclude an equally valid understanding of church as mystical communion. See Avery Dulles, *Models of the Church* (Garden City, NY: Image Books, 1978), 55, 61, 143–44.

Holy Communion model consists in baptism, the acknowledgment of sin, and a profound desire to repent. For all the splendor of the Eucharist as Holy Communion, the pilgrim church still must endure a very imperfect journey towards its goal. The model of the Eucharist as healing remedy therefore makes eminent sense alongside the model of the Eucharist as Holy Communion. Often enough the Eucharist can be the sacrament of Holy Communion because it is first a healing remedy and a sacrament of forgiveness. Indeed, before the priest leads the assembly in declaring, "Lord, I am not worthy," the *Roman Missal* reminds him of the model of the Eucharist as "healing remedy" in the second alternative prayer that the priest says quietly: "May the receiving of your Body and Blood . . . be for me . . . a healing remedy" (131).

When a contrite serious sinner joins the communion line, he or she does not deny the nature of the Eucharist as Holy Communion, a model that retains all its splendor and majesty. All communicants process forward to receive together, because they all desire deeper conversion. Spiritually they all face the same direction. The sinner-communicant needs and even desires what the poet Francis Thompson called "the hound of heaven" to pursue him and bark at his heels.[35] In order to bring himself to make a perfect act of contrition, he still needs "prevenient grace," which is not yet justifying grace, but a sort of preliminary grace that leads to conversion. No sinner comes to sanctifying grace strictly by himself. Grace always precedes conversion. Prevenient grace may come in many forms: a kind word from a friend, a homily that hits home, the wink of an eye, the working of guilt on the soul, or simply looking at one's victim. The sinner urgently needs those graces to gain the courage to make a perfect act of contrition.

This reflection on Communion taken with an act of perfect contrition supports the conclusion of Francis Moloney. After reviewing the positions of many prominent fathers, Moloney observes that "what was required for admission to the Eucharistic table was not sinless perfection but faith in Christ, demonstrated by baptism, a consciousness of sinfulness, and the need for repentance."[36]

---

35. Francis Thompson, "The Hound of Heaven," in *The Norton Anthology of English Literature*, vol. 2, ed. Abrams et al. (New York: W. W. Norton, 1962), 1053–57. The poem portrays Christ as the hound from heaven that relentlessly pursues a sinner until he can say to the sinner, "Rise, clasp my hand, and come!" (line 176).

36. Moloney, *Eucharist as a Celebration of Forgiveness*, 69.

Although many theologians supported the efficacy of a perfect act of contrition, the practice lurked in the background. It relied on a biblically supported pastoral practice that began to change at the close of the patristic era. Moloney reports that roughly around 800 AD, the "biblically inspired reflections on Christian discipline surrounding the Eucharist gradually began to dissipate in the West."[37] At that time, a more legalistic approach started to replace the vibrant biblical, theological, sacramental, and spiritual sensibilities that earlier characterized the church's eucharistic discipline. The Council of Trent's *Decree on the Eucharist* (1551) specifically cited 1 Corinthians 11:27-29, but treated the passage in a way totally removed from its original context, making the moral purity of the communicant a legal precondition for reception of Communion. Nevertheless, the Council also included the possibility of a perfect act of contrition for those who need it.

C. The Contemporary Situation

Pope Francis recognizes the context of Paul's warning to those who might eat at the table of the Lord in an unworthy manner.[38] In 1 Corinthians 11:27-29, Paul warns those who might use the Eucharist as a celebration of arrogant self-satisfaction to the embarrassment of others. This same scenario plays out today when some people join the Communion line while others remain shamefacedly in their seats. The discipline that Francis sets forth marks an advance based on a more authentic interpretation of the Pauline passage.

Matthew Levering thinks that the objective circumstances of adultery alone should disqualify an irregular couple from Communion, regardless of the circumstances. He declares, "Why, then, does the path of mercy not consist—as I strongly think it does—in calling the person to recognize the objective truth of this situation . . . and to end the sexual relationship, despite the (cruciform) suffering this will cause, as a prerequisite for Eucharistic Communion with the merciful Lord of Life?"[39] He does

37. Moloney, 70.
38. See esp. AL 185-186; also Moloney, *Eucharist as a Celebration of Forgiveness*, 72.
39. Matthew Levering, *The Indissolubility of Marriage:* Amoris Laetitia *in Context* (San Francisco: Ignatius Press, 2019), 113. José Granados, Stephan Kampowski, and Juan José Pérez-Soba advance the same arguments in *Accompanying, Discerning, Integrating: A Handbook for the Pastoral Care of the Family According to* Amoris Laetitia (Steubenville, OH: Emmaus Road, 2017), 68-78.

not consider the parental bond which is so important to the healthy development of children, a bond that is put at risk by the practice Levering advocates. In calling for the muting of the spousal bond, he may well undermine the parental bond, depending on the situation the family faces. It may transform a viable family into something more akin to a guardianship arrangement.

Of course, if no children complicate the matter, consideration of the spousal bond alone may indeed be enough to require a couple to separate. It may or may not require heroic virtue. This type of suffering reflects the cross because one absorbs the suffering intelligently, in a creative way. "Cruciform suffering" does not inflict suffering on another. It absorbs the suffering in a redemptive way by ending any further turmoil that it might have otherwise caused. Such a person proceeds with a life of sexual continence while suffering the heartache of a failed marriage and the inability to find fulfillment with another mate. Fair enough.

Francis and those who support the approach he offers in AL do not advocate the invocation of mercy to keep an adulterous relationship alive when they have a viable path to ending it. They do not deny anything of John Paul II's insistence that the indissolubility of marriage reflects "the absolutely faithful love that God has for man and that the Lord Jesus has for the Church."[40] All that remains in place.

But Levering fails to appreciate the dilemmas that can arise. Granados, Kampowski, and Pérez-Soba also refer to couples in irregular marriage who "stubbornly" remain in their unions. They cannot fathom how such people, "living in contradiction to one sacrament (Matrimony) should actually want to receive another sacrament (Eucharist)."[41] Of course, that is true for those who can move out of their adulterous unions, but like Levering, the three coauthors fail to consider those caught in dilemmas. When people have no way out, they are not being "stubborn." People whose hearts seek God and who wish their lives were more consistent with the church's moral teaching can indeed reasonably yearn for the Eucharist even though they cannot rectify their living situations.

40. John Paul II, *Familiaris Consortio* 20.
41. Granados, Kampowski, and Pérez-Soba, *Accompanying, Discerning, Integrating*, 77.

The path of mercy can lead to Communion *precisely because the person recognizes the objective truth of the total situation.* The truth shows itself not simply in the violated spousal bond but also in the violated (and too often ignored) parental bond. Some commentators too quickly conclude that a divorced parent who suffers terribly and soldiers on to raise her or his children through thick and thin must be virtuous. Some are, and some are not. What some might consider as heroic virtue in a single parent might not actually be virtue at all.

A single parent who has experienced a devastating divorce may simply have lost the ability to maintain the virtues needed to raise children well. Some possess the inner resources to manage single parenting well. Others do not. They face not only the task of single parenting, but of doing it while struggling with the pain and rejection of divorce. The experience of abandonment by the spouse who pledged to be one flesh with him or her can understandably be enormously dislocating. The hurt, anger, bewilderment, embarrassment, disappointment, and shock can take months or years to work through. They can seriously distort both parents' relationships with their children. For some, any light-hearted touch vanishes. A parent might not be able to control the onset of tears in front of the young ones. A parent's demeanor may change to the point where the children dread his or her presence. As the single parent loses control, the children may feel abandoned not only by their father, but also, in a way, by their mother. She is physically present, but at the same time emotionally distant. Screaming and shouting replace normal communication. The tension might rise to unbearable limits. The children may reach the point where they feel sinful, as in the Fort Sheridan case considered above. This all weakens the virtues of mothering and fathering. In fact, the divorced single parent may well acquire vices that make his or her abilities as a parent worse than merely poor.

All this sounds harsh. It may well not be the mother's fault. She may simply lack the inner fortitude and the emotional resources to deal with the burdens. What she might have handled with a supportive mate now utterly defeats her. The virtue of motherhood, the excellence of her motherly characteristics and inclinations, for her, have vanished. The same goes for the father. Any joyous carefree interaction with his children becomes heavy, even morose. After a divorce, many times either one or both parents can muster up only a cheap imitation of those virtues that good parenting requires. At times, those virtues can even turn into vices. Virtues produce goodness. Divorced parents often have precious little goodness to show for all the effort they have put into keeping the family together. The situation does not typically present a case of heroic virtue.

Furthermore, the virtue of chastity needs clarification. In the marital context, it refers to the purity of the sexual relationship between the husband and wife. Chastity fosters confidence, stability, unity, and depth in their relationship. Those sorts of qualities radiate onto the entire family. Children more readily feel safe and secure in a home where their parents hold fast to the virtue of chastity. A musical analogy can help to understand this essential aspect of virtue. Philosopher Vladimir Jankélévitch has noted the importance of charm in music.[42] It refers to the "life" of the music. Charm makes beauty both actual and efficacious. It does not come as a result of the technical competence of the musician or the musician's strict adherence to the musical score. Charm displays the soul of music. It prevents the music from becoming a dead letter.

Jankélévitch likens charm to virtue in the moral setting. Both charm and virtue have a transitive effect on others. Virtue should not only enhance one's own life; it ought to improve the lives of others as well. "Greatness is nothing if it does not magnify smallness, if it is not literally magnificent . . . purity is impure if it is not purifying. And conversely, a goodness that improves nothing, a quiescent and idle goodness, is like a flame that does not shine, it does not illuminate anybody, it does not warm anything: this inactive goodness contradicts itself."[43]

At times the chastity of an unusually strong single parent can retain at least something of its qualities that serve to strengthen the children. Women and men whose character, resources, determination, and resilience have reached profound levels can respond to the grace of God and provide a relatively peaceful home in which their children can grow. At other times, distressed parents will attempt a one-sided chastity by the sheer strength of their "technical competence" and their "strict adherence to the musical score." These parents follow the formula, but it does not work for them. Chastity becomes merely abstinence, a dead

42. Vladimir Jankélévitch, *Music and the Ineffable*, trans. Carolyn Abbate (Princeton: Princeton University, 2003), x–xi, 77–129.

43. Jankélévitch, *Music and the Ineffable*, x.

letter that improves nothing, a purity that does not purify. One must ask whether those who claim to uphold chastity in those circumstances might not be living the virtue at all, in spite of their good intentions and dogged determination. It can be like a flame that does not shine and provides no warmth. In considering the relative evils in marital dilemmas, those who weigh the violation of chastity against the necessity to raise the children often neglect the severely diminished form chastity has taken. Might its inactive goodness contradict itself?

When single parents focus on maintaining abstinence where once chastity existed, many of them may be able to provide some stability in the daily life of their children, but others may actually create severe problems for them while trying to feel good about it—as if they were keeping the faith! They may take satisfaction in their adult virtue of chastity and expect their children to suffer too—even while they lack an understanding of the reason for the suffering or how to deal with it. Such myopic adult suffering has nothing to do with heroic virtue. It has nothing to do with cruciform suffering which would protect the children and advance their interests. Depending on the situation, it can be very self-absorbed. Nevertheless, some church leaders, even in the wake of the sexual abuse crisis, fail to regard the pain of children and insist on maintaining an *ersatz* version of chastity that rides roughshod over the rights of the children. If theologians consider only adulterous spouses, the solution seems obvious. If they consider the family unit, the matter becomes much more complicated.

This is not to suggest that some vestiges of chastity can never be maintained when children are involved in a divorce; rather, all the relevant issues need to be weighed to determine the lesser evil. Those sorts of determinations need to proceed on a case-by-case basis. Certainly no one can say that *in every case* a remarriage would save the children. Many times it will not. In other instances, it can nourish and protect the emotional, psychological, and spiritual lives of children who deserve a healthy parental bond. Those sorts of issues do not lend themselves to generalities or universal principles; they must be determined in the concrete. Those burdened with making such decisions deserve the accompaniment of pastoral ministers who can assist them in identifying the issues and clarifying the competing interests at hand in the context of prayer. In every case, ministers offer guidance, but they must leave the ultimate decision to the person involved.

The church intends the denial of the Eucharist to help persuade a sinner to live an authentically Christian life.[44] It constitutes a loving incentive to motivate the person to take the next step in the conversion process. The denial of Communion should encourage the sinner to make a good confession and start moving along the path of conversion. The prohibition from the Eucharist will stop once the sinner takes the next step. The procedure affords them hope. The approach makes a lot of sense. But for those caught in dilemmas, there is nothing they can do. If the denial of Eucharist is intended as a "kick in the pants" to motivate change, the denial simply becomes one kick after another, serving no positive purpose. The Eucharist should always lead to conversion and never be used as pure punishment. Certainly the Gospel offers those caught in dilemmas a more loving and encouraging direction.

Nor does "spiritual communion" represent an adequate consolation prize for those caught in a dilemma. One makes a spiritual communion by calling up the ardent desire to receive the Eucharist in reality. This good and holy practice aims at enhancing the appetite for the Body and Blood of Christ, really present in the Sacrament. It makes sense for those who cannot receive Communion *temporarily* because of the lack of a priest or circumstances that prevent Mass from being celebrated (like the coronavirus pandemic of 2020). Catholics in those circumstances can look forward to the day when that appetite may be satisfied with the real reception of Holy Communion.

The practice makes much less sense for those who are *permanently* relegated to spiritual communion. For those caught in dilemmas, spiritual communion constitutes a punishment that keeps them not only from the Eucharist but also from penance. What happens if such a person commits a serious sin unrelated to the marriage? That person cannot celebrate the sacrament of penance in regard to any sin because they cannot leave the grave objective situation of evil in which they have become trapped. According to this thinking, they cannot make even an act of perfect contrition because they cannot commit themselves to go to confession. This may constitute a "life sentence" for a spouse, depending on which partner dies first. Apart from deathbed

44. See Walter Kasper, *The Message of* Amoris Laetitia: *Finding Common Ground* (New York: Paulist Press, 2019), 43; AL 296–97; and Beal, Coriden, and Green, *New Commentary*, 1550–51.

circumstances, this situation could affect the entire sacramental life of a person caught in a dilemma. In this connection, Walter Kasper calls attention to the fact that, "above all, in light of mercy, one is not permitted to condemn or exclude anyone forever. . . . On the contrary, mercy requires . . . that an opportunity for a new beginning is kept open for everyone."[45] Furthermore, those who engage in spiritual communion as a temporary measure never feel the embarrassment of not joining a Communion line while others in their presence walk in procession up the aisle. Those consigned to spiritual communion on a permanent basis face that awkward reality continually, whenever they attend Mass.

The church's eucharistic discipline can change. Good arguments support the discipline outlined by St. John Paul II and followed by Benedict XVI. John Paul II's 1981 apostolic exhortation *Familiaris Consortio* considered the situation of divorced and remarried Catholics who wished to receive Communion. Before recognizing the various situations represented in such a wide-ranging category, he noted that the church "cannot abandon to their own devices those who have been previously bound by sacramental marriage."[46] Pope Francis would agree. People cannot simply apply mercy to themselves.

Nevertheless, the divorced and remarried have not become separated from the church, which encourages them to attend Mass, pray, do charitable works, and cultivate the practice of penance. And yet, though they are part of the church, "their state and condition of life" prevent them from being admitted to eucharistic Communion.[47] Furthermore, because the faithful would be led into error and confusion about the doctrine of indissolubility if they knew such couples could receive Communion, the church underscores the dilemma for couples caught in impossible circumstances. The parish welcomes them to the meal at which they watch others receive Communion while they can only wish things could be different for themselves. This approach ignores the Eucharist as healing remedy. Ironically, in an effort to include such couples, the directive can tend to produce the very type of community that St. Paul forbade in 1 Corinthians 11:27-29.

45. Kasper, *Message of* Amoris Laetitia, 43. See AL 296–97.

46. John Paul II, *Familiaris Consortio* 84.

47. *Familiaris Consortio* 84.

Reconciliation in the sacrament of penance can be granted to those couples in irregular marriages who, for serious reasons, cannot separate but who live in complete continence. The pope characterizes the "brother-sister" relationship as "a way of life that is no longer in contradiction to the indissolubility of marriage."[48] He does not mention the various ways in which such a relationship does indeed violate a valid marital bond, as we have considered in chapter 3 above. Because the marriage is invalid, he forbids any blessing or other ceremony that might suggest that the union is somehow lawful or approved by the church. It is not; yet the couple can celebrate penance and the Eucharist regularly. As mentioned previously, the faithful accept this pastoral accommodation as a genuine work of mercy. In AL, Pope Francis preserves an expansion of this practice that had already been established in the church.

In 1994, the Congregation of the Doctrine of the Faith elaborated the rationale of *Familiaris Consortio* 84, with its "Letter to the Bishops of the Catholic Church Concerning the Reception of Holy Communion by the Divorced and Remarried Members of the Church." Signed by then-Cardinal Joseph Ratzinger, the future Pope Benedict XVI, the document acknowledges that no bishop proposes open Communion for any and all divorced and remarried Catholics, which remains true in the context of AL as well. The CDF notes that some bishops would like to leave it to the individual conscience of a divorced and remarried Catholic to determine whether, for example, a previous marriage was null after a formal application for nullity was denied. Other bishops had proposed designating an expert priest with whom a couple would consult, leaving the decision to the couple without implying official authorization. The issue would be resolved as a "tolerant and benevolent pastoral solution."[49]

The CDF rejected those solutions to the problem. Even though they seemed to be backed by some fathers of the church, it claimed that they never represented a consensus of the fathers. Relying on the doctrine and discipline of the church, the CDF determined that if the divorced and civilly remarried "find themselves in a situation that objectively

---

48. *Familiaris Consortio* 84.

49. Congregation for the Doctrine of the Faith, "Letter to the Bishops of the Catholic Church Concerning the Reception of Holy Communion by the Divorced and Remarried Members of the Church" (September 14, 1994), 3.

contravenes God's law," they "cannot receive Holy Communion as long as this situation persists."[50] Nevertheless, for serious reasons, a couple may live in the "brother-sister" relationship and receive the sacraments if they live in complete continence. Notably, the document offers no patristic support for that practice.[51] The document reminds the bishops that Pope John Paul II took this position "out of love for the truth."[52] In accord with *Familiaris Consortio*, the letter insists that the divorced and remarried can live in union with the church insofar as they enter into spiritual communion with it, perform works of charity, listen to the Scriptures, and pray—as long as they stay away from the sacrament of penance and the reception of the Eucharist until such time as they can qualify to participate fully in those sacraments.

It reminds readers that marriage is "the fundamental core and an important factor in the life of civil society, [and] is essentially a public reality."[53] This public dimension of marriage makes individual solutions based on individual conscience particularly problematic. Marriage indeed includes a sacramental dimension, an outwardness that puts it on public display and makes it efficacious as a sacrament. The annulment process investigates a marriage and offers a public judgment on its validity, thereby generating a public document that announces the church's judgment on the validity of a marriage. It will either free a party for marriage or prohibit any further attempt at marriage while a valid spouse still lives. The letter notes that eucharistic Communion should never contradict the status of the ecclesial communion of any recipient.

The CDF failed to note that exceptions to this rule do exist, as when a Lutheran, for example, receives the Eucharist in certain limited circumstances. In fact, John Paul II wrote that "it is a source of joy to note that Catholic ministers are able . . . to administer the Sacraments of the Eucharist [and] Penance . . . to Christians who are not in full communion with the Catholic Church but who greatly desire to receive sacraments, freely request them and manifest the faith

---

50. Congregation for the Doctrine of the Faith, "Letter to the Bishops," 4.

51. In fact, the Council of Ancyra (314) seems to argue against the practice in its canon 19: "And, moreover, we prohibit women who are virgins from living with men as sisters."

52. Congregation for the Doctrine of the Faith, "Letter to the Bishops," 5.

53. "Letter to the Bishops," 7.

which the Catholic Church professes with regard to these Sacraments."[54] Presumably a divorced and remarried Lutheran couple would not be turned away on that account. Why would it not also be a source of joy when Communion can be shared with a Catholic who is caught in a marital dilemma?

As we have noted above, Cardinal Christoph Schönborn reported a response by Cardinal Ratzinger in 1994 concerning internal forum solutions. The future Pope Benedict XVI said, "There is no general norm that can cover all particular cases. The general norm is very clear, and it is equally clear that it cannot cover all the cases exhaustively."[55] Precisely. Some of those cases require mercy and simply cannot become the subject of a clearly stated doctrine or law.

Three years later, Cardinal Ratzinger further backpedaled on his letter, revealing that more flexibility exists than it seemed to suggest. As we have noted, he stated in a 1997 interview: "Perhaps in the future there could also be an extrajudicial determination that the first marriage did not exist. This could perhaps be ascertained locally by experienced pastors. Such juridical developments, which can make things less complicated, are conceivable."[56]

Furthermore, the 1994 letter claimed that only a minority of the fathers of the church supported the practices that the letter rejected. Which practices? What doctrine of the fathers was under scrutiny? If the letter was referring to fathers who supported doctrinal exceptions to indissolubility, then his observation is undoubtedly correct, but this is not relevant to AL. Pope Francis himself excludes any exceptions to indissolubility (see AL 300). One should not expect to find many reports among fathers who dealt with specific individual marital dilemmas. When reviewing the cases that survive in ancient records, only the fathers that actually confronted concrete dilemmas would have cause to comment on them. No one was proposing any doctrinal change in cases like those AL features in its chapter 8.

---

54. John Paul II, encyclical letter *Ut Unum Sint* (May 25, 1995) 46. Throughout this treatise, I make no argument for or against ecumenical eucharistic sharing, a topic that exceeds the scope of this study.

55. Antonio Spadaro, "The Demands of Love: A Conversation with Cardinal Schönborn," *America* (August 15–22, 2016): 26.

56. Joseph Cardinal Ratzinger, *Salt of the Earth: The Church at the End of the Millennium* (San Francisco: Ignatius Press, 1997), 207.

The issue concerns a predicament that arises only rarely in the official records of the early church. In truth, most church fathers did not comment on the mercy shown in marital dilemmas, because they either did not confront them or pertinent documentation from them did not survive. For example, Origen mentions the merciful solution of bishops that impressed him as reasonable.[57] We know about that case only through Origen's testimony, not through diocesan archives. Furthermore, canon 8 of the Council of Nicaea (325) required the Novatians to live in peace with those who maintain second marriages. Canon 11 of the Synod of Arles (314) also witnesses to the attempt to make mercy available for those in second marriages in the early church. Add to that the decisions of Popes Innocent I and Leo the Great, a doctor of the church, both of whom upheld the indissolubility of marriage *and* allowed for a merciful tolerance of a second marriage in dilemmas, and a certain consistency in the practice of the fathers becomes clearer. Pope Francis follows their lead to alleviate the misery of those caught in dilemmas in the modern day.

Pope Benedict XVI further clarifies the situation of the divorced and remarried in his 2007 apostolic exhortation *Sacramentum Caritatis*. He reiterates his previous teaching but clearly states that withholding Communion in the case of the divorced and remarried constitutes "the Church's practice, based on Sacred Scripture" (he cites Mark 10:2-12, which concerns divorce, not the eligibility of people to receive communion).[58] Granting or withholding eucharistic Communion in certain circumstances describes a practice having considerable flexibility, as the early church fathers have shown. Although Benedict based eucharistic discipline on an interpretation of the passage from the Gospel of Mark where Jesus forbids divorce, Pope Francis chooses to expand that discipline based on a well-informed interpretation of 1 Corinthians 11:17-33, where Paul admonishes those present at the Lord's Supper not to "humiliate those who have nothing" (1 Cor 11:22).

While the position concerning the eucharistic discipline of *Familiaris Consortio* and subsequent documents is based on reasonable (although not unassailable) arguments, even better arguments can be made to support an *expansion* of *Familiaris Consortio*'s description

---

57. Cited in Reynolds, *Marriage in the Western Church*, 179.

58. Pope Benedict XVI, apostolic exhortation *Sacramentum Caritatis* (February 22, 2007) 29.

of eucharistic discipline to better fit the options available in the tradition as Pope Francis has advocated in AL 305. Of course, the prior discipline remains in place for the divorced and remarried generally speaking. AL's expansion of *Familiaris Consortio* does not extend the tradition; it simply acknowledges what has long been part of the tradition. It applies where an irregular marriage has entered a dilemma and the couple expresses contrition for their situation. Mercy takes over because the partners in an irregular marriage cannot escape the problematic circumstances no matter what they do. While this represents an expansion over what seems permitted in *Familiaris Consortio*, Francis nevertheless relies on resources already available in the tradition.

If partners in an irregular marriage come to Mass and the community regularly shuns them as others receive Communion (despite other efforts to make them feel welcome), pastors cannot expect the couple to return home feeling good that they have received a blessing while others received the Eucharist. What if the couple feels embarrassed, as would seem almost inevitable? Paul disapproves of precisely this circumstance in 1 Corinthians 11:27-29. He would condemn the practice on the same grounds that he criticized the Corinthian community. The more selfless path for couples in a dilemma will oftentimes call for maintaining a normal family life for the children, even though separating or pretending to live "as brother and sister" might ease their consciences. The more cruciform alternative would appear to put the children first. Approaches that see the issue merely in terms of satisfaction of sexual desire severely underestimate the profound love parents can have for each other and for their children.

As the above analysis of the Eucharist has demonstrated, the church has long offered Communion to sinners who desire full conversion. It is food for the journey.[59] It is a healing remedy. It offers nourishment to live the Christian life more fully, more honestly, and with greater charity. It promotes the healing of the soul sickened with sin. It is never a prize for the perfect or a sign that a person has achieved the fullness of being Christian. The eucharistic sign of union appears as

---

59. "The fact that it [the eschatological nature of the Eucharist] names and celebrates that 'we are not there yet' is its own perennial challenge to live the life of God as fully as we can in the time between Christ's ascension and second coming" (Irwin, *Models of the Eucharist*, 214).

an eschatological sign, a sign of that for which we aim. Perfect union lies only in the *eschaton*. Communion for those with lesser sins partially acknowledges this point already. [60] Communion presumes sin. As Francis Moloney has demonstrated, "the Eucharist is always a gift of the Lord to his failing community, a celebration of forgiveness."[61] Patrick Considine captures the spirit of admission to communion in his claim that "Those who could not eat with Jesus were those who rejected him, not those whom he rejected: his welcome was for all those who would respond to him. He made no exceptions."[62]

To the extent the church uses Communion to separate the wheat from the tares (Matt 13:28-29), the saints from the sinners (while imposing suffering for a sin that cannot be amended), it betrays the Lord's message of unity at the Last Supper. To the extent it offers encouragement, nourishment, a healing remedy and solace to those caught in dilemmas, it shows the mercy that lies at the center of the Christian mission.

D. Productive Discomfort

Communion given to people caught in the circumstances of grave objective sin should make everyone uncomfortable, especially those who are trapped. It can give some the incentive they need to move off dead center and to get on with the serious business of conversion in their lives, like the man who could not bring himself to face the annulment process.

Obviously, Communion should not be given in the spirit of false consolation, as if it meant that the person's life needs no adjustment, no alteration, no healing, no strength for the journey—as if one might simply give up. Effective preaching during the liturgy of the Word should

60. It orients the church to the future insofar as it is given in anticipation of the messianic banquet in heaven. See Geoffrey Wainwright, *Eucharist and Eschatology* (New York: Oxford, 1981), 34. Xavier Léon-Dufour, *Sharing the Eucharistic Bread: The Witness of the New Testament* (New York: Paulist Press, 1987), 201: "The Eucharist is therefore celebrated only during the period that precedes the final coming of God's reign; it does not have an absolute value and must always be seen in relation to the 'heaven' which it prefigure but is not."

61. Moloney, *Eucharist as a Celebration of Forgiveness*, 94.

62. Patrick Considine, "Remarriage and the Eucharist," *Priest and People* 3 (1989): 226-27.

preclude that thought. Communion should energize all recipients to come closer to the community and to the Lord in thought, word, and deed. All communicants recite together, "Lord, I am not worthy" prior to receiving. It accurately describes everyone's position.

Reception of Communion by couples in distressed situations will need to be prepared for with catechesis to avoid the impression that indifference has won the day. As Moloney says, none of these thoughts should give rise to a "free-for-all" mentality. The approach to the table of the Lord should remind one of Vatican II's image of the church as a mother who holds sinners close to her heart.[63] Certainly Pope Francis intends to heal divisions at Communion time and avoid its attendant embarrassment for those caught in the objective circumstances of grave sin. AL 305 tries to bring present eucharistic discipline more in line with Paul's conception of the worthy reception of the Eucharist he envisioned in 1 Corinthians 11:27-29.

---

63. *Lumen Gentium* 8; see also Moloney, *A Body Broken for a Broken People*, 229.

Conclusion

"Why, what a wasp-stung and impatient fool
. . . tying thine ear to no tongue but thine own!"
—Northumberland in *King Henry IV, Part I* 1.3.11

Patience hopefully has rewarded the reader.

Impatient reading, like impatient listening, can put the reader at the mercy of only his or her own thoughts. As Northumberland upbraided Hotspur, impatience can tie "thine ear to no tongue but thine own."

Many people have approached the text of AL with an open mind. They give it a genial reading, sincerely interested in the pope's insights. They prefer to mine its riches, not spot its flaws. The text richly rewards those who can do that.

Other readers approach the text anxiously, either looking for points to criticize or looking for ways to make it blend with their own beliefs. Any text can be distorted to the point of parody, including this one. I am also aware that I can fall into the same trap of misreading others, and I hereby take this opportunity to ask for forgiveness if I have distorted the thought of anyone. In any event, impatient reading serves no one. If impatience has intruded, perhaps rereading the text in more peaceful circumstances would help.

Throughout the course of this treatise, I have attempted to analyze the issues surrounding AL in ways that are faithful to Catholic teaching. I hope that I have clarified several points. Among them are the following:

1. As Paul contends, the faithful need to de-absolutize the law and treat it as a pedagogue (Gal 3:24). If they never let go of the

pedagogue, the slave who is taking them to school, they will never meet the Master, Jesus Christ. The law presents itself as a much more subtle phenomenon than most people suspect. The rule of law does not imply the law of rules. The law must be discerned, not simply applied in a "one-size-fits-all" fashion. Such an exercise requires prudence, which demands that one pay attention to all the circumstances, as AL insists. Divorced and remarried people do not form a single monolithic group. All the various solutions remain available to be applied in appropriate circumstances, including the "brother-sister" relationship, separation, divorce from the illegitimate partner, and so on.

General principles simply cannot take all the concrete factors into account when people apply those principles to particular incidents. Usually principles function well enough, but, as Aquinas taught, abstract principles exist in a vacuum; concrete moral action never does. Only by faith can one discern the proper course of action. Of course the rules count. They are part of faith. They give direction, just as the pedagogue does. The rules, however, do not constitute the destination, nor does the pedagogue, only the Master. Those who naively remain at the level of the abstract become cruel in the application of the law.

2. *Mercy is not opposed to the law; it is a way of applying the law.* Too often Christians want to apply mercy as pagans saw it applied, only where strict justice could still be maintained. They view mercy as something done instead of the law. At times they risk applying the law in a harsh fashion. The Lord expects mercy.

3. AL does not change the law on divorce, nor does it claim that irregular marriages can be "justified." The church's teaching on the indissolubility of marriage remains in place. AL does claim that mercy can tolerate what the law cannot allow in order to prevent a greater evil. Hence, in certain circumstances, namely dilemmas, mercy can tolerate an irregular marriage and let it remain in place.

God does indeed will that some invalid marriages continue. When breaking up the invalid marriage would produce greater evil, the couple has a duty to stay together—even though they cannot solemnize their union as if it were a valid marriage. God does not will only what is intrinsically good. God also wills what, for now, is the best that a person can do, given present circumstances. This means that the formation and guidance of conscience become enormously important along with accompaniment.

4. Both the spousal bond between husband and wife (arising from the unitive aspect of marriage) and the parental bond between parents and children (arising from the procreative aspect) need protection. Both constitute indissoluble bonds, and both have claims to make. The divorced parent who faces a dilemma must discern where the lesser evil lies and try to achieve it.

5. Mercy is always bestowed by another. It is not something that one claims for oneself. AL does not authorize any couples to absolve themselves and to proceed as if their irregular marriages were regular. Various issues will typically arise while a priest accompanies the irregular couple. The irregular partners will most likely complete the accompaniment in the sacrament of reconciliation.

6. Scripture and history show that the church has acted in ways that manage the marital bond. Paul began doing this before the evangelists even wrote the Gospels. Pope Francis continues pastoral practices that were started by Paul, continued through the Council of Nicaea, sustained by St. Leo the Great, and extended through many other popes, right to the pontificate of St. John XXIII in modern times.

7. Pope Francis does not extend the discipline of those who may receive Communion beyond what the tradition already allows. He adopts a more reliable interpretation of 1 Corinthians 11:27-29 in accordance with the best of modern biblical scholarship. He properly applies the church's tradition to allow people who are caught in a dilemma to enjoy the benefit of the sacraments after receiving the accompaniment and guidance of competent pastoral ministers.

Those are some of the main thoughts that I hope emerge from the text. I submit them in hopes that the church may become more the place of mercy envisioned in *Lumen Gentium* 8.

Some Catholics might consider the theological and historical arguments presented above, and, nevertheless, reach contrary conclusions as a matter of personal piety. Perhaps the personal devotion of some Catholics encourages such views, but they do not thereby become part of the teaching of the church. At a minimum, Catholics need to live at peace with those living in second marriages. Scripture and tradition teach that mercy can rescue an irregular family from a dilemma. Pastoral care of the people living as a family may tolerate an invalid marriage. The official church has been given the power to manage the marital bond through the power of the keys. In AL, Pope Francis has acted well within the church's teaching and its history. Distressed families deserve the aid of the sacraments for their difficult journey. Such an interpretation of AL is not only possible but is commanded on the basis of church tradition.[1]

One further issue deserves attention. Possibly because of the haphazard way that the press has sometimes reported on the contents of AL, tensions have grown to the point where some have spoken of a possible schism. Reporters have characterized the pope's action as "playing down traditional teachings on marriage," and they have portrayed his eucharistic discipline as "a departure from traditional doctrine."[2] Both claims badly distort AL.

Some critics assume that schism must lie ahead unless the pope capitulates. One would hope that deference to magisterial authority would prompt opponents to reexamine their own positions with more care.

Scripture testifies to the great importance that Jesus placed on unity (see John 17:22; 1 Cor 12:12-27; etc.). Paul noted that factions in Corinth arose because of the immaturity of the Corinthians (1 Cor 3:1; 14:20). More productive ways exist than schism. When the faithful disagree, theologian Bernard Lonergan, SJ, contended that they must enter into dialectics until problems can be resolved.[3] An honest discussion may reveal not a need for schism but a need for thinkers to reread

---

1. Walter Kasper, *The Message of* Amoris Laetitia*: Finding Common Ground* (New York: Paulist Press, 2019), 45.

2. See, for example, Francis X. Rocca, "Pope Francis Doesn't Fear Schism," *The Wall Street Journal* (September 11, 2019): A-9.

3. Bernard Lonergan, *Method in Theology* (New York: Seabury Press, 1972), 235–66, esp. 242–44.

AL so as to ensure that their comments pertain to the actual text. Many commentators need to reexamine the text. Too often polemics have subverted attempts to restate AL accurately. Tensions have sometimes interfered with calm, rational, and respectful language that should produce works that can be read with equanimity and appreciated by all sides. Prayer and charity need to inform conversations on the neuralgic topics raised in AL. Who knows what creative solutions or explanations may lie in the future unless respectful dialogue takes place?

A decision to enter into schism amounts to a refusal of the bonds of spiritual kinship. It is not the natural result of conversation; it is its failure. Stubbornness simply leaves all parties in the dark. Finally, it should be noted that there is something unseemly about Catholics objecting to the church showing mercy to contrite sinners who have encountered dilemmas in their lives. Misery should draw Christians closer to those who suffer, not send them farther away, and it certainly should not divide them.

We long for the day when we can truly rejoice as one in the Lord. Getting there will not be easy, but the faithful need to persist and endure the trials that surely will come. In his earlier letters, Paul writes of hope quite consistently. But in Titus 2:2, after he has gone through much suffering, he calls hope something else.

Patience.

A Postscript

This treatise has attempted to capture the pope's teaching on marital dilemmas in *Amoris Laetitia*. I offer it as a friendly contribution to a discussion that has at times become testy.

I am aware that some bishops and even cardinals will disagree. Many local bishops have already issued their own directives, some supporting the pope's efforts and others resisting. Still other bishops may need more time "to work out criteria that are tailored to the respective concrete situation" in their local dioceses.[1] Indeed, the implementation of AL poses a pastoral challenge, not a doctrinal one.

One of the bishops' tasks demands that they oversee "public relations": they must present the message of the church in an attractive way that minimizes any possible distortion. Particularly in the United States, journalists look for "sound bites," short, catchy phrases that summarize both the news and the preferred response people ought to have. When news of chapter 8 in AL reached the media, the headlines invariably got it wrong. They proclaimed that the church now admitted the divorced and remarried to Communion. Even some scholars mistook the message. Life should not proceed on the basis of sound bites—although political campaigns try their best to do just that. Some journalists want easy copy. They yearn for something easily written and easily read. Nothing too subtle or complex will do. What can bishops do when their message deals precisely with such subtle complexities?

---

1. Walter Kasper, *The Message of* Amoris Laetitia: *Finding Common Ground* (New York: Paulist Press, 2019), 45.

While this problem seems to present a dilemma of its own, doing nothing would simply relinquish authority to the sound bite mentality. Bishops have the responsibility to work diligently, using all the means at their disposal, to investigate magisterial teachings and to give them suitable expression according to the specific pastoral situations present in their dioceses. The pope has called for mercy and forgiveness in marital dilemmas. He has asked bishops to consider those values that occupy such a central position in the church's teaching. It may take some bishops more time to navigate those very difficult waters. In any case, readers should follow the directives given to them by their local ordinaries.

Obviously respectful and charitable dialogue should improve the climate for bishops and other ministers to provide pastoral care that includes the merciful accompaniment of those caught in distressed marriages. As the issues continue to be considered from various theological viewpoints, I hope this commentary will help to stimulate theologians to add insights from their areas of expertise in defending AL in the days to come.

GJB

Index